Mergers and Acquisitions

Mergers and Acquisitions

A Guide to Creating Value for Stakeholders

─────

Michael A. Hitt
Jeffrey S. Harrison
R. Duane Ireland

OXFORD
UNIVERSITY PRESS
2001

OXFORD
UNIVERSITY PRESS

Oxford   New York
Athens   Auckland   Bangkok   Bogotá   Buenos Aires   Calcutta
Cape Town   Chennai   Dar es Salaam   Delhi   Florence   Hong Kong   Istanbul
Karachi   Kuala Lumpur   Madrid   Melbourne   Mexico City   Mumbai
Nairobi   Paris   São Paulo   Shanghai   Singapore   Taipei   Tokyo   Toronto   Warsaw

and associated companies in
Berlin   Ibadan

Copyright © 2001 by Oxford University Press, Inc.

Published by Oxford University Press, Inc.
198 Madison Avenue, New York, New York 10016

Oxford is a registered trademark of Oxford University Press

Library of Congress Cataloging-in-Publication Data
is available
ISBN 0–19–511285–7

1 3 5 7 9 8 6 4 2
Printed in the United States of America
on acid-free paper

To Frankie. I love you. We share everything.
MAH

To my angel, Marie.
JSH

*To my wife, Mary Ann, and our children, Rebecca and Scott.
I love each of you deeply. Thank you for being there for me the time
or two that I have fallen behind. I'll always be there for you, too.*
RDI

Contents

Preface

The number and size of mergers and acquisitions being completed continue to grow exponentially. Once a phenomenon seen primarily in the United States, mergers and acquisitions are now taking place in countries throughout the world. It is clear that acquisitions have become one of the most important corporate-level strategies in the new millennium.

Because of the importance of acquisition strategies to firm growth and success in the twenty-first century, we have written this book as a guide to help managers navigate a successful merger or acquisition. We explain the actions and processes of executing effective mergers and acquisitions. We also describe some of the major problems confronting managers who are planning such strategic actions.

Our book is grounded in research on many firms in a number of industries and we describe multiple examples of successful and less successful mergers and acquisitions. Although their number and size are increasing, many mergers and acquisitions fail—or at least do not reach their potential. Furthermore, some of these failures have been highly publicized. To explain these less-than-intended outcomes, and, more important, to describe actions that lead to merger and acquisition success, we were motivated to write this book. We have conducted research on mergers and acquisitions for the last 15 years. While the basis for our book is grounded in this research, the book goes beyond our prior research. Our goal was to write a complete guide for executing successful mergers and acquisitions. We explain how to conduct an acquisition and also how to avoid major potential pitfalls. The book describes the due diligence process and how acquisitions are financed. We explore how firms find partners/targets for acquisitions that have complementary resources, an important characteristic for acquisition success. The process of seeking and finding cooperative mergers and achieving integration and synergy are explored in two separate chapters. The next two chapters describe how learning from experience enhances acquisition effectiveness as well as deciding when and how to acquire innovation. We examine the potential hazards of diversification found in mergers and acquisitions and how to avoid them. The next two chapters explore cross-border acquisitions, a growing trend (more than 40 percent of all acquisitions are cross-border) and ethical approaches to M&As. Finally, we explain how to "beat the odds in the M&A game."

While we must accept responsibility for the contents of this book, we owe a debt of gratitude to many people who contributed to it directly or indirectly. First, we thank Herb Addison, our editor at Oxford. Herb was duly patient with us in the book's development and provided excellent guidance and feedback as we revised it. The book is most assuredly better because of his sage advice and guidance. We also thank our colleagues at Texas A&M University, Arizona State University, University of Central Florida, Baylor University, and University of Richmond. We have had many teachers over the years, too numerous to mention here; we have learned from them and owe them all a debt of gratitude.

We hope that you will derive as much pleasure from reading this book as we did in writing it. More important, we hope that you find the guidance useful and that it helps you make a successful acquisition.

March 2000   M.A.H.
                                                             J.S.H.
                                                             R.D.I.

Mergers and Acquisitions

1

The World of Mergers and Acquisitions

Many companies' stocks badly underperform the market after a big merger. The 30 largest deals of the past five years have on average underperformed Standard & Poor's 500 stock index.... Yet the trend is more complicated than that number suggests. It includes some spectacular successes ... and some spectacular fumbles.

—Greg Ip

In 1998, there were a large number of "blockbuster" mergers and acquisitions that made past mergers and acquisitions look small by comparison. For example, the largest announced mergers in 1998 were the marriage between Citicorp and Traveler's Group estimated at approximately $77 billion in value and Exxon's acquisition of Mobil for an estimated $79 billion. Closely following were transactions between SBC and Ameritech valued at approximately $61.8 billion and between Nations Bank Corp. and BancAmerica Corp. valued at approximately $60 billion. AT&T announced the acquisition of Tele-Communications, Inc. valued at approximately $43 billion. One of the largest industrial mergers and acquisitions, between Chrysler Corp. and Daimler-Benz AG valued at $45.4 billion, was also announced.[1] These were all larger than the acquisition of MCI by WorldCom announced in 1997 and characterized as a megamerger by many at approximately $37 billion.[2]

The size and number of M&A transactions continue to grow worldwide. For example, one of the largest mergers in history was announced in 1999. MCI WorldCom and Sprint agreed to a merger valued by

3

analysts between $115 billion and $129 billion. But it did not receive regulatory approval and the respective boards of directors called off the merger agreement in July 2000. Had the merger been completed, the combined firm would have been the second largest global telecommunication company behind only AT&T.[3]

Importance of Mergers and Acquisitions

The 1980s produced approximately 55,000 mergers and acquisitions in the United States alone. The value of the acquisitions during this decade was approximately $1.3 trillion. As impressive as these numbers are, they are small in comparison to the merger wave that began in the earlier 1990s, approximately in 1993. The number and value of mergers and acquisitions have grown each year since 1993. For example, in 1997, there were approximately 22,000 mergers and acquisitions, roughly 40 percent of the total during the whole decade of the 1980s. Perhaps more important, the value of mergers and acquisitions in 1997 was $1.6 trillion. In other words, the acquisitions completed in 1997 were valued at $300 billion more than all acquisitions during the 1980s. Interestingly, the 1980s were often referred to as a decade of merger mania. The year 1998 was no different, as noted by the huge M&A transactions listed earlier; it was predicted to be another record year.[4] Interestingly, the 6,311 domestic mergers and acquisitions in 1993 had a total value of $234.5 billion for an average of $37.2 million, whereas the mergers and acquisitions announced in 1998 had an average value of $168.2 million for an increase of 352 percent over those of 1993.[5] Approximately $2.5 trillion in mergers and acquisitions were announced in 1999, continuing the upward trend.[6]

The mergers and acquisitions in the 1990s represent the fifth merger wave of the twentieth century and their size and number suggest that the decade of the 1990s might be remembered for megamerger mania. With five merger waves throughout the twentieth century, we must conclude that mergers and acquisitions are an important, if not dominant, strategy for twenty-first century organizations.[7]

The purpose of this book is to describe effective actions and processes as well as some of the primary pitfalls (ineffective actions and processes) of executing mergers and acquisitions. This book is based on a program of research over a 15-year period in which we have studied the mergers and acquisitions of many firms. Furthermore, we have carefully read the primary research on mergers and acquisitions as well as case studies and reports of mergers and acquisitions in the popular business press. This work, then, represents a compilation and synthesis of our research, the research of others, and the experience of many firms and executives.

Acquisitions Often Fail

Despite their popularity and importance among large and small firms alike, many acquisitions do not produce the financial benefits expected or desired for the acquiring firm.[8] In fact, one often quoted study by a prominent financial economist, Michael Jensen, showed that shareholders of the acquired firms often earn above-average returns from the acquisitions but that shareholders of the acquiring firms earn returns, on average, close to zero.[9] There have been a number of other studies, some by scholars and others completed by think tanks and prominent consulting firms, showing problems with the performance of acquisitions. For example, one study by McKinsey & Co. found that approximately 60 percent of the acquisitions examined failed to earn returns greater than the annual cost of capital required to finance the acquisitions. In fact, the McKinsey study found that only 23 percent of the acquisitions examined were successful. Other studies have shown that a high percentage (30–45 percent) of acquisitions are later sold and often at prices producing a loss on the investment. Recently, it has become common for these low performing acquired businesses to be spun off into independent companies (e.g., the NCR spin-off by AT&T).[10] The point is that there clearly are risks involved in mergers and acquisitions.

There have been several poorly performing acquisitions. For example, Quaker Oats bought Snapple Beverage Co. for $1.7 billion in 1994. However, it sold the Snapple business three years later in 1997 for only $300 million, for a loss of $1.4 billion. Similarly, Novell, a computer network company, lost approximately $700 million (50 percent of the purchase price) within a year of its 1994 acquisition of WordPerfect Corp. More recently, Boeing Co. bought McDonnell Douglas Corp. in 1997. In three years prior to the acquisition, McDonnell Douglas' stock had quadrupled in value. However, in the months following the McDonnell Douglas acquisition, Boeing stock declined in value by 15 percent.[11] Some of Boeing's performance problems are related to manufacturing inefficiencies. However, it has had to eliminate several unprofitable airplanes from the McDonnell Douglas line. Additionally, as McDonnell Douglas planes are phased out, Boeing plans to shut down 27 million square feet of production line by 2003.[12]

Based on figures compiled by CommScan LLC, an investment banking research firm, even megamergers are no guarantee for success. CommScan tracked the stock values of the 15 largest acquisitions for 1995 through 1999. It discovered that, on average, the merged firms performed 9 percent below the S&P 500. The worst performing acquisitions relative to the S&P 500 were USA Waste's acquisition of Waste Management (80 percent below) and Walt Disney's acquisition of Capital Cities/ABC (78 percent below).[13]

This is not to suggest that all mergers and acquisitions produce negative results. Indeed, in a recent study that we conducted, we found several high-performing acquisitions. Understandably, many of the acquisitions in our study produced negative results; however, some of the positive acquisitions produced high returns for the acquiring firm. For example, Citigroup, the merger between Travelers and Citicorp, has performed 75 percent above the S&P 500 since completion of the merger in 1998. Thus, acquisitions can be a highly profitable strategy with positive results for both shareholders and the long-term health of a firm.[14] Taken further, Federal Reserve Chairman Alan Greenspan said that the current national wave of megamergers produces no sign of economic danger. In fact, he strongly recommended that the government respect the dynamism of modern free markets.[15] Thus, mergers and acquisitions do not pose a major threat to the domestic or global economies, nor do they have to produce negative results for acquiring firms. Nonetheless, many studies demonstrate that mergers and acquisitions are likely complex and challenging strategies for top executives to implement. Furthermore, they must be managed effectively, beginning with the selection of an appropriate target firm for acquisition, in order for them to succeed.

Avoiding Acquisition Pitfalls

Although the merger wave of the 1980s was fueled largely by the need to restructure and focus on core and related businesses, the fifth merger wave in the 1990s has been mostly the result of a desire to achieve economies (e.g., of scale and scope) and market power in order to increase competitiveness in global markets. This is true in the United States, Europe, and Asia.[16] In addition, in some industries, firms are attempting to prepare for a future in which dramatic changes occur in the industry, often due to technological developments (e.g., in the telecommunications industry). Even though many acquisitions made in recent times are between firms in the same or related industries and potential economies or synergies are clearly evident, there are many other potential pitfalls in mergers and acquisitions. Often an unintended consequence of mergers and acquisitions is reduced innovation.[17] Firms engaged in multiple acquisitions over time are likely to introduce fewer new products to the market. This is because they often overemphasize financial controls and become more risk averse. These firms then seek to make acquisitions in order to supplement their innovations. It becomes a self-fulfilling prophecy. As they bring new firms into the fold with new products, they integrate them into a system that discourages innovation, and thus they must continue to buy other firms with innovative new products to compete, to the extent that the industries in which they operate require new products to meet customer demand.[18] This is important because increasingly firms are seeking to introduce new and innovative products rapidly as a means of competing success-fully in fast-changing and unpredictable markets.[19]

Other pitfalls relate to the potential for managerial hubris that may preclude an adequate analysis of the target firm or may produce substantial premiums paid for firms that are acquired. CEOs have been involved in several highly publicized acquisitions such as Sony's controversial $5 billion takeover of Columbia Studios in which Walter Yetnikoff paid almost $800 million to acquire two producers from their contract at Warner Brothers. This was part of a battle with Warner Brothers' then current CEO, Steven Ross. Yetnikoff convinced his superiors at Sony that the two producers would earn millions of dollars for the firm. Unfortunately, the two set new records in Hollywood for underachievement.[20] Similarly, the final price of the MCI acquisition by WorldCom was fueled by a personal battle between WorldCom's CEO, Bernie Ebbers, and Charles Lee, CEO of rival GTE.

Another potential pitfall is the problem of integrating two large and complex firms that often have diverse cultures, structures, and operating systems.[21] In the race for global competitiveness, some firms trying to achieve economies and market power may not effectively analyze their target firms prior to acquisition and may make mistakes when attempting to integrate the acquired firm into the acquiring firm. Examples of such errors can be seen in the Union Pacific acquisition of Southern Pacific Railroad. Union Pacific hastily cut costs by laying off thousands of Southern Pacific employees primarily in consolidating the two railroads. These actions resulted in substantial railroad congestion and many problems. The Southern Pacific Railroad was a weak and poorly managed firm, suffering from inadequate investment and poor performance. There were multiple delays, derailments, and equipment breakdowns after the consolidation. As many as 10,000 railroad cars were stalled on Union Pacific railroads at a given time. This caused substantial problems for Union Pacific customers. The costs to customers have been estimated as high as $1.3 billion because of lost business related to the delays or inability to ship their goods.[22]

Interestingly, the current merger and acquisition wave could extend several years into the future. Although it has been fueled by strong stock markets and high valuations of firms, even a negative change in some markets, especially outside the United States, may not severely dampen the current merger and acquisition binge. Most of the current mergers and acquisitions are financed with stock. However, many corporations have built up large amounts of cash. Thus, they may change the financing from stock to cash.[23] Furthermore, government actions support increasing numbers of transactions, thereby providing a stimulus to mergers and acquisitions.[24] Regardless of the pitfalls previously noted and the fact that many acquisitions do not produce the success desired, we see a strong market for mergers and acquisitions.

Because of this continued strength in numbers, top executives and others need to fully understand the requirements for success in mergers and acquisitions, as well as the potential problems that can lead to failure or at least lower than desired performance from the implementation of this major strategy. Therefore, top executives must make effective decisions and implement effective procedures throughout the acquisition process to enjoy the benefits of successful acquisitions.

The Requirements for Success

Each chapter of this book focuses on an important issue related to making effective mergers and acquisitions. We should note that most of these discussions concern acquisitions. The reason for this emphasis is that mergers represent a transaction between two firms that agreed to integrate their operations on a relatively coequal basis. However, these are rare. Most of the transactions represent acquisitions in which one firm buys up to 100 percent controlling interest in another firm, thereby making the acquired businesses a part of its portfolio.[25]

In the following paragraphs, we provide an overview of the content and discussions in the chapters that follow.

Exercising Due Diligence

Because the acquisition process begins with the selection of potential acquisition targets, the second chapter focuses on performing due diligence on potential target firms and avoiding managerial hubris. Careful and deliberate selection of target firms and conduct of negotiations can produce mergers and acquisitions with the best complementary assets and the highest potential synergies. Additionally, careful analysis produces effective knowledge that will reduce the probability of paying an inappropriate premium to acquire a target firm. An inappropriate premium significantly reduces the probability that the acquisition will lead to enhanced financial performance. Investment bankers play a key advisory role providing assistance in the due diligence process, particularly in the decision regarding the price paid. While logical and almost "commonsensical," it is not uncommon for firms to inadequately analyze target firms prior to acquisition. Sometimes, the lack of evaluation can be attributed to managerial hubris, which reflects managers' overconfidence in their own abilities to manage the assets being purchased. Earlier, we provided examples of the effects of managerial hubris in M&As. Poor selection of target firms could also be the result of simple managerial ineptitude. Managers should not be surprised by any characteristics, processes, or outcomes of the target firm operations after the acquisition has been consummated.[26] In this chapter, we explain how to conduct an effective due diligence process.

Financing an Acquisition

Another critical element is the financing of the acquisition. In the 1970s, cash was a popular medium for financing acquisitions. However, in the 1980s, emphasis was placed on the use of debt as a primary means of such financing. Unfortunately, sometimes due to the extensive use of debt and its high costs (particularly those using high-interest financing sometimes referred to as junk bonds), M&As produce high financial risks and lower performance or even bankruptcy.[27]

The use of debt to finance acquisitions has declined dramatically with the high valuations of firms in the stock market. As a result, stock is used to acquire firms in many transactions in the 1990s. Studies have shown that firms maintaining financial flexibility, such as financial slack (which includes a moderate debt position, thereby allowing future use of debt if necessary), generally produce more effective acquisitions. As a whole, such acquisitions entail less financial risk and allow the flexibility to pursue other strategic opportunities as they become available.

We explore the various factors that affect the choice of financing mode for an acquisition. Among those are tax implications, accounting treatments, managerial control, market psychology, returns to shareholders, and amount of the firm's slack. Finally, we recommend steps to achieve successful acquisition financing.

Searching for Complementary Resources

Acquiring and target/acquired firms that have assets/resources complementary to one another often produce the most successful acquisitions. The operative word is *complementary,* in which the assets/resources of the acquiring and target firms are not the same. Instead, the resources are different but mutually supportive of one another, thereby increasing the probability of achieving synergy. In some cases, the complementary assets/resources may entail businesses operating in related but different markets that in effect feed one another. Such complementary businesses can be observed in the marriage of Morgan Stanley and Co. and Dean Witter Discover and Co. in 1997. Both were securities firms, but Morgan Stanley was a primary developer and provider of financial products, whereas Dean Witter was a strong distributor. Additionally, the two firms' primary product/service lines were highly complementary. Thus, both businesses gained new product/service lines to market.[28] Perhaps the most value-creating complementarities are those that can produce positive synergy but are difficult to observe by others. As a result, they are less easily imitated by competitors.

In this chapter, we explore the importance of synergy and the managerial challenge of achieving it. We examine the value of complementary resources and their effect on organizational learning and emphasize how economies of scale and scope and the skills lead to synergy.

Seeking a Friendly and Cooperative Merger

The decade of the 1980s was one of hostile takeovers. Supposedly, these takeovers were aimed at firms underperforming the market and thus assumed to be poorly managed. The purpose was to acquire firms whose assets were undervalued and institute new and more effective managerial processes, which, in turn, would increase the firm's stock market valuation. In some cases this approach worked; in others it did not seem to be as effective as argued. One study showed that as many as 50 percent of the hostile takeovers were not aimed at underperforming firms, but at those outperforming many in their industries. As a result, the takeover and change in managerial processes in previously high performing firms actually produced a reduction in performance, as opposed to an increase.[29] Furthermore, hostile takeovers can result in relatively negative feelings between the management and professional groups of the two firms. In other words, it can produce a hostile culture in which integration and synergy are difficult to achieve. Friendly takeovers, if between firms that have complementary assets, may instead produce an environment in which cooperation leads to an easier and faster integration of the two firms and a higher probability of achieving synergy. Interestingly, when target firm managers resist hostile takeover bids, the price eventually paid for the acquired firm is generally higher. Thus, it may be likely that hostile bids actually promote resistance that, in turn, increases the price that must be paid to acquire the firm. When a premium is high, it reduces the ability of the acquiring firm to earn an appropriate return on its investment in the new business.[30] Therefore, we argue that while some hostile takeover attempts may be appropriate and lead to successful outcomes, in general, friendly mergers and acquisitions have a higher probability of producing positive long-term results.

We discuss the importance of and how to develop a friendly and cooperative climate after the merger of two (or more) firms. Of course, cooperation begins with the acquisition negotiation process or even before. We examine causes of resistance and how to overcome them. Finally, we present guidelines for achieving a friendly deal.

Achieving Integration and Synergy

As synergy is linked to the creation of value in mergers and acquisitions, successful integration of the two firms after the transaction has been completed is critical to the achievement of synergy. First, there must be potential synergy. Undoubtedly, the existence of complementary assets/

resources contributes to the potential for synergy from mergers and acquisitions. Furthermore, integration is facilitated by friendly mergers and acquisitions and a healthy culture that recognizes and rewards the value of contributions made by parties from both firms.

Fortunately for some firms, potential integration problems are discovered prior to the consummation of the particular merger or acquisition. This was evident, for example, in the collapse of discussions between KPMG Peat Marwick and Ernst & Young on their previously announced merger. Although both firms were receiving pressure from regulatory agencies expressing concerns about the potential market power a merger between the two accounting giants would create, the primary reasons for ending the discussions were the expected problems in combining the two firms' cultures. The chairman of Ernst & Young, Philip Laskawy, observed that during the negotiations it became evident that both firms had noticeably different cultures. For example, Ernst & Young partners tend to be more entrepreneurial, while KPMG partners more commonly worked with relatively risk-averse clients (e.g., the United States government).[31]

Similarly, two pharmaceutical giants ended their talks primarily because of disagreements over who would manage the combined company. SmithKline Beecham PLC broke off merger talks with Glaxo Wellcome PLC. The market had reacted positively to this potential merger because of the combination of the two firms' financial and market power to create blockbuster drugs, as well as their combined scientific acumen and marketing prowess. However, SmithKline managers expressed concern about Glaxo's intent to acquire SmithKline rather than to make it a merger of relative equals. SmithKline managers took special note of the aftermath of Glaxo's hostile takeover of Wellcome PLC several years earlier. Few of Wellcome's top executives held major positions after the firm was acquired. Essentially, SmithKline executives were expressing a concern about the potential integration of their firm into Glaxo Wellcome.[32] To achieve the synergies from complementary resources and foster learning and continued development from an acquisition, effective integration of the two businesses after the deal is consummated is essential.[33]

In this chapter, we examine how integration of merged firms can best be accomplished. The importance of strategic fit in achieving integration and synergy is emphasized. We also explore the effects of organizational fit on integration. In addition, we discuss managerial actions and value creation as foundations for synergy.

Learning from Experience

If firms have experienced acquisitions in the past and learned from those experiences, it may improve the processes used to select target firms, negotiate the transaction, and implement the acquisition (i.e., achieve synergy) to gain a competitive advantage. Furthermore, firms can learn new skills and knowledge from the acquired firm if they can effectively integrate the acquired business into theirs. It may require special processes that are developed over time through experience and learning from past acquisitions.[34] In particular, studies have shown that firms can learn from diversity; thus, having different but complementary skills may not only aid a firm but may help it develop new skills as well.[35] Additionally, firms having recent experience with acquisitions may already be in a fluid state and therefore more easily adaptable to changes required by a new acquisition. In other words, the firm's systems, structures, processes, culture, and even internal politics may be more flexible.[36] For an effective integration of two separate businesses, substantial change in both firms may be required. Therefore, flexibility should facilitate post-acquisition integration.[37] In fact, any previous experience with large-scale change may help a firm be more flexible in adapting to another company. The key for change experience to contribute to more effective acquisitions is organizational learning. Thus, firms must learn from prior change and apply that learning to the process of selecting and/or integrating the acquired firm.

In addition to the ideas presented here, we explore the facilitation of organizational learning. In particular, we examine knowledge acquisition and diffusion along with the development of organizational memory. Finally, we explain how to take advantage of learning opportunities.

Deciding When and How to Acquire Innovation

Innovation is becoming increasingly important for global competitiveness in multiple industries. One study of United States, European, and Japanese firms over a 10-year period found that those firms bringing more new products to the market were the highest performers.[38] With the growing importance of innovation, even outside high-technology industries, the ability to maintain an emphasis on innovation while following an acquisition strategy is crucial. On average, firms following an acquisition strategy often become less innovative over time, as previously mentioned.[39] Thus, firms must consciously emphasize innovation when following an acquisition strategy. They may do this by continuing to make healthy investments in research and development, maintaining an innovative culture, providing incentives for continuing innovation, and searching for partners that either have a similar culture or complementary innovation skills.

Firms also complete acquisitions to gain access to innovation in the acquired firm. In these cases, firms are likely using the acquired innovation as a substitute for producing innovation from their own R&D

operations. If handled carefully, this approach may also be successful. We examine both approaches to innovation through acquisition in this chapter.

Avoiding the Hazards of Diversification

Although complementary skills and resources do not necessarily have to come from the same or similar lines of business, they are more likely to result from related businesses than unrelated businesses. Related businesses provide stronger opportunities to gain economies of scope and develop synergy than unrelated businesses.[40] Therefore, firms are more likely to gain value when they acquire companies that operate in industries similar to or the same as their own. Some firms have been able to operate successfully as a conglomerate (with a series of highly unrelated businesses in their portfolio), but most have not been able to do so. Financial synergies represent the primary opportunity in unrelated acquisitions. However, related acquisitions provide more opportunities for complementary managerial and knowledge-based assets, as well as economies that can be gained through physical assets and other functional forms (e.g., joint marketing activities). Managers often do not have the specific knowledge to manage an unrelated business, and thus they use financial controls as a substitute for more strategic means of managing that business. When they do so, they are less likely to achieve performance gains.[41] Alternatively, it is more difficult to manage related acquisitions in order to achieve the necessary integration and obtain the potential synergies between the firms. Thus, related acquisitions do not guarantee the achievement of synergy. Firms can learn from diversification. Acquired firms may hold knowledge useful to other businesses in the acquiring firm's portfolio. Of course, firms are more likely to learn from acquired businesses that are related to current businesses in their portfolio. In particular, learning new technological capabilities may be useful. Managers must focus on learning in order to gain knowledge, however.

Acquiring or Merging Across National Borders

Executives are developing a global mindset. Consequently, the number of cross-border acquisitions has been increasing. For example, approximately 40 percent of the acquisitions in 1999 were across national borders, doubling the percentage of cross-border acquisitions in 1998. The number of cross-border acquisitions is relatively equally balanced across Asia, Europe, and North America. Reasons for cross-border acquisitions include increased market power, overcoming market entry barriers, covering the cost of new product development, increasing the speed of entry into a market, and greater diversification. Cross-border acquisitions can produce both economies of scale and economies of scope. They help a firm enter new international markets and thereby enhance their ability to compete in global markets. Of course, cross-border acquisitions are even more challenging to complete successfully than acquisitions of domestic firms. Thus, while their numbers are growing, they are likely to become increasingly complicated.

Taking an Ethical Approach to Mergers and Acquisitions

There has been much written about agency problems with mergers, yet most of it has focused on avoiding managerial decisions such as product diversification that do not enhance shareholder value. This is, indeed, an important issue, but other issues may be prevalent with regard to acquisitions. For example, acquisitions should not be made to enhance the power of a top executive or because of a top executive's hubris. However, we have found that acquisitions are sometimes undertaken for these reasons.[42] For example, some acquisitions may involve decisions made for opportunistic reasons. Additionally, there have been examples when executives have acted in unethical ways to enhance the perceived value of companies, either before acquisitions (to make the firm more attractive for acquisition) or after. Accounts of the firing of CEO Al Dunlap from his position at Sunbeam Corporation suggest that there may have been inappropriate decisions made and actions taken to enhance the short-term financial performance of the firm after it made several acquisitions. For example, Dunlap acquired three firms almost simultaneously, but was unable to improve Sunbeam's overall stock price for the long term. In fact, the stock price eventually experienced a significant decrease. Because inventory numbers were at unusually high levels, decisions were made to provide lucrative terms to dealers to ship products aggressively. It was referred to as a build and hold strategy. It made short-term profits seem attractive but led to losses over time.[43]

Other problems may include negative actions taken by either the acquiring or acquired firm's executives that harm the reputation of the overall merged firm. Reputations can play important roles in holding current and recruiting future customers; therefore, actions that harm the overall reputation can have a dampening effect on the firm's performance over time. For acquisitions to work effectively, opportunistic and/or potentially unethical actions must be avoided. Of course, this is likely true in the conduct of all business, not just acquisitions. Executives making acquisition decisions must be diligent and careful to watch for such actions by their own staff and by the managerial team in the target firm as well.

We examine the importance of governance and oversight during the acquisition process. Members of the board of directors must be especially vigilant during this time. The ethical implications of hostile takeovers are also explored. Hostile takeovers are not necessarily unethical. However, if they are targeted at high-performing firms, they may harm rather than enhance shareholder value.

Beating the Odds in the M&A Game

The final chapter in this book emphasizes the key lessons to be learned from acquisitions. In it, we articulate how to undertake and complete successful acquisitions. Furthermore, we review the important trends in mergers and acquisitions for the twenty-first century. In summary, this book describes the critical characteristics that determine the success and failure of mergers and acquisitions. We begin the journey with a discussion of exercising due diligence.

2

Exercising
Due Diligence

Diligence is the mother of good fortune.

—Cervantes

According to Mark Sirower of the New York University, all effective acquisitions begin with a strategic vision. He argues that management's vision of an acquisition should be clear to the firm's many constituent groups and adaptable to many potentially unknown circumstances. Further, he suggests that a strategic vision is one of the cornerstones of a firm's ability to achieve synergy from an acquisition.[1] Warren Helman, former CEO of Lehman Brothers, suggests that because so many mergers and acquisitions fail, we should presume failure with each one. He argues that decision-makers in the acquiring firm should have the burden of proof to show that they can provide positive outcomes.[2] There are multiple reasons for acquisition failure, including the lack of appropriate due diligence.

An example of concerns about due diligence can be found in the problems discovered following the HFS, Inc. and CUC International, Inc. merger to form the new company Cendant Corp. CUC was the leading membership-based consumer services company. It provided members access to shopping, dining, and travel, particularly vacation exchange services. HFS was a leading franchiser of well-known hotels (e.g., Ramada Inn, Days Inn, Howard Johnson), residential real estate (e.g., Century 21) and car rentals (e.g., Avis). It also owned the world's largest time-share vacation exchange, Resort Condominiums International. The merger of the two companies produced a virtual monopoly on full-ser-

17

vice timeshare exchange services. However, several months after the two firms merged, potential accounting irregularities were discovered in CUC's books. In short, auditors from Arthur Andersen & Co. found what they described as "widespread and systematic" practices of overstating or possibly fabricating results. In effect, the problems discovered would require the reduction of 1997 net income by $200 to 250 million. Likewise, net income for 1995 and 1996 had to be revised for the same reasons. This caused considerable problems within the merged company, and in particular between the two top executives who were the CEOs of the formerly independent firms, Walter Forbes of the former CUC and Henry Silverman of the former HFS. Within a span of four months after the announcement, Cendant's stock price had fallen from $41 to $17. CUC's former auditor Ernst & Young stated that it appeared that efforts had been made to deceive the auditors. Considerable turmoil within the firm resulted from these actions.[3]

Appropriate due diligence could have avoided the problems in Cendant Corp. As the size of mergers and acquisitions continues to grow and their pace increases, due diligence may be harmed. For example, some of the huge acquisitions announced in the last few years have been put together in a very short period, some as little as one week. This does not leave much time for the variety of people involved in the due diligence process to complete their work effectively.[4] According to Jack Levy, head of mergers and acquisitions at Merrill Lynch & Co., "The level of M&A activity is clearly stressing the system." Benjamin McCleary, partner in McFarland Dewey & Co., an investment bank, states that "there are a lot of value judgments, depending on the speed (of a deal)." Finally, Mark L. Mitchell of the Harvard Business School suggests that "we are going to see more . . . deals that turn out to be bust, in part, because of the lack of due diligence."[5]

In this chapter, we begin with an explanation of how to conduct an effective due diligence process. We follow this discussion by examining problems related to the conduct of due diligence (i.e., managerial hubris may cause executives to overlook critical problems). Next, we explore the role of investment bankers in the due diligence process. We end the chapter with a presentation of managerial implications related to due diligence.

The Due Diligence Process

A thorough due diligence process covers hundreds of items in such areas as balance of equity and debt capital, sale of assets, transfer of shares, environmental issues, financial performance, tax issues, human resources, and many other business aspects.[6] The due diligence process is generally performed by accountants, investment bankers, lawyers, and other specialized management consultants. There may also be a number of additional internal specialists who will help with this process. Due diligence is a highly complex process when conducted correctly.[7]

The most effective due diligence processes begin with the earliest stages of the acquisition. For example, the due diligence process should help a firm select a target for acquisition. It should aid in choosing a target that will facilitate the firm obtaining a long-term competitive advantage and thereby increasing shareholder wealth. In fact, if the wrong target firm is selected for acquisition, the rest of the due diligence process may have less value.

Dynamic Due Diligence

Dynamic due diligence begins with an empowered due diligence team that has the responsibility and authority to obtain information and analyze the data in order to integrate them into a vision for the merger or acquisition. Effective due diligence goes beyond the financial numbers and inventories to include the culture, human resource attitudes, and other critical attributes that may affect the vision. Thus, one critical outcome of effective due diligence is the assessment of the viability of the post-merger integration of the two firms.

Clearly, an important part of the due diligence process is analyzing the firm's financial resources. This should include a return on assets per employee, economic value added, percentage of revenues and profits from new businesses, and a quantification of lost business revenues. Lost business revenues relate to missed business opportunities (e.g., beaten to the market by competitors, new product failures, etc.).

A dynamic due diligence process also carefully and completely analyzes customer- and marketing-related issues. For example, customer relationships should be fully evaluated and detailed, a customer satisfaction index should be developed, and market share relative to competitors must be examined, along with other characteristics such as the number of sales calls per customer.

Another important area of due diligence is the analysis of major processes (e.g., manufacturing, provision of service). This analysis may include measurements of cycle times and improvements over time, achievement of quality goals, assessment of the effectiveness of management information systems, and administrative expense per employee (overhead expense).

Finally, an effective due diligence process will also analyze the human resources of the firm. These analyses may be more qualitative and thus difficult to complete. Included may be an evaluation of management capabilities, investment in human resources (e.g., amount of training per employee), and indices on leadership, motivation, and employee empowerment.[8] Human capital is critical to the success of firms in general, but especially to mergers and acquisitions.[9]

The due diligence team members are likely to specialize in different types of analyses. However, the reports from each of the specialized areas must be integrated into a final overall set of conclusions based on the due diligence process. Unfortunately, because this is a complex and often time-consuming process, many of the current and larger acquisitions do not entail dynamic due diligence as we have described.[10] Although analyzing the two cultures of the potential merger partners and their compatibility is important, it is also crucial to evaluate the compatibility of the two firms' information systems. In fact, a complete analysis of each firm's information system may be a critical element in the achievement of effective integration after the merger has been consummated.[11]

Of course, the due diligence process is further complicated by cross-border acquisitions. This is because of the differences in legal structure, tax rates, accounting practices, environmental laws, and so forth that may exist in the separate countries. For example, firms must carefully analyze the potential to transfer money easily across borders—some countries do not allow the free movement of currency across their border (e.g., China, Russia).[12]

In the end, the due diligence process must be thorough and conducted with integrity.[13] The due diligence process involves both ethical and legal obligations for corporations and their agents (e.g., investment bankers). Ineffective, unethical, and illegal practices should be identified and disclosed.

Inadequate Due Diligence

Inadequate evaluation of the target firm occurs in most of the unsuccessful acquisitions. For example, inadequate due diligence was evident in Datapoint's purchase of Inforex. Inforex filed for Chapter 11 bankruptcy the year prior to the acquisition by Datapoint because it could not meet its semiannual debt payment. The second year after its acquisition of Inforex, Datapoint suffered a 95 percent reduction in net income from the previous year. Managers blamed this reduction on the recession but, in fact, total revenues were higher than in the previous year. Therefore, one would surmise that the problem was an inability to control costs that may not have been foreseen prior to the acquisition.[14]

Lee Iacocca described Chrysler's acquisition of AMC as similar "to swallowing a whale." One might ask why this was not anticipated prior to Chrysler's completing the transaction. American Motors was in the same industry as Chrysler and had multiple well-publicized problems in its production, labor relations, and organization. Not unsurprisingly, Chrysler suffered reductions in overall productivity after the acquisition and experienced substantial production overcapacity. While Chrysler attempted to turn around the fortunes of AMC's cars, it was unsuccessful. AMC generally had a poor image—its customers constituted less than

1 percent of the United States automobile market. Its manufacturing plants were outmoded and unprofitable and the firm had negative working capital in the year preceding the Chrysler acquisition. It seems that a knowledgeable observer of the industry could have easily predicted the outcomes experienced by Chrysler even without a thorough due diligence process.[15]

Chrysler did obtain access to the Jeep brand and subsequently leveraged it into a profitable product line. However, Renault, the company that sold AMC to Chrysler, was experiencing substantial financial problems at the time of the sale. Chrysler could thus have purchased only the Jeep assets instead of all AMC assets if it had desired. At least the profitable Jeep product line has partially offset the costs and losses Chrysler suffered from the acquisition of AMC.

In 1999, DaimlerChrysler strongly considered acquiring Nissan Motor Company. The chairman of DaimlerChrysler, Jurgen Schrempp, seemed to be keenly interested in acquiring Nissan to increase his firm's market share and access to the global automobile markets.[16] However, others were critical of Schrempp's interest in Nissan. For example, Robert Lutz, retired vice chairman of Chrysler Corporation, stated that "they might as well take $5 billion in gold bullion, put it in a huge container, spray paint the word Nissan on the side and drop into the middle of the Pacific Ocean."[17] The primary concern was with Nissan's $22 billion worth of debt. Nissan also has considerable other problems. A number of external analysts urged DaimlerChrysler to analyze the potential Nissan acquisition very carefully. In other words, they suggested that Daimler-Chrysler should conduct a thorough due diligence process. Fortunately, DaimlerChrysler decided not to undertake the acquisition. Interestingly, France's Renault decided to buy an equity stake in Nissan to gain access to United States and Asian markets where its presence was weak. It is unclear, however, if the benefits of this transaction will outweigh the considerable costs involved.

Due Diligence Problems

Due diligence involves a comprehensive analysis of all important target firm characteristics to include its financial condition, management capabilities, physical assets, and other intangible assets relevant to the acquisition.[18] In the conduct of the due diligence process, it is important to detect potential liabilities arising from the acquisition. Liabilities that are undetected prior to the acquisition can create significant financial problems after the acquisition is consummated. The purpose of the due diligence process is not to discover why a deal should not proceed. Rather, it is to obtain a more complete understanding of the financial, operating, human, and legal implications among others of a merger or acquisition.[19] Examples of unsuccessful mergers and acquisitions abound in which ineffective due diligence was conducted. Quaker Oats acquired Snapple Beverage Co. in 1994 for $1.7 billion. In 1997, it sold Snapple for only $300 million, less than 18 percent of the original purchase price. AT&T bought NCR Corporation for $7.5 billion in 1991. Thereafter, NCR produced almost $4 billion in net losses before AT&T spun it off as a separate company. Novell lost almost $700 million on its acquisition and then sale of WordPerfect two years later. Sometimes, acquiring companies paid too high a premium. In other cases, the firm should never have been acquired. A critical reason for these problems is the acquirer's lack of knowledge about the target firm prior to acquisition.[20]

Managerial Hubris

A major potential due diligence problem is that of top management hubris. Managerial hubris may lead firms to do a less than adequate job of due diligence or to ignore the information received from the due diligence process. A recent study conducted by Mathew Hayward and Don Hambrick, both of Columbia University, showed that managerial hubris was a major cause of high premiums paid for acquisitions. Hayward and Hambrick focused on the CEO. They found that premiums were higher when the acquiring firm had experienced more recent success in its financial performance, when the media had recently praised the CEO, and when CEOs rated their own self-importance highly. Thus, their research supported the hubris hypothesis. Furthermore, they found that the premiums paid were exacerbated when there was weak corporate governance, such as more inside directors, and when the CEO was also the chair of the Board of Directors.[21]

There are several prominent cases in which the effects of managerial egos on acquisitions are evident. For example, managerial hubris was operative in Sony's controversial $5 billion acquisition of Columbia Studios. The primary strategist involved in the acquisition was Walter Yetnikoff, CEO of Sony's record division. His superiors questioned the payment of $800 million to obtain the release of two producers, Peter Guber and Jon Peters, from their contracts with Warner Bros. Yetnikoff had allowed the deal to become a personal issue with Steve Ross, the CEO of Warner Bros. He argued that these two producers were going to make billions of dollars for Sony and his superiors then agreed to the huge payment. However, Guber and Peters and Columbia Studios were substantial underachievers for a number of years following the acquisition. Other battles of CEO egos were evident in the attempted takeover of ITT by Hilton Hotels and a battle between Viacom and QVC for Paramount. Rand Araskog, CEO of ITT, and Steve Bollenbach, CEO of Hilton Hotels, refused to talk to each other but traded insults in the press. Unfortunately, these battles often lead to the payment of "irrational premiums."[22] Such overpayments usually have a negative effect on shareholder wealth.

Whether egos are at work or not, when there are multiple bidders, thereby creating an "auction," premiums paid for acquiring the target firm are likely to be much higher. Emotions often enter the decision arena and lead to ineffective decisions. At one point, Mario Gabelli, whose Gabelli funds were one of the largest Paramount shareholders, exclaimed "Let the auction begin!" At the time, Paramount had just received a $9.5 billion offer to be acquired by QVC, $2 billion above Viacom's prior offer.[23] Likewise, MCI was in the enviable position of being courted by three powerful companies, British Telecom, GTE, and World-Com. The premiums paid were staggering as the bids more than doubled over the course of the "auction." Although target firm shareholders clearly benefit from multiple bidders, acquiring firm shareholders often lose under these conditions.[24]

Shareholders clearly lost value on the Bank One acquisition of First Chicago in October 1998. By October 1999, one year after the acquisition, Bank One's stock had decreased in value by 13 percent and also had underperformed the S&P 500 by 42 percent.[25] As a result, longtime CEO John McCoy announced in December 1999 that he was taking early retirement at age 56. One analyst suggested that it was a positive change; the company was in need of new leadership.[26]

Managerial hubris can also continue after the acquisition and thereby harm the firm. For example, the merger of Daimler-Benz and Chrysler has not performed as well as expected. One year after the acquisition was completed, DaimlerChrysler's stock price had decreased by 8 percent and underperformed the S&P 500 by 25 percent. Yet sources suggest that Chairman Jurgen Schrempp purged several senior executives because they represented a threat to his dominance in the firm. The most critical casualty was Thomas Stallkamp, president of the firm's United States operations. Stallkamp played a key role in Chrysler's performance rebound in the early 1990s. He was also considered the firm's "spiritual" leader, helping to smooth the transition and integration for thousands of Chrysler employees after the acquisition.[27]

An Incomplete Due Diligence Process

Sometimes, firms conduct effective financial due diligence but do not consider other factors that are related to organizational, cultural, or possible human barriers in the process. For example, acquiring firms should carefully examine the list of customers and the length of time that customers have been buying products from the target firm. Additionally, the costs and revenues for continued operation or provision of the services should be forecasted. The target firm's culture should be examined.[28]

Often, potential synergies may seem significant on the surface, but existing organizational and cultural barriers may be less evident. We explore the concept of synergy further in Chapter 6.

If firms do not conduct a thorough due diligence, they may take actions immediately following an acquisition that produce harmful effects rather than positive outcomes. One example is Union Pacific's acquisition of Southern Pacific. Union Pacific implemented substantial cost-cutting actions immediately after its acquisition of Southern Pacific. It laid off thousands of experienced workers and consolidated the railyards of the two companies. However, multiple problems ensued. For example, three major train crashes shortly followed these actions. Cargo was lost and there was substantial chaos on the Union Pacific railways, leading to significant delays in the delivery of customers' goods. In short, the Union Pacific railways experienced gridlock. Union Pacific simply had not effectively analyzed the Southern Pacific Rail Corporation and the importance of its experienced employees in operating its lines. It was very difficult for Union Pacific to overcome this error. Many of its customers lost millions of dollars and were extremely angry about the railroad delays. In fact, one customer, Dow Chemical Co., filed a suit against Union Pacific, claiming that its delays had cost the company more than $25 million in a nine-month period. Similarly, Entergy Corporation also filed a suit for losses incurred because of delays in service. To overcome some of the problems experienced after the 1996 merger, Union Pacific hired almost 2,300 new employees in the first five and one-half months of 1998. Although Union Pacific claims that it has reduced derailments and improved its service, customers continue to complain about the poor service provided by the company.[29]

Among these horror stories are also examples of proper managerial action and effective due diligence that have paid dividends. Symbol Technologies, Inc. attempted to acquire Telxon Corporation in 1998, but managers at Telxon rebuffed the acquisition attempt. A few months later, Symbol Technologies provided a new offer to Telxon's management. The CEO of Telxon, in turn, communicated that his company might be willing to accept the offer if the deal was negotiated quickly, within a three-day period, and without the normal evaluation of the financial statements and supporting documents of Telxon. Symbol executives were unwilling to move that quickly without examining Telxon's books. Therefore, they insisted on a full due diligence process. Symbol's due diligence process showed that Telxon made some controversial and questionable decisions that effectively boosted its revenue by $14 million and provided a rich profit. In effect, Telxon had included in its sales revenues and profits a sale of $14 million of equipment to a computer equipment distributor. However, there was no purchase agreement with an end buyer. The financing of the computer distributor's inventory was backed by Telxon's suggesting that the transaction should not be reported as a sale. As a result, Telxon had to restate its earnings. This restatement showed that revenue was flat and profitability about at the break-even point. Immediately following the restatement, Telxon's stock decreased by 45 percent. Because of the due diligence, Symbol Technologies did not acquire Telxon. Clearly, the effective due diligence process followed by Symbol Technologies avoided substantial problems had the acquisition been consummated.[30]

External parties—especially investment bankers—are often hired to help acquiring firms avoid these errors and problems. Next, we examine the role and effect of investment bankers in mergers and acquisitions.

The Role of Investment Bankers

Mergers and acquisitions have become a major business for investment banking institutions. The top five investment banking institutions providing support for mergers and acquisitions are Merrill Lynch, Morgan Stanley Dean Witter, Goldman Sachs, Salomon Smith Barney, and Credit Suisse First Boston (CSFB). The role of investment bankers has increased even more in recent years because of large cross-border deals and the growing number of mergers and acquisitions in Europe (e.g., especially in Germany).[31] We examine cross-border acquisitions in greater depth in Chapter 10.

Investment bankers can add value to an acquisition by identifying appropriate acquisition targets and helping to value the acquisition. Thus, by finding appropriate acquisition targets that can provide increased economies of scope, economies of scale, and other types of synergy, investment bankers provide value. Additionally, their assistance in determining the acquisition price, and thus the appropriate premium to pay for a target firm, can be especially beneficial.[32]

Although investment banking has been criticized for its role in the merger and acquisition process, studies have shown that these institutions produce higher value for their acquiring firm clients, relative to the fees paid. However, studies also show a variance in the quality of advice provided by prominent investment banking institutions.[33] Therefore, choice of an investment banking advisor may be an important part of the due diligence process.

Investment Bank Fees and Advice

As noted, there has also been considerable criticism of investment banking firms. One criticism has aimed at the fees charged for providing services and advising acquiring firms. In fact, corporate executives have been some of the primary critics of what they believe to be exceptionally high fees.[34] One problem with these fees is that they are often contingent on the price paid for the target by the acquiring firm. This fee arrangement provides the wrong set of incentives for the investment banking firm and allows the opportunity for conflict of interest. A recent study showed a positive relationship between the premium paid for a target firm and the compensation given investment bankers. Because there are investment bankers on both sides of the acquisition, providing assistance to both the target and acquiring firms, this type of arrangement is not always undesirable. It is appropriate for the investment banking firm advising the target firm to attempt to achieve the highest price possible. In this case, target firm shareholders gain value from the investment banker. Alternatively, when investment bankers advising the acquiring firm earn more money because of a higher price paid by the acquiring firm, questions could arise about the propriety and appropriateness of the advice given.[35]

Another study, however, showed that the average investment banker advisory fee was 1.29 percent of the value of the completed acquisition. This is below the levels often represented in the popular business press. However, according to the contractual arrangements, most fees are largely contingent on the outcome of the acquisition negotiations, thereby offering investment bankers significant incentives to ensure that the acquisition is completed.[36]

There are a few examples of investment bankers abusing their advisory roles. One instance involves the acquisition of Republic Bank Corporation by InterFirst Corporation in the late 1980s. Goldman Sachs & Co. advised InterFirst, Morgan Stanley & Co. was an advisor to Republic Bank. Prior to the acquisition, InterFirst and Goldman Sachs & Co. obtained information that Republic Bank was overvaluing its $1 billion plus loan portfolio. Because of this, Republic Bank was actually much weaker than projected on paper. There is even evidence that this information was shared with Republic Bank's investment banker, Morgan Stanley & Co. None of these parties shared this information with investors. About $6.5 million was paid to Goldman Sachs and Morgan Stanley for providing fairness opinions. In total, Wall Street firms were paid approximately $13 million in fees, commissions, and other expenses. Regardless of the fees paid, First Republic Bank (the name of the bank after the two banks were merged) failed only 14 months after the acquisition was completed. First Republic shareholders, bondholders, and the Federal Deposit Insurance Corporation lost approximately $3 billion because of this transaction. While it is unclear how much information was shared between the investment banks and their clients, it is clear that none of it was shared with InterFirst stockholders. Obviously, if the information known to the investment banks had been revealed prior to the acquisition, it would never have been completed. After the bank failed, a number of investigations were conducted. It was shown that the due diligence process in this acquisition was questionable. In fact, the investment bankers conducted surprisingly little analysis on their own.[37]

Investment Banks and Competition

Today, there is increasing competition for the investment banking business. As a result, investment banks are now taking actions to ensure their lucrative business in the merger and acquisition market. In particular, investment banking institutions now focus on building an effective relationship with firms, particularly those active in the merger and acquisition market. For example, Peter J. Solomon Company served as an advisor to Office Depot in its $3.4 billion merger with Staples, Inc. Although Solomon is not a large investment banking firm, it cultivated a relationship with Office Depot's chief executive, David Fuente, over a period of approximately seven years. The relationship is so strong that Peter Solomon is a member of Office Depot's Board of Directors. As a result, Solomon has served as an advisor to several of Office Depot's major acquisitions including Office Club and Eastman, Inc.[38]

A recent study showed that investment banks' reputation may be critical to their long-term business. The study indicated that the banks' ability to build a reputation for truth and accuracy enabled them to be credible providers of information and advice in major merger and acquisition deals.[39] This is evident in the relationship that CSFB developed with Chrysler Corporation through over a decade of work for the automaker. Because of this long-term positive relationship, CSFB played an important role in the merger between Chrysler and Daimler-Benz. Similarly, Goldman Sachs developed a relationship with Daimler-Benz over several years and thus played a key role in advising that company in the DaimlerChrysler merger. The roles of both investment bankers were critical because of the complexity of this international merger.[40]

Nevertheless, the lucrative merger and acquisition business has drawn competitors. For example, auction houses and transaction advisors threaten to take over some of the investment bankers' business. In these cases, each type of business is much more specialized than the investment bankers. The transaction advisor basically helps a client sell or buy other properties. These advisors do provide a large amount of support in these activities, however. They collect raw data, calculate reserve reports, and negotiate final terms, as well as handle closings of the deals. These advisors may also provide marketing efforts to bring together buyers and sellers. The competition tends to be relatively fierce over small and medium-sized mergers and acquisitions. The investment bankers still hold the primary market for the larger mergers and acquisitions.[41]

While the larger more complex deals may require investment bankers, some of the smaller transactions that tend to be less complicated and more straightforward may not need the assistance of investment banks. Thus, some firms are attempting to handle the due diligence process internally to avoid the large investment banking fees. One study showed that firms conducting the due diligence process internally, compared to those using investment banks, achieved higher returns from the acquisitions. [42]

To combat competition, some investment banks have begun to market their services in a variety of ways. For example, the Japanese investment bank Yamaichi Securities has its own Web site in which it posts merger and acquisition activities for both buyers and sellers. This is the first attempt by a major investment bank to market its services to buyers and sellers on the Internet.[43]

We conclude from our analysis of investment bankers' involvement in mergers and acquisitions that they do add value to the transaction. Studies show that acquiring and target firms that employ top-tier investment bankers for advice on the transaction achieve higher returns than firms that do not use such investment banking firms for this purpose.[44]

Managerial Implications

We have presented information on the potential problems of conducting an inadequate due diligence process, as well as the competitive benefits available from a thorough due diligence process. Due diligence is often overlooked because of managerial hubris and the rush to complete the transaction. However, the due diligence process should help the acquiring firm avoid paying too high a premium or making an inappropriate acquisition. Our analysis of the due diligence process used in mergers and acquisitions leads us to the following recommendations.

1. Top executives must take special care to avoid managerial hubris in mergers and acquisitions.[45] Of course, the best way to avoid managerial hubris is to ensure a thorough due diligence process before making a decision to acquire another firm.
2. Acquiring firms should carefully choose those organizations and individuals from whom they seek advice on the acquisitions they undertake. For example, acquiring firms should only choose investment banking firms (whether large or small) that have strong positive reputations. That is, investment banking firms should be considered to have high integrity and only offer effective advice, even if that means advising a firm not to complete an acquisition (thereby reducing the amount of fees the investment bank is likely to earn).
3. While it is appropriate and potentially effective to link the fees paid to investment bankers to the acquisition price for the target (acquired) firm, the fee paid to investment bankers and other advisors by the acquiring firm should not be tied to the acquisition price. In these cases, linking the fees paid to the acquisition price produces the wrong set of incentives. It encourages these advisors to keep the acquisition price high.

4. Acquiring firms should follow a dynamic due diligence process such as that described in this chapter in all acquisition decisions.
5. Firms that are active in the market for corporate control (acquisition market) should pay careful attention to changes in governmental regulations and other standards in the approaches used in completing acquisitions. For example, in 1999, there was considerable emphasis in the United States on proposed accounting rule changes for valuing assets in mergers and acquisitions. In particular, the Financial Accounting Standards Board (FASB) considered a relatively controversial plan to limit the "pooling-of-interest" method of accounting for merged assets. Less than 5 percent of all United States domestic acquisitions involved this method, yet it was used in the largest mergers (amounting to 52.5 percent of the value of all mergers and acquisitions during 1998). [46] As described in Chapter 12, the FASB has eliminated this method effective January 1, 2001. Some acquiring firms may use advisors to provide them with the current information in this regard, but we recommend that acquiring firms stay abreast of such developments because they may affect their decision to make acquisitions.

Due diligence may be one of the most important activities for ensuring successful acquisitions. In the next chapter we examine the financing of acquisitions. In the 1970s, cash was the primary means of making an acquisition. In the 1980s, debt was the most popular financing mode. However, the 1990s were the decade of equity financing. Each means of financing has advantages and disadvantages.

3

Financing
an Acquisition

> If a company takes on debt to make an acquisition and the deal goes
> sour, it runs into financial trouble and the executives are replaced.
> But if an equity-backed deal goes wrong, the stock price simply
> underperforms and nobody can be sure why. One thing is certain—
> unwise acquisitions abound in this market.
>
> —Michael H. Lubatkin and Peter J. Lane

Even the best-intended acquisitions can result in financing-related corporate indigestion. For example, Hilton Hotels absorbed a $125 million loss to restructure debt after its acquisition of Bally Entertainment. Furthermore, a financing arrangement that makes sense for one combination may not work elsewhere. When First Union agreed to acquire Signet Banking in a stock transaction, the share prices of both companies fell. On the other hand, both Travelers and Citicorp enjoyed increases in their share prices when they agreed to join forces in an all-stock deal.[1]

In this chapter, we review recent acquisition financing trends. In addition, we explore the psychology of the market with regard to choice of financing methods and the dangers associated with the increased debt that often accompanies acquisitions. This chapter ends with a review of important considerations when planning to finance an acquisition.

Financing Trends

Acquisitions are financed through a cash purchase, an exchange of stock, or a combination of cash and stock. Among these three alternatives, cash is by far the preferred medium of exchange. Cash became a popular financing medium for mergers and acquisitions during the 1970s, when the percentage of takeovers for cash grew steadily from less than 20 percent in the late 1960s to over 50 percent by 1978.[2] As Figure 3.1 illustrates, pure cash transactions have dominated the other two methods over the past decade. Most recently, an increase in the incidence of pure stock exchanges was accompanied by a reduction in combined stock and cash transactions, but not pure cash transactions. The largest multibillion dollar deals typically are financed with stock. Because these deals receive a substantial amount of attention from the media, they might lead one to believe that stock deals are now more popular than cash deals. However, these megadeals do not account for a very large percentage of the total number of transactions. In large deals (over $100 million), cash transactions are still the most popular form of exchange, accounting for nearly 50 percent of the total.[3]

Several considerations guide the selection of a medium of exchange. Among the most important are tax considerations, accounting treatment, managerial control issues, financial returns to shareholders, and the existence of slack, which we define here as unused financial resources.[4]

Figure 3.1   Merger Financing Method

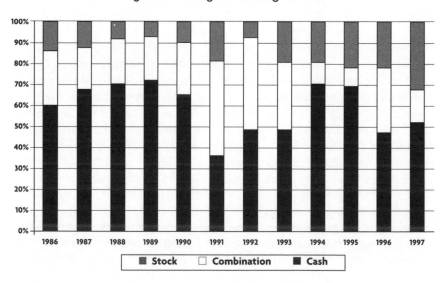

Note: Figures are as a percentage of all mergers in which method of financing was reported. Source: *Mergers and Acquisitions*, 1987–1998.

Tax Implications

The popularity of cash exchanges is surprising, especially in the United States, where taxes have favored stock transactions for many years. If at least 50 percent of a target's shares are exchanged for stock, the Internal Revenue Code has traditionally classified the acquisition as a "continuity of interests," which means that the transaction is nontaxable (tax deferred) to the target firm shareholders.[5] The $83 billion megamerger between Travelers and Citicorp was a nontaxable transaction. Also, United HealthCare's acquisition of Humana for $5.38 billion and British Petroleum's takeover of Amoco were nontaxable transactions.[6] Given the high premiums typically associated with an acquisition, the potential tax savings to target firm shareholders were enormous. Consider, for example, Ahmanson's unsolicited takeover proposal for Great Western Financial. The $6 billion deal by the nation's number one thrift to take over the number two firm in the industry represented a premium of approximately 24 percent over the previous market price of Great Western.[7] The taxable gain on the transaction, not counting any prior appreciation in stock price in anticipation of the announced acquisition, was over $1 billion to Great Western shareholders.

From the perspective of the acquiring firm, there may be a marginal difference in favor of a taxable transaction, because ownership rights are considered sold and the acquiring firm is allowed to step up the depreciation basis of the assets acquired. However, target firm shareholders are likely to expect a larger premium if they know their gains will be taxed. Brown and Ryngaert argue that, all things considered, "stock is at worst tax neutral and at best an advantage" in an acquisition.[8] Accounting convention and managerial control issues also favor a stock transaction.

Accounting Treatment

The medium of exchange influences the way an acquisition is treated for accounting purposes. Existing research evidence does not support the superiority of one type of accounting convention over another.[9] However, as a practical matter, stock transactions may allow accountants to create a more favorable picture with regard to future performance. Typically, stock deals may be accounted for as a pooling of interests, which means that the assets of the two firms are combined at book value (this ruling is changing, as we discuss in the final chapter). Pooling interests eliminates goodwill charges, thus boosting future earnings. On the other hand, all cash deals must be treated as a purchase, which means that excesses associated with the purchase price over the book value must be reported as goodwill in financial statements. To make matters worse, the goodwill is not deductible for tax purposes.

Investors who are trying to evaluate the performance of an acquisition should exercise caution due to these and other accounting variations. We are familiar with a situation that occurred recently in a Fortune 100 company. The president of a major division of the company was actively pursuing an acquisition target and target firm executives seemed anxious to sell. During the due diligence process, accountants at the acquiring firm uncovered several accounting "irregularities" in the target firm's statements that greatly reduced its reported financial performance. The potential acquirer backed away from the deal.

One common method for inflating future earnings is taking a huge, one-time, "restructuring" charge at or shortly after the time of acquisition. Stock traders tend to forgive companies for huge one-time charges. According to *Business Week*, "that's got investors and the SEC worried that companies are burying all sorts of normal operating expenses into their restructuring charges."[10] If normal operating expenses can be written off in advance, then future earnings will be higher.

In-process R&D charges may provide the greatest potential for accounting manipulation. These are charges representing the estimated value of research and development within the target firm at the time of acquisition. Since the R&D may prove worthless, some acquiring firms write it all off. However, any revenues that are gained from the R&D in the future will boost earnings. Since the expenses have already been written off, this is pure gain. For example, America Online tried to take a $20 million charge for in-process R&D associated with its $29 million acquisition of NetChannel. The SEC questioned the action (the Financial Accounting Standards Board is also attacking this accounting procedure, as we will discuss in the last chapter). Rather than delaying its quarterly earnings statements until the SEC challenge was resolved, AOL released incomplete figures. The market responded by reducing AOL's share price 5 percent.[11]

Managerial Control

If target firm managers value control in the combined company, they will prefer to receive stock. This point is especially relevant in targets with high levels of management ownership. In fact, receiving stock may be one way to increase the likelihood of job retention for target firm managers after the merger is complete because high executive turnover is common in acquisitions. For example, in the proposed stock-financed merger of Chrysler and Daimler-Benz, each firm was expected to receive the same number of board seats in the new company and the two current chairmen were to serve as co-chief executives for three years.[12] Also, Ghosh and Ruland demonstrated that managers of target firms are more likely to keep their jobs after acquisition when stock is the medium of exchange. In addition, they found that stock exchanges are common when managerial ownership of the target company is high.[13]

Managers of acquiring firms tend to favor stock financing when they have greater investment opportunities. Martin discovered that the greater the potential for growth in the acquiring firm, the more likely that managers will finance an acquisition with stock.[14] In these cases, the acquiring firm may want to conserve cash and borrowing potential to finance future growth. In addition, Martin found that stock financing is more common when the acquiring firm has experienced higher than normal stock returns prior to the acquisition. Both factors probably motivated the managers of Compaq Computer to finance the acquisition of Tandem Computers with stock. Compaq, once thought of as only a PC company, was aggressively expanding its product lines into complementary areas. Industry analysts noted that using stock instead of cash for the acquisition of Tandem preserved Compaq's flexibility to buy other companies.[15]

So far, these arguments all suggest that stock financing should be the preferred medium of exchange in acquisitions. Why then is cash so popular? The answer may be found in market psychology and the size of the premiums to the target firm shareholders.

Market Psychology

The psychology of market participants helps explain the popularity of cash transactions. Wansley, Lane, and Yang and others offered evidence that the choice of financing sends signals to the market. When management of the bidding firm believes that its own stock is overvalued, securities are the preferred form of payment.[16] For example, bidding firm managers may have unfavorable private information about their equity value. However, the market will read this signal and adjust its evaluation of the bidder accordingly. For example, BancOne's stock experienced a decline of 8.9 percent after announcing the share exchange rate to be used in its acquisition of First USA. A $7.3 billion sale became a $6.65 billion sale, an immediate loss of $650 million for First USA shareholders.[17] Consequently, target firm shareholders may prefer a fixed payment, as opposed to absorbing a stock price devaluation if the market considers the purchase price too high.

Some of this market psychology has to do with information that one firm has that the other doesn't. According to Hansen, "When a target firm knows its own value better than a potential acquirer, the acquirer will prefer to offer stock, which has desirable contingent-pricing characteristics, rather than cash."[18] In other words, the acquiring firm will reduce its risk of incorrect payment by causing the target firm shareholders to absorb a portion of this risk. In these situations, the future of both firms is linked through joint ownership. However, target firm managers and owners may be reluctant to absorb the risk.

Market psychology thus favors cash transactions. Stock-financed acquisitions lead to increased risk for target firm shareholders. Also, acquiring firm managers may be concerned that they are providing the wrong signals to the market. When acquiring and target firms are public and reliable information is available on the target, a cash transaction is often preferable for both companies. In addition, cash deals provide higher immediate returns to both acquiring and target companies.

Financial Returns to Shareholders

Wachovia Corp., a very conservative southern bank, experienced a decrease in its stock price when it agreed to buy Central Fidelity Banks. So also did Columbia/HCA Healthcare when it signed an agreement to acquire Value Health. When Bell Atlantic and GTE confirmed plans to merge, both stock prices dropped.[19] All these deals were pure stock transactions and all are indicative of the type of stock returns to be expected when stock-financed transactions are announced. The market often penalizes both companies for stock deals, perhaps due to the psychological factors discussed previously.

For acquiring firms, abnormal (unexpected) stock price adjustments often are negative for the period immediately surrounding the announcement of an acquisition. Many years of research on mergers and acquisitions have demonstrated almost overwhelmingly that higher than normal stock returns for acquiring firms are unlikely. However, stock transactions perform even worse than cash transactions.[20]

Target firm stock returns are also higher in cash transactions. Target firms experience abnormal stock price increases of almost 34 percent in cash acquisitions, compared to approximately 17 percent in stock deals.[21] In the 1990s, for example, premiums over market value averaged between 25 and more than 50 percent for target companies.[22] However, this is a significant reduction compared to the early 1990s, when average premiums were over 50 percent. Of course, premiums can reach as high as 100 percent, as seen in Hercules' agreement to purchase BetzDearborn.[23] The large premium was explained as the result of a then current general slump in stock prices in the industry, which meant that BetzDearborn was undervalued. Although this may have been true, the excessive premium was at least partially a result of Hercules' anxiousness to complement its existing paper products lines with those obtained from BetzDearborn as well as a desire to expand into new segments. As a result of high premiums, institutions such as mutual fund managers and banks that own large blocks of stock in a target company encourage target firm managers to seek cash transactions.[24]

Conventional wisdom and some early research evidence suggest that tender offers, in which the bidding firm makes a public offer to purchase outstanding shares directly from shareholders, provide the highest returns for target firm shareholders. However, research has demonstrated that the difference in returns is due to the high incidence of cash as the medium of exchange in tender offers, as well as the tendency for target firms to resist unexpected tender offers.[25]

Also, while cash deals lead to higher shareholder returns when the target is a publicly owned company, this does not hold for private targets. When targets are privately held, bidding firms experience abnormal increases in their share prices. No increases were observed when the proposed acquisition was for cash.[26] Several factors explain these surprising findings. First, there may be limited competition for a private target because the stock is not publicly held; therefore, potential acquiring firms must strike a deal directly with the owners. Second, an acquisition of a private company for stock creates a group of shareholders that hold large blocks of stock. These blockholders may be better monitors of the management in the combined company. Finally, much of the negative effect from market psychology may disappear because more accurate and complete information is passed between the bidding firm and the target.

The available evidence regarding shareholder returns supports a strong trend in favor of cash as the preferred medium of exchange in acquisitions. Shareholders of both acquiring and target firms gain higher returns (or, in the case of the acquiring firm, less negative returns) in cash transactions compared to stock deals. A final factor, slack, may also lead to a higher incidence of cash transactions.

Slack

The Swiss drugmaker Roche agreed to pay about $11 billion to acquire Corange, the parent company of the German company Boehringer Mannheim GmbH, the number two diagnostics company in the world. Although this was a lofty sum for a cash transaction, Roche had a cash balance of five billion Swiss francs ($3.54 billion U.S.) and ample ability to obtain the rest of the money without issuing stock.[27] Therefore, Roche had considerable slack in the form of unused financial resources.

Acquirers with higher cash balances seem to prefer cash-financed acquisitions; however, some evidence exists to the contrary.[28] The issue is a subject of debate. Michael Jensen of the Harvard Business School argues that free cash flow is invested in projects with negative net present value rather than paying it out to shareholders. If managers have access to substantial amount of cash, they may engage in unprofitable or hasty acquisitions to spend it. Jensen's argument has found some support from researchers who study acquisitions.[29] However, two countervailing forces are at work. The existence of slack, whether in the form of large amounts of cash or excess borrowing capacity, may cause managers to seek an acquisition. However, it also can facilitate the acquisition process, in essence making an acquisition easier to digest.

In our own research, we discovered substantial financial slack in nearly half of the most successful acquisitions. Slack was commonly in the form of large amounts of available cash or a highly favorable debt position, which allows potential significant borrowing with minimal stress (e.g., low interest rate). In one of the highly successful acquisitions, Unilever had $1.5 billion in cash and obtained a bank credit line of up to $3 billion to purchase Cheesborough-Ponds. The $3.7 billion transaction included $2.2 billion in new debt; however, Unilever quickly reduced this burden by selling some of Cheeseborough-Ponds' nonrelated businesses. Not only did these sales make sense financially, they allowed Unilever to focus available resources on a narrower group of businesses. In another of the most successful acquisitions, the *target* company had significant slack. Signal Companies had a low debt-to-equity ratio of only 25 percent when acquired by Allied.[30] Consequently, the debt-to-equity ratio of the newly combined company was lower due to Signal's pre-merger financial position.

In a well-known work, Jay Bourgeois argued that slack can allow an organization to adapt successfully to changes inside and outside the company. He also pointed out that slack can facilitate strategic change.[31] Acquisitions require enormous internal changes associated with integrating factors such as management systems, information systems, organization structures, schedules, routines, accounting methods, pensions, and compensation systems, to name only a few. They also require adjustments to strategy. The existence of slack can reduce pressure during these integration processes. In essence, slack allows managers to catch their breath.

To summarize the significant points of this chapter so far, we first documented the popularity of cash as the medium of exchange in acquisitions. This trend is surprising given the favorable tax treatment of stock deals in the United States. Also, managerial control and longevity favor stock. Nevertheless, cash deals provide higher stock returns for target firm shareholders and less negative returns for bidding firm shareholders. Market psychology also favors use of cash because the use of stock may signal that acquiring firm management believes its stock is overvalued. In addition, high levels of slack can motivate managers to use cash financing. The existence of slack is closely related to a firm's debt position. Debt, which is discussed in the next section, has a profound influence on the success or failure of an acquisition.

The Importance of Debt

In our study of highly successful and unsuccessful acquisitions, debt was the only factor important to both groups. Eighty-three percent of our successful acquisitions had low to moderate debt while 92 percent of the unsuccessful acquisitions we studied had large or extraordinary debt.[32] As might be expected, the successful acquisitions that demonstrated slack also had low to moderate debt levels. Other acquisitions kept debt levels low through the use of stock. We noticed that some acquiring firms used high levels of debt financing for the acquisition, but then paid the debt down quickly. For example, Textron's debt-to-equity ratio was only 16 percent prior to its acquisition of AVCO, which indicates substantial slack with regard to borrowing potential. After its $1.4 billion acquisition of AVCO, Textron's debt-to-equity ratio jumped to 70 percent. However, Textron sold off businesses, most from its own firm and a few from AVCO, to reduce its ratio to 40 percent.

Some of the unsuccessful acquisitions compiled truly extraordinary debt. For example, Ecolab increased its total debt 265 percent in its $500,000 purchase of Chemlawn. After the purchase, Ecolab had a debt-to-equity ratio of 2.13, which led to dismal financial performance for several years. Similarly, Kratos borrowed $49 million in its acquisition of Keuffel & Esser, resulting in total debt of $72 million. The $49 million was borrowed at an interest rate of 17.75 percent, making its annual interest payment on the new debt greater than the combined annual net income of the two companies. Ultimately, Kratos delayed installment payments on its debt due to inadequate cash flows. U.S. Steel used $3 billion of debt to purchase Marathon Oil, resulting in two reductions in its debt rating by Standard & Poor's within a nine-month period. Similarly, Kleer Vu's acquisition of Nestle-Lemur led to a debt-to-equity ratio approaching 2.0. Each of the acquiring firms mentioned experienced significant net losses after their acquisitions due, at least in part, to significant financing costs.

These examples demonstrate the important role debt plays in acquisition financing. In the sections that follow, we describe the sources of debt in acquisitions and the negative influences high debt levels can have on acquisition performance. Finally, we recommend the means to maintain minimum debt levels in an acquisition and how to determine if an acquisition has a low probability of contributing to competitive success at any price.

Sources of Debt in Acquisitions

Acquisitions can be very expensive in the best of circumstances. However, several factors make acquisitions even more expensive. Premiums, which often average over 30 percent, are a major source of additional expense. The fact that organizations routinely pay huge premiums above market value is alarming. The stock market is not entirely accurate, but it is at least semi-efficient in establishing the differential value of securities. From one perspective, premiums paid for targets represent an estimate of the value added from the combination that could not be achieved separately. However, the evidence cited throughout this book does not support such a view.[33] In fact, Jay Barney argued that without the rare presence of a unique synergistic opportunity between the buyer and seller that is unavailable to other potential buyers, the acquiring firm will bid up the price to a value that is equal to or greater than the value of the target firm.[34] Consequently, a high premium probably is more closely related to managerial motivations associated with power, pride, or control (described in Chapter 2) than to shareholder interests.[35]

High premiums are easy to find. Marsh & McLennan, the world's largest insurance broker, agreed to a 57 percent premium for Britain's Sedgewick, the third largest broker, in an effort to increase its dominance in the U.S. insurance brokerage industry. The 100 percent premium Hercules paid to acquire Betz-Dearborn was mentioned earlier. These were both cash transactions, but premiums are also high in stock deals. Cardinal Health agreed to buy Owen Healthcare in a stock swap with a value of about $484 million. This represented a 59 percent premium.[36] Premiums are even higher when there are multiple bidders for the same target.

Target firm resistance also can lead to high premiums. Lotus Development agreed to be acquired by IBM for $64 per share after offering resistance to a $60 per share unsolicited offer. The $64 price is nearly a 100 percent premium from Lotus's market value before IBM's initial offer. Vodafone originally offered a 12.5 percent premium in its bid for Mannesmann. However, after the offer was rejected by Mannesmann's supervisory board, Vodafone sweetened the deal an additional 16 percent. Also expensive are "white knight" situations, in which an acquiring firm emerges to "save" the target from an unwelcome or undesirable suitor. The thirteenth largest acquisition in 1997, the $6.8 billion "white knight" acquisition of Great Western Financial by Washington Mutual, was nearly 4 percent higher than a hostile bid from Ahmanson & Co.[37]

Mark Sirower describes excessive premiums as anything over 25 percent. "Because synergies are so difficult to achieve even with a sound strategy, once you cross the 25 percent threshold, you're really piling on the risk." In the meantime, "the clock is ticking on the extra money you've paid." Sirower estimated that to recover a 50 percent acquisition premium, an acquirer would have to increase the return on equity in the target firm by 12 percent in each of the years two through nine after the acquisition.[38]

Premiums, while potentially very expensive, are only one of many costs associated with acquisitions. Consultants, investment bankers, and law firms all receive large fees for their roles in acquisitions. Advisory fees have been rising steadily. In 1997, the average total advisory fees were $6.78 million per deal, up from $2.82 million in 1996. The $6.78 million figure was about 3 percent of the average price of an acquisition for the same year.[39] The 3 percent in fees buys nothing tangible, nor does it disappear with a stock-only transaction. Furthermore, there is potential for a conflict of interest between investment bankers and the acquiring firms they represent. When a high premium is paid by an acquiring firm, investment banking advisors' fees are also often high. This does not represent a problem for target firms because high premiums are advantageous to target firm shareholders. However, it does create a misalignment of objectives between bidding firms and the bankers representing them.[40]

Post-acquisition costs are also a significant factor in acquisitions. These costs are associated with such items as legal fees, plant closings, relocations, layoff of redundant employees, and integration of information and accounting systems. Tenet Healthcare reported $467.7 million in charges mainly related to its acquisition of OrNda Healthcare. Similarly, Foundation Health Systems recorded $405.9 million in charges and costs related to the merger of the two companies that created it. This amount was about double expectations. Underestimating integration costs is very typical in acquisitions. Mattel took a charge of $175 million to integrate Tyco, which included about $60 million in legal, accounting, and investment banking fees for the transaction. Tyco only cost Mattel $755 million, so these expenses are nearly one-quarter of the cost of the target.[41]

The expenses described so far in this section have an indirect effect on debt. That is, they reduce slack and create the need to assume more debt. These types of costs are especially detrimental to organizations because they are unproductive—they do not lead to production of the goods and services provided by the organization. Acquisitions also have a direct effect on debt. Obviously, a cash transaction can result in higher debt levels, as an organization borrows money to make the purchase. Price Communications only had about $41 million in cash and $60.5 million in working capital when it decided to acquire Palmer Wireless for $506 million, plus the assumption of $380 million in debt. Price was relying on a syndicate of lenders for a $500 million loan and also planning to issue over $200 million in high yield debt often referred to as "junk bonds" to cover the rest of the acquisition costs.[42]

Typically, acquisitions also involve the assumption of a significant amount of debt from the acquired firm. For example, AT&T announced that it would acquire TCI for $37.3 billion in cash and securities, plus the assumption of $11 billion in debt. News of the deal reduced AT&T's share price 8.2 percent. Westinghouse bought American Radio Systems for $1.6 billion, plus the assumption of $1 billion in debt. Westinghouse was already mired in debt from a $7.5 billion bank loan associated with its acquisition of CBS.[43]

Pure stock financing does not eliminate the effect of an acquisition on debt levels. Transaction and integration costs are still absorbed by the acquiring firm in a stock deal. Also, the assumption of large amounts of debt is common in stock transactions. For example, PhyCor assumed $1.2 billion in debt related to its stock swap acquisition of MedPartners. PhyCor's stock lost three-quarters of its value during the year after the MedPartners merger and the company lowered its earnings forecasts several times.[44] Sometimes the value of the debt assumed can exceed other consideration. For instance, JP Foodservice paid $689.2 million in stock for Rykoff-Sexton, but also assumed $700 million in debt.[45]

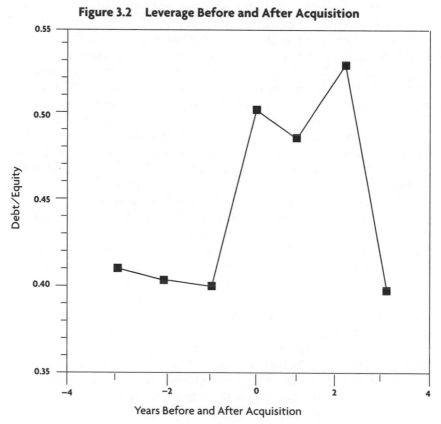

Figure 3.2   Leverage Before and After Acquisition

Years Before and After Acquisition

Note: M. A. Hitt, R. E. Hoskisson, R. D. Ireland, and J. S. Harrison, 1991. Are acquisitions a poison pill for innovation? *Academy of Management Executive* 5(4): 26.

In summary, acquisitions are expensive. In addition to any borrowing that may occur in a cash transaction, both cash and stock transactions typically involve the assumption of large amounts of debt. High premiums, advisory fees, other transaction costs, and post-acquisition integration expenses can lead to even higher debt levels. In one of our earlier studies, we discovered an average increase in debt to equity of over 25 percent in the year of acquisition, including stock, cash, and combination deals.[46] As illustrated in Figure 3.2, debt did not return to normal levels in the combined firms for three years. We will discuss the negative effects of high debt levels in the next section.

Influences of Debt on Acquisition Performance

Time assumed approximately $14 billion in new debt to acquire Warner Communications. Following the transaction, Time Warner chairman Gerald Levin felt a great deal of pressure from shareholders to reduce debt. Similarly, Disney added $10 billion in new debt to acquire Capital Cities/ABC. Disney Chairman Michael Eisner admitted that taking on that much debt was one of the toughest business decisions he has made in his career. Herbert Allen of Allen & Co., a major consulting firm, warns that in some cases these highly leveraged companies "will be fighting their way out of it for years to come."[47] Debt servicing costs can reduce earnings performance directly. Since acquisitions are associated with such high debt levels, it is an uphill battle to make them profitable.

High debt levels also increase the likelihood of bankruptcy, which can lead to a downgrade in the firm's credit rating from rating agencies such as Standard & Poor's or Moody's. This makes future debt more difficult to obtain (i.e., at higher interest rates). Such was the case with Mallinckrodt's purchase of Nellcor Puritan for $1.9 billion, saddling the combined company with "a significant financial burden." Fears about "financial flexibility" and "business uncertainties" led both Standard & Poor's and Moody's to review Mallinckrodt's debt for a possible downgrade in its rating. Although Nellcor would have added to Mallinckrodt's strong position in healthcare products, leading industry experts to conclude that the deal made strategic sense, the market still responded by bidding down the price of Mallinckrodt's stock by nearly 4 percent on the day of the announcement.[48]

Debt servicing associated with acquisitions may also divert resources away from other important areas. Activities with short-term costs but long-term payoffs such as human resource training and research and development are among the first to be reduced. Advertising and quality control may also be cut. In addition, the need to reduce payrolls to cover debt payments can lead to layoffs. Mattel, after acquiring Tyco, planned to lay off 2,700 employees in the combined company. The total number of employees at Tyco was only 2,200, so Mattel had to cut deeply into its own workforce to achieve the required number.[49] While layoffs sometimes are designed to eliminate redundancies and achieve economies of scale in a newly combined company, these layoffs appeared excessive relative to these objectives.

With regard to debt's negative effect on research and development, we discovered that acquisitions are associated with both reductions in R&D activities and reductions in the patents resulting from R&D. We believe that reductions in innovative activities are, in part, a result of the diversion of funds away from R&D to service debt. However, the higher leverage also causes managers to be more risk averse. Basically, they cannot afford to fail in a risky R&D project because they know that the firm has to service its debt. Also, some of our own research demonstrates that firms may use acquisitions as a substitute for internally driven innovation. In fact, our research shows that firms reducing their investment in R&D and bringing fewer new products to the market often acquire other firms to gain access to their R&D and new products. This is similar to a make-or-buy decision. Rather than generating new ideas and products internally, acquiring firms buy new ideas and products in the form of an acquisition.[50]

In contrast to the negative effects associated with high levels of debt, low levels of debt, a form of slack, can mitigate the negative effects from an acquisition. Some scholars have argued that debt is necessary as a disciplinary force for managers.[51] We do not accept this view as it relates to mergers and acquisitions. For example, research found that too little slack, in general, discouraged experimentation in 264 functional departments of two multinational corporations.[52] While the research also found that too much slack fostered complacency with regard to innovation, organizations involved in an acquisition are unlikely to have too much slack. The often substantial expenses associated with the acquisition absorb it. Consequently, we do not see a downside with regard to slack in acquisitions, either in the form of low debt levels or high levels of cash. Low to moderate debt levels may also allow managers more strategic flexibility, which is necessary for success in a dynamic and hypercompetitive environment.[53]

This section has outlined the sources and negative effects associated with high debt levels and the potential positive effects of low debt and slack. High debt levels are related to acquisitions because of borrowing associated with the purchase price, which can be much higher in auctions, "white knight" situations, or when the potential target resists acquisition. Debt levels in the acquiring firm also can increase dramatically due to the assumption of debt from the target company. Interest costs associated with acquisition-related debt reduce potential gains from the combination of companies. In addition, the fund used to service debt may be diverted away from activities with long-term payoffs such as research and development. In the final section, we offer suggestions that will help minimize debt and increase the probability of a successful acquisition.

Successful Acquisition Financing

In this chapter, we have outlined acquisition financing trends and the consequences of various financing tactics. As a summary of our analysis, we offer the following specific recommendations about acquisition financing:

1. Try to keep premiums low. Avoid auctions. Don't be a White Knight. If the target firm resists, be willing to walk away. Don't let ego lead to a foolish price.
2. Try to keep advisory fees at a minimum. When Disney acquired Capital Cities/ABC, it used Wolfensohn & Co. and Bear Stearns & Co. instead of selecting merger titans at Goldman Sachs or Morgan Stanley. CEOs, who know more about the value of their companies than bankers and other external advisors, should act as the primary negotiators.[54]
3. Seek a private company if possible. If the target is private, finance with stock to keep debt levels lower.
4. Be wary of potential accounting manipulations that may lead to a distorted picture of the value of a target or, from the perspective of investors, mask the actual performance of an acquisition.
5. Expect, and plan for, large post-acquisition integration expenses. Unexpectedly high post acquisition costs can lead to ineffective behaviors that may be detrimental to the long term, such as cutting R&D, selling off strategically valuable assets, or instituting painful human resource reductions.
6. Keep debt at manageable levels. If debt increases substantially as a result of an acquisition, pay it down as soon as possible. Maintaining a low debt level does not necessarily require using a stock transaction because cash deals tend to have higher short-term stock returns for both acquiring and target companies.
7. If the bidding firm has substantial financial slack, whether in the form of cash or additional borrowing capacity, strongly consider a cash purchase.
8. If stock financing is used, be extra careful about the premium paid. If an acquiring firm pays too much, its stock will be devalued in the market and the target firm shareholders will lose much of their value in the purchase.
9. If a company already has high debt levels, it should not consider

making an acquisition. Even a pure stock deal can lead to higher debt due to transactions costs, post-integration costs, and debt assumed from the target. Clearly, junk bonds should not be used. The detrimental effects on activities with long-term consequences such as R&D, combined with the relatively high interest expenses, make these types of acquisitions a higher probability for failure.

If these recommendations make a potential acquisition seem unwise, other alternatives may still be pursued. Texaco and Shell Oil agreed to merge much of their marketing and refining businesses through a joint venture. A joint venture is an excellent way to experience some of the same potential synergies that are available in an acquisition, but without all the additional costs. Likewise, Germany's Krupp suspended its takeover proposal for rival Thyssen, but the firms agreed to discuss combining their steel businesses.[55]

Partial acquisitions are another way to limit market influences associated with auctions or market psychology, much like a private firm acquisition. For example, Pacific Gas & Electric agreed to acquire only the natural gas business of Valero Energy. Similarly, Merrill Lynch bought a division of Barclay's Global Investors.[56] Some partial acquisitions include contingent payments, which can keep the initial price low. Contingent payments mean that the seller continues to receive income from the divested business, based on future performance, in exchange for a lower sales price. According to *Mergers & Acquisitions*, there were only 105 deals with contingent payments in 1997. However, this was a 44 percent increase over the 1996 total of 73. This change may be an indication that the popularity of this financing alternative is increasing.[57]

Acquisitions are an expensive and high-risk strategy. However, organizations with sufficient slack, including low debt levels, are more likely to enjoy performance increases through acquisition than highly leveraged firms with little or no slack. Organizations with high leverage should not consider acquisitions. However, joint ventures, partial acquisitions, and other alternatives might achieve some of the same purposes with less financial strain.

Many merger experts believe that the key to a successful acquisition is similarity between acquirer and target. In the next chapter, we will demonstrate that this common prescription for good fortune may not be so wise after all.

4

Looking
for Complementary
Resources

I am confident that by combining R&D excellence with marketing
strength and financial power, Glaxo SmithKline will lead the industry into the future. This will give us a major competitive advantage
to succeed in the fast-changing healthcare environment.

—Jean-Pierre Garnier of SmithKline Beecham

The two companies (Glaxo and SmithKline) have complementary
drug portfolios, and a merger will let them pool their research and
development funds and will give the merged company a bigger sales
and marketing force.

—a comment from a business analyst

Finalized in February 1999, the $4 billion merger between Oryx Energy
Co. and Kerr-McGee Corp. is an example of a transaction that company
executives believe will allow the sharing of complementary resources. As
the world's fourth-largest independent oil and gas exploration and
production company, the merged firm (with Kerr-McGee Corporation as
its new name) is thought to have the potential needed to increase shareholder value. At the time of the merger's announcement, Luke R.
Corbett, the chairman and CEO of Kerr-McGee, suggested the expectation of enhanced performance. In Corbett's view, "This strategic merger
creates value for both Kerr-McGee and Oryx shareholders. The companies have complementary skill sets and assets, particularly in the Gulf of
Mexico and the North Sea. Kerr-McGee brings a strong balance sheet,

exploration and exploitation opportunities and development expertise [while] Oryx brings a significant inventory of exploration prospects and technical expertise, particularly in the deepwater area of the Gulf of Mexico."[1] Financial analysts supported the position that this merger allowed the melding of complementary resources. In fact, their consensus was that Kerr-McGee would indeed benefit by gaining access to Oryx's expertise in oil exploration and development. Complementing these resources and skills were Kerr-McGee's financial resources; resources that would support the development of energy sources that Oryx owned in Asia, South America, and the Gulf of Mexico. Early results from the merger of these two firms were positive. Speaking to this matter, company officials observed in early 2000 that the newly created firm was on track to reach its target of $100 million in annualized pretax savings. Thus, in this instance, the combining of complementary resources was helping the firm improve its performance and reach its performance-related objectives.[2]

In this chapter, we discuss the pursuing and using of *complementary resources*—the third of the attributes that we found in our study to be associated with effective merger and acquisition activity. We consider *resources* in a broad and comprehensive sense. Drawing from the work of those studying this topic, we believe that a firm's resources include "all assets, capabilities, organizational processes, firm attributes, information, knowledge, etc. controlled by a firm that enable the firm to conceive of and implement strategies that improve its efficiency and effectiveness."[3] As special assets, skills, and capabilities, resources are the unifying thread through which firms seek to develop the innovative goods and services that are required for success in the highly competitive global marketplace.[4] Strategically valuable resources are those that allow the firm to exploit specific environmental opportunities or to protect itself from environmental threats.[5]

Complementary resources exist when the resources being combined between the acquiring and target firms are different, yet mutually supportive. In contrast, *resource similarity* indicates a situation in which there is a significant overlap between the resources of the acquiring and the acquired firms. Such overlap can exist in terms of both the types and quantities of resources possessed by the two firms.

The experiences of companies and the work of those studying merger and acquisition success indicate that the melding of *complementary* rather than *highly similar* resources between firms involved in a merger or an acquisition increases the probability that economic value will be created.[6] A key reason for this is that firms with highly similar resources also have highly similar strategic capabilities and vulnerabilities in the marketplace.[7] Thus, a merger or acquisition that combines highly similar resources can result in a newly created firm that will encounter larger quantities of virtually the same environmental opportunities and threats that they faced as independent entities. Given this evidence, it is economically rational (within the constraints of limited information, cognitive biases, and causal ambiguity) for firms in the pursuit of competitive advantages and marketplace success to seek combinations of complementary instead of highly similar or even identical resources.[8]

As with the merger between Oryx Energy Co. and Kerr-McGee Corp., the merger between Citicorp and Travelers demonstrates the joining of resources that are different, yet mutually supportive. This $70 billion merger created a megabank with over $700 billion in assets. The primary intent of this transaction was to combine these firms' resources to create a financial institution that would be, as the world's first universal retail bank, a unique global franchise.[9] As a merged entity, Citigroup is the product of combining a global bank (Citicorp) with insurance (e.g., Travelers Life & Annuity) and brokerage-related products and services (e.g., Salomon Smith Barney). By integrating different, yet complementary financial products (e.g., Citibank's certificates of deposit and Salomon Smith Barney's indexed stock funds) with different, yet complementary distribution channels (e.g., bank financial counselors with insurance representatives), Citigroup expects to gain increased percentages of customers' total financial transactions. The ability to effectively combine the resources that were owned by the formerly independent firms is thought to be critical to Citigroup's ability to gain the competitive benefits that accrue through the use of complementary resources.[10]

In early 2000, John S. Reed and Sanford I. Weill, then Chairmen and Co-Chief Executive Officers of Citigroup, observed that resources were being combined successfully. In their words, "The year that has passed since the group-breaking business combination that created Citigroup has been marked by significant achievements. Our integrated businesses are performing exceptionally well, revenue building and cross-selling efforts are well underway and demonstrably successful, and the expense reductions and integration efficiencies achieved to date provide a solid foundation for incremental earnings growth in 2000."[11] Supporting this positive assessment of the value being created by combining complementary resources were the increase of 250 percent in core income per diluted share on a year-to-year basis between the third quarters of 1998 and 1999 and the earning of a return on equity (ROE) of 21.9 percent in 1999's third quarter. This ROE level exceeded the stated goal of a 20 percent return.

Competitive benefits through the use of complementary resources are gained when synergy has been created. Synergy has an important relationship with complementary resources *and* with the successful integration and operation of firms once a merger or acquisition has been completed. We discuss the first aspect of synergy in this chapter; we consider the second aspect in Chapter 6.

Pursuing Synergy—A Critical Objective
of Merger and Acquisition Activity

Firms engage in merger and acquisition activity for many reasons. Effective mergers and acquisitions can, for example: (1) serve as a platform for corporate growth, (2) lead to increased market share, (3) provide the foundations required to generate and gain advantages from economies of scale (these are benefits that accrue when the firm is able to use its resources to drive costs lower across multiple products; scale economies are acquired primarily at the operational level) and economies of scope (these are benefits realized through using one unit's resources in the operations of another unit), and (4) reduce organizational expenses by eliminating duplication and transferring knowledge between and among business units and/or individual product lines.[12] The increasing amount of acquisition activity occurring among car dealerships in the United States demonstrates intentions to help firms achieve one or more of these desirable outcomes.

Paying four to six times pretax earnings for choice targets, firms acquiring automobile and truck dealerships typically seek the additional market share and profitability that are associated with the target's brand name and physical location. For example, to increase the size of its markets and to share complementary resources across dealerships to gain economies of scale, Republic Industries Inc. acquires firms that sell different brands (including products from General Motors, Nissan Motor Company, and BMW, among others). These newly acquired dealerships are located in various states such as Georgia, Texas, Florida, and Washington.[13] As a further indication of its desire to share resources in the pursuit of economies of scope, Republic also continues to acquire car rental companies. Currently, Republic is the only firm that has "integrated retail sales of autos with rentals within the same house."[14] However, benefiting from the attempt to combine what appear to be complementary resources is proving difficult. Observing this reality, some analysts concluded that AutoNation's used car concept (a concept in which customers would select from massive inventories of carefully selected cars) was flawed. Accounting for the concept's ineffectiveness is the fact that the firm had to buy most of its used cars at auctions where it had to pay as much as the smallest dealer. Thus, the combining of brands and locations as complementary resources to compete in the used car business did not yield the return the firm anticipated resulting in a change in the firm's strategy.[15]

The Importance of Synergy

Firms gain intended benefits from merger and acquisition activity, including those mentioned above, when the merger or acquisition creates *synergy*. Frequently elusive, synergy is pursued diligently by executives leading most companies, especially large ones.[16] Although challenging, pursuing synergy is enticing in that, when managed well, synergy allows firms to create additional value through the combination of existing resources.

Gripped in what one analyst called "synergy fever," Wall Street reacts favorably when it believes that a merger or acquisition will create synergy. Increases in the value of firms' stock demonstrate a favorable reaction. This was the case following the announcement of the merger between Chemical Banking and Chase Manhattan. Chase shares increased by almost 11 percent while Chemical shares increased roughly 9.6 percent immediately following the announcement of the firms' intentions. Among others, one reason for this positive outcome for both firms' shareholders was the expectation that the sharing of Chase and Chemical's complementary resources would result in significant cost reductions, increasing the newly created firm's operational efficiency as a result.[17] In commenting about Walter V. Shipley's legacy when he retired as Chairman of Chase Manhattan Corp. in 2000, analysts spoke quite favorably about the performance of the combined firm, noting that following its creation in 1996, "the combined bank had become a huge multinational institution with leading businesses in retail banking, wholesale lending, underwriting and loan syndications, trading, advisory and venture capital."[18]

Mergers and acquisitions are sometimes completed because the melding of two firms' complementary resources will allow the newly created company to create synergy through the filling of geographic and/or product gaps that existed in the independent entities. The merger between Daimler-Benz and Chrysler Corporation is a case in point.

Through the firm's assets, skills, and capabilities, Daimler-Benz's cars had become known widely for their luxury and sterling engineering. Using its resources, Chrysler had become renowned for its low-cost manufacturing of minivans, sport utility vehicles, and trucks. In terms of geographic coverage, Chrysler had chosen to remain virtually a domestic producer, deriving 93 percent of its sales from the United States market. Daimler-Benz, on the other hand, had developed distribution channels in multiple countries. In fact, at the time of the merger, Daimler-Benz was generating 63 percent of its revenues throughout all of Europe rather than only in Germany, its domestic market.

One intention of this merger was to allow each of the formerly independent companies to strengthen its position in its partner's home market through the sharing of complementary resources. Similarly, Chrysler's low-cost production expertise was to be melded with Daimler-Benz's superior engineering skills to generate new products for both companies.[19] Juergen E. Schrempp, Chairman of the Management Board of Daimler-Benz, labeled this sharing of complementary components and technologies as critical to the merged firm's success. In Schrempp's words, "Both companies have dedicated and skilled workforces and successful products, but in different markets and different parts of the world. By combining and utilizing each other's strengths, we will have a pre-eminent strategic position in the global marketplace for the benefit of our customers . . . and shareholders."[20]

Analysts and company officials alike consider this merger to be bold and profound. A merger or acquisition of a significant magnitude such as the one between Daimler-Benz and Chrysler can affect the nature of competition within an industry. Daimler-Benz's Juergen Schrempp believes, for example, that the merger between his firm and Chrysler was historic in nature and that it would change the face of the automotive industry. Analysts seemed to be in agreement with this perspective. *Business Week* writers, for example, offered the following opinion about this merger: "By combining forces, Daimler, Germany's biggest industrial concern, and Chrysler, America's No. 3 carmaker, bring a range of hot-selling models and formidable financial muscle under one garage roof. Simply said, DaimlerChrysler is set to transform the way the auto industry operates worldwide."[21] In the forest products' industry, Finland's Enso merged with Stora of Sweden. This transaction created the world's largest forest products' company (to be called Stora Enso; the company is based in Finland). Analysts viewed this merger as a deal that established a new "high-water mark in a growing transnational consolidation process among forest producers that is quietly transforming a previously stolid sector."[22] Thus, when companies observe an increase in merger and acquisition activity that involves major firms and/or major resource combinations, they should anticipate potentially significant changes in the dynamics of competition within the industry or industries in which they compete.

Sometimes, the changes to industries and their structural characteristics created through mergers and acquisitions engender regulatory review. At the end of the 1990s, for example, the U.S. government decided to marshal the resources required to complete a broad review of concentration in U.S. business. This decision was influenced by some government officials' belief that merger and acquisition activity was significantly redefining competition in various settings, including the airline, defense, financial, telecommunications, and automobile manufacturing industries.[23] Consider, for example, that according to observers of activity that occurred in a particular segment of one industry, "the decade-long consolidation juggernaut actually picked up steam (in 1997) in commercial banking, with nearly $42 billion worth of transactions."[24] In general, United States governmental policy supports business decisions, including those that involve mergers and acquisitions, when the net outcomes of firms' actions "promote competition, protect consumers, and preserve innovation."[25] Thus, when seeking synergy through mergers and acquisitions, firms should be aware that significant changes to an industry's structural characteristics—changes that can be brought about through the effective merger of complementary resources—may invite scrutiny by regulators.

Next, we define synergy. As we have noted, firms seek synergy when combining complementary resources through a merger or an acquisition.

What Is Synergy?

Derived from the Greek word *synergos*, which means working together, synergy "refers to the ability of two or more units or companies to generate greater value working together than they could working apart."[26] Typically, synergy is thought to yield gains to the acquiring firm through two sources: (1) improved operating efficiency based on economies of scale or scope; and (2) the sharing of one or more skills.[27] For example, Call-Net Enterprises, a Canadian long-distance carrier, acquired Fonorola, another long-distance carrier, for C$1.8 billion. Because of expected operating efficiencies from economies of scale, Call-Net estimated that the integration of Fonorola's complementary resources with its own would result in savings of over C$600 million in the first five years alone.[28] Acquisitions are also taking place in the golf leisure industry to create economies of scale. Given the highly fragmented nature of the industry, multicourse operators such as National Golf Properties and Golf Trust of America are moving aggressively to gain synergies by acquiring and integrating the resources owned by course properties. The slight differences in operational methods and target customers between the acquiring firm and the companies being acquired permit the melding of complementary resources.[29] Paying a premium of 28 times the firm's earnings, Johnson & Johnson's executives believed that its $3.5 billion acquisition of DePuy would create synergies through skill transfers. At the time it was acquired, DePuy was the world's oldest orthopedics company. The firm's primary products were hip, knee, and spinal implants. Johnson & Johnson decision-makers concluded that DePuy's world-class products would blend effectively with items in its own orthopedics division. The transferring and sharing of resources, particularly in terms of the two firms' complementary but not identical distribution channels and managerial skills, was expected to create valuable synergies.[30]

In managerial terms, synergy exists when managers find ways for the combined firm to create more value as compared to the summed value that had been created by the companies when they acted as independent entities. For shareholders, synergy exists when they acquire gains that they could not obtain through their own portfolio diversification decisions.[31] Some note that this is difficult for firms to achieve because shareholders can diversify their ownership positions more cheaply simply by grouping stakes in a set of companies.[32]

Similarly, firms must compare the value to be created through a merger or an acquisition with the value that could be created through alternative courses of action. Disney's merger with Capital Cities/ABC, for example, has been criticized. In the words of one observer of this transaction, "All of the ballyhooed synergies being talked about in this merger could as well be accomplished through nonexclusive strategic alliances between the companies."[33] Thus, for both companies and individual shareholders, the value of synergy that is to be created through merger and acquisition activity must be examined in relation to value that could be created through other strategic options.

The Managerial Challenge of Achieving Synergy

Synergy is difficult to achieve, even in the relatively unusual instance when the acquiring firm does not pay a premium. However, when a premium is paid, the challenge is more significant. The reason for this is that the paying of a premium requires the creation of greater synergy to generate economic value. Given this reality, it is interesting to note that the premiums paid in the 1990s exceeded, on average, those paid in the 1980s. Thus, the management of an acquisition is critical to the acquiring firm's efforts to create economic value. Those managing GE Capital Services, a firm that completed over 100 acquisitions during the five-year period between 1993 and 1997, are thought to have superior skills in terms of their ability to create synergy through the integration of each additional acquisition into the firm.[34] Because the topic of interest is the *integration* of resources, how GE Capital managers complete acquisitions is considered in greater detail in Chapter 6, our other chapter dealing with synergy as an attribute of successful mergers and acquisitions.

The failure rate of acquisitions demonstrates the managerial challenge that is associated with creating synergy. Following a review of academic research, one observer concluded that the record of portfolio strategies is dismal and that mergers and acquisitions generally reduce shareholder value.[35] In one study, for example, it was found that of the large acquisitions (those worth $500 million or more) completed in the United States over a recent 10-year period, fewer than one-half generated returns that were superior to the industry average. Results such as these influenced a conclusion advanced by *Business Week*: "The surge of consolidations and combinations is occurring in the face of strong evidence that mergers and acquisitions, at least over the past 35 years or so, have hurt more than helped companies and shareholders."[36] More recently, a survey completed by KPMG mirrored those reported previously. Based on results from its survey, KPMG estimated that 83 percent of the mergers it analyzed produced no shareholder value. Moreover, the consulting firm found that more than half of corporate mergers actually reduced shareholder returns.[37] The outcomes achieved through merger and acquisition activity that was undertaken by Quaker Oats and Kimberly-Clark may demonstrate the conclusion that was reached by *Business Week's* writers.

Even though the sharing of complementary resources (e.g., different types of distribution channels) between Quaker Oats' Gatorade and the drinks manufactured by Snapple when Quaker acquired that firm seemed reasonable, managerial mistakes may have contributed to the acquisition's failure as well as to Quaker's subsequent divestiture of Snapple.[38] Among the most critical errors, some analysts believe, was the failure to focus on the types of sales and marketing activities that were required by Snapple's products.[39] The decision to divest Snapple and refocus on what had been its creative and successful marketing-related activities that were directed to the Gatorade brand served Quaker Oats well. The brand enjoyed strong volume gains in Latin America and Europe. With annual sales growth of 10 percent, the sports drink is outpacing the U.S. food industry's growth.[40]

Counting on the creation of synergies, especially in terms of the sharing of skills associated with slightly different distribution channels, Kimberly-Clark executives believed that the strategic decision to acquire Scott Paper Co. for $9.4 billion was appropriate. However, the expected synergies are proving elusive. A key reason for this may be Kimberly-Clark's lack of managerial experience and expertise regarding the management of an acquisition the size of the Scott Paper transaction.[41] Historically, Kimberly-Clark has been able to effectively integrate acquisitions of smaller companies into its portfolio of businesses. The firm's executives are again focusing on smaller acquisitions. Kimberly-Clark's experiences mirror those of some other firms, in that acquiring firms have more success with future acquisitions when the newly acquired companies are similar to those that the firm acquired previously.[42] Thus, the importance of the link between managerial experience and merger and acquisition success should not be underestimated.

The Value of Complementary Resources

When combining resources through mergers and acquisitions, the firm seeks to develop a sustainable competitive advantage.[43] Competitive advantages are built through the use of firm-specific resources that are difficult, if not impossible, for competitors to imitate.[44] The company that learns how to complete mergers and acquisitions successfully across time becomes capable of developing new competitive advantages faster than competitors can learn how to duplicate the benefits of its current ones. More specifically, this desirable capability is developed when a combination of two firms' resources has made it more difficult for competitors to compete against the joined businesses of the acquiring and acquired companies than it was to compete against them when they were individual entities.

Resource Complementarities or Product Similarities?

When considering a merger or an acquisition, firms should focus on resource complementarities rather than relatedness among the product offerings of the acquiring and target firm. The reason for this is that in the rapidly developing and constantly changing global economy, the acquisition of special assets, skills, and capabilities that are difficult if not impossible for competitors to imitate is the pathway to the continuous development of competitive advantages and marketplace success.[45] As suggested by the following commentary, it is the alignment of comple- mentary resources rather than the combining of what may be similar products that firms should seek when engaging in merger and acquisi- tion activity: "companies often err by expanding into market segments that appear to be related to their existing businesses but in fact are quite different. In particular, they tend to make this mistake when they define relatedness according to product characteristics rather than resources."[46]

Consistent with this suggestion, our research shows that unique, yet complementary differences between the resources possessed by the acquiring firm and its target have a higher probability of creating syner- gies and competitive advantages, and enhancing the firm's value as a result, as compared to combinations based on resource and/or product similarities.[47] For example, in our work, we found that Quaker Oats decided to acquire Anderson Clayton for the expressed purpose of gain- ing control of the firm's Gaines pet food business. The Gaines pet food business had well-known and established national brands such as Gaines Burgers, Gravy Train, Top Choice, and Cycle dog foods. The integration of the Gaines pet food business with Quaker Oats' pet foods division doubled the size of that division and significantly increased Quaker Oats' market power in the pet foods business. Additionally, economies of scale, which resulted from efficiencies that were made possible by combining the complementary resources of the two business operations, enhanced the profitability of the newly created Quaker Oats' pet foods division. In fact, the division's market share in the pet foods business increased from 5.9 percent to 13.1 percent through the acquisition of Anderson Clay- ton. This acquisition also prevented the market leader, Ralston Purina, from dominating the market through its attempted purchase of Ander- son Clayton. Even after three years of retaliatory responses (e.g., signif- icant price reductions) from Ralston Purina and other competitors, Quaker Oats maintained market shares of over 50 percent in the moist dog food segment and 80 percent of the soft-dry dog food segment. Both of these strong market share positions were a product of effectively integrating the complementary resources of the two formerly independent dog food business operations.

We now turn our attention to the role organizational learning can play in understanding relationships between acquiring and target firms' resources. A desirable skill that can result from such learning is the ability to identify synergies that can be created through the combining of complementary resources. We present a comprehensive discussion of organizational learning's role in effective merger or acquisition activity in Chapter 7.

Complementary Resources and Organizational Learning

The ability to determine the set of resources that, when combined through a merger or acquisition, can be expected to create synergies and competitive advantages is a critical skill for organizational members (especially those in top-level managerial positions) to possess.[48] With respect to resource complementarity, the interest is to learn how to configure complementary resources such that newly created competitive advantages will allow the firm to match the requirements of a changing external environment.

Complex in nature, organizational learning encompasses both cognitive and behavioral changes. Organizational learning is a phenomenon through which cognitive and behavioral skills and knowledge are acquired and developed. This type of systematic learning facilitates sometimes profound and durable modifications that are made in the firm's operations.[49] Moreover, learning results in the creation of new knowledge. Knowledge, which can be thought of as information whose validity has been established through tests of proof, endows the firm with the skills it needs to understand how to compete successfully.[50]

In terms of complementary resources and organizational learning, firms benefit when personnel acquire the skills needed to identify ways to uniquely combine mutually supportive resources and develop the commitment and capabilities required to change their work behaviors appropriately. To facilitate this type of learning and behavioral change, managers must provide visible and tangible support. Through continuous support and the learning it can engender, personnel can become highly skilled at integrating complementary resources in ways that create superior value propositions for customers.

In summary, the successful acquisitions that we examined in our research study were ones in which complementary resources existed between the acquiring and target firms. In our view, these findings indicate that significantly related acquisitions (with relatedness a function of resources rather than products) make it easier for the merged firm to identify complementarities between resource sets and exploit positive synergy as a result of being able to do so. We found that even conglomerate firms (i.e., companies that are composed of groupings of highly unrelated businesses) were able to complete acquisitions successfully, as long as the target firm was related to some of the acquiring firm's businesses. The key to success appears to be the ability to identify complementarities and take specific actions to achieve positive synergy. This ability was noticeably absent in our study of unsuccessful transactions. Thus, resource complementarities are of greater importance than the product/market relatedness of a specific acquisition. This finding regarding the importance of resource complementarities shows that successful merger and acquisition activity leads to the creation of one or more of the following desirable outcomes: economies of scale, economies of scope, and the sharing of skills in patterns that are difficult for competitors to understand and certainly to imitate. In turn, attainment of one or more of these outcomes—outcomes that are possible because of the creation of synergy—results in a competitive advantage for the firm.

Examples of firms pursuing competitive advantages through scale economies, scope economies, or the sharing of skills are described in the next several sections. However, it should be noted that firms often seek to simultaneously reach more than one of these outcomes. For example, an acquiring firm may desire to create both scale and scope economies when merging with or acquiring another company. Thus, our analyses of firm-specific merger and acquisition activities focus on what appears to be the primary reason for the acquirer to pursue its target and eventually to complete its intended transaction. Because of our belief that it is difficult to assign a single reason (in terms of the goal of creating synergy) for the completion of a merger or an acquisition, we also present a few examples of transactions that appear to have been completed in the simultaneous pursuit of both scale and scope economies through the combining of complementary resources.

Synergy Through Economies of Scale

Unilever is a large multinational firm headquartered in Great Britain. Historically, European sales had been critical to the firm's competitive success. In light of its declining effectiveness in efforts to introduce new products into the European market, Unilever decided to acquire Cheseborough-Ponds. Because 75 percent of Cheseborough-Ponds' sales were in the United States, this acquisition provided Unilever with quick access to a large and vital market. Through a combination of complementary resources, the newly created firm was able to expand its global operations more effectively than had been the case for each of the independent entities. In fact, the economies of scale that were created, coupled with the successful skin product lines from Cheseborough-Ponds (such as Vaseline and Vaseline Intensive Care) and the new international markets that the transaction permitted, combined to create positive synergy for the merged firm.[51] For similar reasons, Unilever acquired Best Foods in 2000.

Brunswick Corporation is the largest United States manufacturer of recreational and leisure products.[52] Among its well-known lines are Zebco, Remington camping gear, Roadmaster, and American camper. The firm has long relied on an active acquisition strategy to continue expanding its product lines. In recent times, a primary objective of this strategy has been to add brand-name sporting goods and outdoor equipment to the fold. Brunswick acquired Igloo Holdings Inc. for this reason. As a famous maker of ice chests and beverage coolers, Igloo was thought by Brunswick decision-makers to be a strong fit with its concentration on the sports-oriented customer. Contributing to the high expectations of synergy to be gained through the completion of this transaction was the intention of developing scale economies by using the full set of distribution channels owned through Brunswick's acquisitions, including Igloo. The common thread among Brunswick's customers is their enthusiasm for sports-oriented activities. Campers, bicyclists, and fishing enthusiasts can benefit from use of ice chests and beverage coolers. Identically, those interested in coolers and ice chests can be exposed to opportunities to purchase an array of sporting equipment.[53] Thus, slightly different yet mutually supportive distribution channels can be used to cross-sell Brunswick's array of products.

Following the acquisition of its major rival Computer City from Tandy Corp. in September 1998, CompUSA became the only national superstore chain in the United States that specializes in personal computers. Although a challenging business, CompUSA's CEO believed that the acquisition would help the firm deal with its competitive issues. None of these issues were more significant to CompUSA than the continuing decrease in the prices of personal computers. Although a boon to consumers, these price reductions were squeezing the profit margins for all parties in the computer industry.

In light of declining prices, an ability to operate even more efficiently could prove to be critical to CompUSA's future competitive success. To improve the efficiencies of its operations following the acquisition of Computer City, CompUSA converted 36 of Computer City's stores to its own retailing format; 58 other stores were closed. Among other areas, the opportunity to advertise across a larger number of stores within individual markets was expected to create economies of scale. Another value proposition in this acquisition was the opportunity to meld Computer City's *selling* expertise with CompUSA's *service* expertise. Service-related skills required for training, computer upgrades, repairs, delivery, and installation were a competitive advantage for CompUSA. Melding complementary service skills (possessed by CompUSA) with sales skills (possessed by Computer City) was expected to create synergy for the new firm.

The immediate returns from CompUSA's attempts to integrate and exploit complementary resources were not encouraging. For example, sales for the second quarter of the firm's fiscal year 2000 decreased approximately 21 percent for the comparable period in the previous year. To respond to this decline, CompUSA concentrated on what it termed Retail Initiatives to improve its core business operations—operations that are at least partly grounded in ongoing efforts to create value through integrating what continue to be thought of as complementary resources between CompUSA and the former Computer City chain. Far more definitive evidence that these complementary resources were not sufficient to create value is suggested by the January 2000 acquisition of CompUSA by Grupo Sanborns SA, a large Mexican retail company. Grupo Sanborns acquired CompUSA because "we think there's a lot of potential to develop e-commerce in CompUSA." Simultaneously, however, the acquiring firm's chairman also admitted that there was a great deal of work to be done to strengthen the retail side of CompUSA. Thus, CompUSA's attempt to create synergy through combining its resources with those of Computer City failed to create value sufficient to prevent further declines in CompUSA's performance.[54]

The production of circuit boards has become a mature business. Unlike previous times, competition in this arena is now based primarily on price rather than technology. A specialist in computer circuit boards, Hadco Corp. acquired Zycon Corp. in what some viewed as an attempt to consolidate this segment of the computer industry. In fact, an analyst suggested that through this acquisition, Hadco "obtained mass and economies of scale in a market that is increasingly becoming commodity-oriented yet remains a sector of high demand as a basic product during the age of information technology."[55] Thus, it seems that the synergies generated through the combination of these firms' complementary resources can be expected to yield scale economies and a competitive advantage for the newly created company.

Synergy Through Economies of Scope

Clorox bleach is a product known to many consumers. The firm that produces this venerable product, Clorox Co., is recognized as a specialist in managing mass-market consumer brands. This core competence has been particularly effective for Clorox in the general area of cleansing products. One indicator of this effectiveness is market share. Recently, Clorox held the number-one share of the market in liquid bleach, water filters, drain openers, abrasive and dilutive cleaners, scrubbing tools, and charcoal.[56]

To expand its reach in the cleansing product area, Clorox acquired Armor All. Almost identical to Clorox, Armor All is known widely for the quality and breadth of a line of cleansing products. In this instance, the products are geared toward the automotive market. This acquisition served the interests of both parties well. Clorox was able to purchase a firm with widely distributed products that it could make even more successful through its managerial skills. The value to Armor All was that, with Clorox, it became part of an organization with extensive distribution channels. These channels were important with respect to ongoing efforts to broaden Armor All's customer base.[57]

Cole National Corp. operates several specialty-retailing businesses. The optical departments located in Sears, Roebuck and Co. and other large stores are one of these business concepts. Until recently, Cole did not have units operating in the freestanding store segment of the retail optical market. Because of a belief that this segment has great growth potential, Cole decided to acquire Pearle Inc. (at the time of this transaction, Pearle was a subsidiary of Grand Metropolitan PLC). As is the case with some of its competitors, Pearle seeks synergies through the creation of scale economies in its operations by providing quick and reliable service to an increasingly expanding customer base. The acquisition of Pearle affords Cole an opportunity to use its optical-related skills in multiple segments of the total optical-care market, yielding benefits from scope economies as a result of doing so.[58]

The defense contracting industry has become increasingly competitive. The result has been a set of decisions by some major companies to exit this business segment. Long known as a major player in this field, Rockwell International agreed to an acquisition of its aerospace and defense operations by Boeing Co. The acquisition of what analysts viewed as a premier business operation provided Boeing with the foundation needed to gain economics of scope. Boeing intends to develop scope economies by using its own resources with the complementary ones owned by Rockwell's aerospace and defense unit in the manufacture of both military and commercial products.[59]

Synergy Through Economies of Scale and Scope

Wal-Mart is committed to succeeding in global markets. In the early 1990s, for example, the firm expanded into Mexico. Currently, Wal-Mart is the largest chain store operating in Mexico. One of the primary factors contributing to the firm's success in this country was the decision to purchase a majority ownership position (53 percent) in Cifra S.A. Under the Cifra name, Wal-Mart controls 350 outlets, including a chain of 176 restaurants. By melding its renowned distribution channel capability and its enormous buying power with Cifra's slightly different yet complementary distribution channels, buying relationships and keen understanding of local taste preferences, valuable synergies have been created in the operation of discount stores and restaurants. To date, competitors have not been able to match the synergy/competitive advantage that Wal-Mart and Cifra possess through the scale and scope economies that are being generated by combining the firms' complementary resources.[60]

Interestingly, Wal-Mart is now in the process of entering the grocery supermarket business directly through the opening of units called Wal-Mart Neighborhood Market.[61] Wal-Mart executives noted that these stores are intended to "fill some of the gaps between its big, out-of-town Supercenters, which sell a mix of general merchandise and groceries, and supermarkets." To support this attempt to gain additional synergy and competitive advantages in a different market, Wal-Mart intends to create economies of scale and scope through the decision to have the "new store chain piggyback on its existing distribution system and benefit from its unmatched buying power."[62] In time, Wal-Mart executives may decide to acquire ownership positions in existing grocery chains to grow this business just as the firm chose to acquire a majority ownership position in Cifra S.A. to expand its operations in Mexico.

The $37 billion WorldCom merger with MCI Communications catapulted WorldCom from the fourth-largest to the second-largest position in the long-distance market. The intent with this merger was to combine WorldCom's local facilities with MCI's long-distance traffic. In terms of economies of scale, this combination was expected to create a cost savings of $20 billion over the first five years of the newly created firm's life. In addition, the economies of scope that could be generated by applying each unit's skills in the other one were anticipated to be substantial. In fact, Jeffrey Kagan, founder of Kagan Telecom Associates, suggested that this merger would "change the way people think about the telecom business."[63]

Synergy Through the Sharing of Skills

SmithKline Beecham (known as SmithKline at the time of the acquisition we studied) develops, manufactures, and markets prescription and OTC pharmaceutical and consumer products. This firm's acquisition of Beckman Instruments appears to be an example of *private synergy*. In essence, private synergy can be created when the acquiring firm has knowledge about the complementary nature of its resources with those of the target firm that is not known to others. The most valuable of all types of synergy, private synergy exists when it is possible for two firms to combine their complementary resources in a way that creates more value than would any other combination of the firms' resources.[64] Through continuous study and analysis, firms are able to learn how to identify private synergies.

The intent of the SmithKline/Beckman Instrument's transaction was to combine SmithKline's skills in pharmaceuticals and healthcare with

Beckman Instrument's diagnostic technology skills. The synergy that was created from the sharing of the two firms' skills was expected to result in a competitive advantage in terms of biomedical research. Moreover, the cash being earned from SmithKline's pharmaceutical business, particularly from the sales of its extremely successful Tagamet anti-ulcer drug, was to be used to finance research and development activities within Beckman. Because both companies were committed to the pursuit of research in molecular biology and biotechnology, it was possible for the newly combined firm to produce more R&D-related value than would have been generated through the organizations' independent actions or other combinations of each firm's resources with resources owned by yet another company.[65]

United States Filter Corp. used an aggressive acquisition program to achieve its objective of transforming the world's water treatment industry. Between 1991 and 1998, U.S. Filter acquired 130 companies on a worldwide basis. Through these acquisitions and the operations of them, the firm grew from annual sales of roughly $23 million in 1991 to an annualized rate of $35 billion in 1998. At that time, U.S. Filter was "the only company in the world that can design, manufacture, install, service, finance, and operate nearly every product and technology needed to treat water." With its strong positions in the industrial and municipal water-treatment businesses, the firm believed that it had the skills required to develop economies of scope by using its complementary resources to move into residential and consumer water businesses. In the long term, the firm sought to fully integrate its expertise, resources and product offerings into what the CEO called a "single, seamless source."[66] If developed, such a source would likely generate significant synergies and value for the firm's shareholders. Partly because of its skills, U.S. Filter was acquired by Vivendi.

In the next and final section, we offer recommendations that should be considered when evaluating the degree of complementarity between the resources owned by an acquiring firm and its target.

Complementary Resources and Merger and Acquisition Success

In this chapter, we have discussed the role complementary resources play in merger and acquisition success. As a summary of this analysis, we offer the following recommendations:

1. Remember that mergers and acquisitions are complex transactions. In terms of resource complementarity, this complexity calls for detailed study and careful analyses before deciding to complete either a merger or an acquisition.

2. Seek targets that possess resources that are slightly different, yet mutually supportive of the resources in your firm. Complementary resources have a higher probability of creating valuable synergy than the joining of resources that are highly similar or even virtually identical.

3. Look for private synergy when examining target firms. This type of synergy is possible when information about the ability to uniquely combine the complementary resources of the involved companies is known only by those working within the acquiring firm. Private synergy provides value because it is extremely difficult for competitors to understand how it was created. An inability to understand the causes of value creation stifles and often prevents imitation by competitors.

4. Recognize that opportunity costs are associated with mergers and acquisitions. Carefully evaluate and compare the value that can be created through combining the slightly different yet mutually supportive resources of the acquiring and target firm with the value that could be created through the exercise of other strategic choices.

5. Support the need for personnel to allocate their time to learn how to identify and then integrate complementary resources. Through practice, personnel have opportunities to gain the skills that are needed to quickly identify how to create economic value by combining their company's resources with the mutually supportive resources owned by the firm that has been acquired.

Some acquisitions are hostile. In those instances, what are often substantial disagreements surface between the acquiring and acquired firm. In the next chapter, we describe the value and goodwill that are created when all aspects of a merger or acquisition transaction are completed in a "friendly" manner. Among other positive outcomes, friendly transactions increase the probability of firms finding the complementary resources they seek when acquiring another company.

5

Seeking a Friendly and Cooperative Merger

Assuming that the person did all his homework, and the financial, the strategy and the concept made sense, I would tell him to treat the other company and the people in the other company with respect. Lots of times acquisitions are of companies that are doing poorer than you are doing. And it usually is not the fault of all the people in the organization. Usually it is the fault of the leadership. You shouldn't punish everyone for that.

—Sanford I. Weill

As the preceding chapters have demonstrated, mergers and acquisitions can challenge even the most adept managers. Some of the best combinations require enormous amounts of goodwill, cooperation, and planning. Consider the recent acquisition of Netscape by America Online. Netscape, the pioneer in Internet access, employed some of the brightest minds in the software industry. AOL was best known for providing access to users who are largely computer illiterate. However, at the time of the deal, AOL was moving in the direction of technological sophistication and Netscape had been having problems due to Microsoft's strong competitive position. The companies needed each other, yet industry observers were concerned that a combination would scare away many of the talented minds that were Netscape's greatest strength.[1]

America Online's acquisition of Netscape is an illustration of how a friendly deal can work. As a start, both companies were backed by Kleiner Perkins Caufield & Byers, a leading venture capital firm in Silicon Valley. Kleiner companies come together annually for a private conference. At the

June 1998 meeting, Stephen Case, Chairman of AOL, told James Barks-dale, Netscape's CEO, that AOL should have bought his company years ago. Discussions began shortly thereafter. By November, the companies were considering a wide range of possible partnerships, including a deal that would embed Netscape's browser into AOL's software.[2] The ultimate deal was dependent on a venture with yet another Kleiner company, Sun Microsystems. To sell Netscape's talented employees on the benefits of the acquisition, AOL entered into an agreement with Sun to purchase $500 million in computer systems and services over three years in exchange for access to Sun's sales force of 7,000. This is a huge increase over the 700 salespeople Netscape had previously employed. Another important aspect of the deal was the vocal support of Netscape principals, especially those of the target firm. Marc Andreessen, co-founder of Netscape, reflecting on the combination, said, "America Online has really changed from a closed on-line service for novice users to an Internet media and technology company with a diverse set of brands. These two companies have been moving in the same direction, and the fit is good."[3] A jubilant Mr. Case noted in an interview, "We can build the service, run the service and promote the service, all in one."[4] A year later, the SunNetscape Alliance launched the iPlanet Commerce Integration Suite, which ties together all of a company's E-commerce-related computer systems.

Success in acquisitions, financial or otherwise, can be elusive in even the most favorable circumstances. This chapter is about those circum-stances. In our in-depth study of some of the most successful and unsuc-cessful acquisitions of the 1980s, every one of the successful acquisitions was friendly. We are using the term "friendly" to mean a situation in which target firm top executives are in favor of the acquisition and there-fore cooperate during and after negotiations. For example, in 1998, Seibe PLC and BTR PLC of Great Britain agreed to merge into a company that will be a world leader in controls and automation. "Both companies say they wanted to do the deal so they could improve cross-selling in comple-mentary product lines and build on global presence in key controls and automation markets."[5]

In this chapter, we provide many examples of friendly deals and explain why we believe that "friendliness" is essential to merger success. We also discuss types of resistance and why it can destroy the potential of what might otherwise be a successful combination. Finally, we offer a few guide-lines that help managers know when to back out of a deal and how to increase the probability that an acquisition will be friendly and successful.

Friendliness

Successful acquisitions require thoughtful selection, diligent planning, and appropriate financing, but these actions are not enough. Success also requires cooperation. Merging two companies is complicated and requires much work by many people such that an uncooperative spirit in the target firm can lead to disastrous results. There simply are too many things that can go wrong. Dennis Kozlowski, CEO of Tyco International and a major dealmaker, says, "It's like landing a plane. You can't make any mistakes."[6] Imagine landing a plane at an airport with unco-operative air traffic controllers and ground crew.

Under Kozlowski's leadership, Tyco International has landed 110 planes over the past few years at a combined value of about $28 billion. He has an outstanding track record. Most of his transactions are winners, which helped increase Tyco's market capitalization from $1.6 to $49 billion at the end of 1998. One of Kozlowski's cardinal rules is that he never makes hostile bids. Because his approaches are always friendly, Tyco gains access to a lot of private information during due diligence, such as auditors' work papers. Kozlowski also makes sure that transitions are as friendly as possible. For example, Tyco closed down a factory after the acquisition of Professional Medical Products in 1996. The company gave employees a year's notice, offered retention bonuses, conducted job fairs, and paid unusually large severance bonuses.[7]

Friendliness can help potential merger partners overcome a multitude of obstacles that might otherwise lead to problems during negotiations and post-merger integration. In some cases, a friendly climate can even save a deal that would otherwise have to be cancelled. For example, Fenway Partners Inc. of New York was able to complete its acquisition of the bedding maker Simmons Co. despite a lack of support from creditors. To make this transaction work, Fenway, a private-equity investment firm, committed more equity, sharply cut the size of a bridge loan, and added more senior bank debt and junior subordinated debt. The price of Simmons was lowered from the originally agreed amount of $497 million to approximately $483.5 million. Although modifying the terms of the deal was important, the key to successful completion was "a continued desire on both sides to get it done despite the market turmoil."[8] On the other hand, the planned megamerger between American Home Products and Monsanto collapsed due to a lack of cooperation. "Senior executives at the two companies had clashed in recent weeks over virtually every issue under discussion."[9]

Three related aspects of friendliness are reviewed in this section. One important aspect is the creation of a cooperative acquisition climate. In addition, friendliness seems to be easier to achieve if the acquirer and target have previously pursued ventures together. Finally, we discuss the pros and cons of being a white knight.

A Cooperative Acquisition Climate

A key to creating an appropriate climate for acquisition negotiations is to understand the mindset of the acquiring and target firm managers.

According to Mitchell Marks and Philip Mirvis, merger consultants, "The acquirer often will have a 'victor' attitude and will tend to dominate the action. The target, the 'vanquished,' often feels powerless to defend its interests or control its fate. Target management may respond with hostility, or withdraw in defeatism."[10] Marks and Mirvis have heard target firm managers in hostile takeovers refer to the process as rape and their buyers as barbarians. Even in friendly deals, acquired firm managers talk of being "seduced" by promises or having been taken advantage of during the process.

Such attitudes obviously are counterproductive during the negotiation process; however, they can produce longer-term disadvantages as well. Executive turnover is much higher than normal in acquired firms.[11] One of the great mysteries associated with the popularity of acquisitions is that the executives of acquiring companies pay a premium for the assets of a target, yet they understand that some of the most valuable of those assets—human talent—will be gone within the first few years! The level of turnover in the acquiring firm is influenced by the nature of merger negotiations.[12]

One of the keys to a successful acquisition, then, is to avoid a win–lose climate that may eventually lead to high levels of turnover among the most valuable managers and employees. At the beginning of this chapter, we described America Online's deliberate approach to reducing the potential for turnover in Netscape through simultaneous negotiation of a joint venture with Sun Microsystems. Being aware of and responding positively to what is most important to the target firm is an excellent first step toward creating an atmosphere of trust and cooperation.

Acquiring firm executives should be sensitive to the culture of the target and the strength of that culture.[13] Organizations that have been successful in the past are much more likely to have strong cultures, which requires greater adjustments and sensitivity on the part of acquiring firm executives. Other actions that can help include jointly creating goals and a business plan for the combined firm, beginning transition planning before the deal is completed, announcing a transition team, and allowing transition team members to be present and participate in the final stages of the negotiation process.[14] These actions can help create shared purpose and greatly reduce integration problems after the deal is signed.

Many executives involved in mergers agree that the most important success factor is not the apparent synergies that exist between buyer and target, but the existence or absence of excellent managers who have the ability to catalyze the merger process.[15] Consequently, while there may be an inclination on the part of the principals to a merger transaction to select senior managers for the combination with whom they are familiar and feel comfortable, in reality the best possible team should be selected. Senior managers should be selected in an efficient and open manner to prevent delays and foster trust.[16]

Another critical aspect of creating a friendly and cooperative climate is effective communication. Direct communication with customers is essential to retaining them through the merger process.[17] Employees also should not be left in the dark. One of the most effective ways for managers to reduce anxiety among employees is to communicate with them as soon as possible about all the anticipated effects of the change. Realistic merger previews reduce dysfunctional outcomes after the acquisition is complete. For example, researchers conducted a study in two plants engaged in light manufacturing. Both plants were owned by Fortune 500 companies and both were involved in mergers. The employees of one plant were given a realistic preview of the changes that would take place, while employees in the other plant were given no such preview. The employees of the plant in which the preview was given experienced less stress, less uncertainty, and significantly higher job satisfaction, commitment, and performance. In addition, they perceived that the company was more trustworthy, honest, and caring.[18]

Potential merger partners may also find it easier to achieve a friendly and productive relationship during the acquisition process if they have worked together before. Some of the highly successful acquisitions we studied were natural extensions of earlier joint ventures.

Pre-acquisition Ventures

One of the most successful acquisitions we studied was the combination of General Dynamics and Cessna Aircraft in 1986. General Dynamics bought 500,000 shares of Cessna in 1983, as part of an agreement in which the companies would share technology. By 1984, engineers began meeting together and discussing ways to introduce advanced materials and aerodynamics into Cessna products. By the time merger talks began in earnest in 1985, both companies saw many advantages from coming together. General Dynamic's military marketing could help Cessna rebuild its once-sizable defense business. General Dynamic could offer strong financial backing for Cessna while Cessna provided an opportunity to diversify out of defense. The companies saw opportunities to cross-utilize facilities. This list of advantages was reinforced as the companies worked together for the three years prior to merger. They got to know each other. After the merger, Cessna was reorganized and a major loss at Cessna during 1986 was turned into a profit by the year immediately following the acquisition. Familiarity allowed the newly combined company to take immediate action.[19]

Germany's Hoechst AG and France's Rhone-Poulenc SA developed a merger in a similar fashion. In late 1998, they announced the creation of the largest life sciences company in the world, with $36 billion in assets. They created the company by combining their pharmaceutical and agrochemical businesses into an equally owned venture. According to executives at both companies, the new company, called Aventis, was the initial step toward a full merger of Hoechst and Rhone-Poulenc. They changed their names to Aventis Hoechst and Aventis Rhone-Poulenc and installed nearly identical management teams for both companies.[20]

The acquisition of Union Camp by International Paper represents a different type of working familiarity that likewise can facilitate the acquisition process. Craig McClelland, Union Camp's CEO, was head of Hammermill Papers when IP acquired it in 1986. The success of the Hammermill acquisition paved the way for friendly negotiations between IP and Union Camp. Commenting on the acquisition, John T. Dillon, IP's chairman and CEO, stated, "We're doing this because we have a hand-in-glove fit. There's no baggage."[21] Less than a year later, John T. Dillon, International Paper's chairman and CEO, announced that the company increased its estimates of cost savings from the Union Camp acquisition to $425 million from the $300 million the acquisition was originally expected to produce.[22]

Adequate time together seems to be a critical factor to keeping a deal friendly, even if the time is not spent in a formal business venture. As we mentioned in our chapter on due diligence, executives should avoid rushing into deals. Taking time to study a potential combination allows the principals from both firms to get to know each other. For example, executives from Lucent Technologies and Ascend Communications, both computer network companies, held discussions for 18 months "to make sure that there was a proper fit between the two companies."[23] The initial offer by Lucent was accepted by the Ascend board the day after it was made public.[24]

Of course, there is no particular reason why merger negotiations should be announced publicly. In fact, going public about a deal too soon can invite additional bidders to the table, thus increasing price, or result in competitor retaliation and legal battles. Consequently, the best possible scenario is one in which the companies privately work together, either as partners in a venture or simply during a careful due diligence process. Such was the case in 1994 when Lockheed Corp. and Martin Marietta combined in what was, at the time, the largest aerospace merger. Daniel Tellep and Norman Augustine, chairmen of Lockheed and Martin Marietta, respectively, had worked together two years previously in a failed attempt to buy LTV Corp. Early in 1994, the two came together to talk about industry consolidation and possibly teaming up to buy another company. Negotiations from that point on were uncharacteristically private. By the time the merger was announced on August 30, both boards had already agreed to the terms of the deal. The announcement, which surprised the industry, resulted in share price increases for both companies, although Lockheed gained much more than Martin Marietta.[25] The consolidated Lockheed Martin experienced high growth in stock value for several years after the combination, although recent problems have led some analysts to wonder if perhaps the company should now be broken up.[26]

In this chapter we have reviewed many of the advantages of a friendly acquisition. These advantages fall into two broad categories. The first category is associated with the cooperation that comes from working together both during negotiations and afterward. These can be called cooperation benefits. The second general category of advantages we refer to as financial benefits. If both companies want to merge, they should be able to strike a fair financial deal, including reasonable terms and a fair price. These benefits are enhanced if negotiations are private. White knight transactions are also friendly, but they do not enjoy all the benefits of a privately negotiated deal. They gain many cooperation benefits, but not necessarily financial ones.

White Knights

The imagery associated with acquisitions is fascinating. Barbarians raping helpless victims. Potential targets selling off "crown jewels" to become less attractive to potential suitors. Target firm executives bailing out of a plane with "golden parachutes." Perhaps the most appealing imagery is that of a courageous knight galloping into the scene to save a kingdom from ruin. Firms that rescue a target from unwanted suitors are called white knights.

White knight transactions obviously are friendly. They enjoy benefits associated with securing the cooperation of target firm managers. In our study of highly successful acquisitions, US Gypsum served as a white knight for Masonite. In 1981, Belzberg bought a 5.1 percent stake in Masonite as a prelude to an acquisition bid. Masonite bought the stock back from Belzberg at a premium. This type of transaction has come to be known as paying "greenmail." In 1982, Masonite fought another acquisition attempt, this time by the Pritzker family. Then, in 1984, General Felt attempted a takeover. Masonite filed a legal suit to block the acquisition and sought a white knight through its financial advisor. This is when USG entered the picture. USG had products, markets, and a business philosophy complementary to Masonite, but offered Masonite managers the opportunity to maintain a certain degree of operating autonomy while also providing the potential for synergistic benefits.[27] The merger led to immediate financial success. USG earned return on assets of 13 percent and return on sales of 9.6 percent in the year following the merger, compared to 6.7 percent and 5 percent for the year prior to merger. Masonite's returns were 5 percent for ROA and 3.7 percent for ROS just prior to merger, so the financial results were not merely a result of adding Masonite's figures to those of USG. Furthermore, growth in sales for the combined entity were 15 percent higher than the combined sales of both companies prior to merger.

However, the benefits associated with cooperation often come at a high cost that, contrary to the USG/Masonite combination previously described, are not always warranted. In all the acquisitions we have studied to date, we never recall a situation in which a white knight paid less for a target than earlier suitors. This is because white knight transactions involve bidding wars, which we discuss in the next section.

Resistance

In March 1998, WHX Corporation, the holding company for the Wheeling-Pittsburgh Steel Company, announced that Handy & Harman, an industrial manufacturer, had agreed to be acquired for $35.25 per share. Just 10 months earlier Handy & Harman rejected a bid from WHX for $30.00 per share.[28] In late 1990, House of Fabrics offered to buy Fabricland for $43.2 million. Fabricland was very vocal in opposing the acquisition, invited other bidders, charged House of Fabrics with violating federal securities laws, and even claimed that a third party was negotiating to buy the company, although the third party was never identified. The company reported that it spent over $100,000 fending off the acquisition. However, the payoff was enormous. House of Fabrics ultimately paid $58 million for Fabricland, a huge $14.8 million difference between initial offer and final bid.[29] A study of takeovers from 1988 to 1996 conducted by Frederic Escherich of JP Morgan Securities demonstrated a 66 percent higher premium when the acquisition was hostile.[30]

Resistance to mergers comes in a variety of forms and degrees of intensity. All resistance is disadvantageous to a potential acquirer; however, some tactics are more damaging than others. Furthermore, various forms of resistance have differential effects on the target firm and its shareholders. In this section, we discuss two general types of resistance: auction-inducing resistance and competition-reducing resistance. Auction-inducing resistance has as its ultimate goal the achievement of a higher sales price. Typically this type of resistance is considered in the best interests of the target firm shareholders. However, competition-reducing resistance is often associated with management entrenchment, typified by incompetent managers attempting to thwart possible acquisition attempts because of fear of job loss or a desire to keep their high salaries and perks despite their own inadequacies.[31]

Auction-inducing Resistance

Perhaps no other single management decision can have such a profound and immediate effect on the value of a firm's securities as the decision of how to respond to a takeover bid.[32] January Investments Ltd., the bidding vehicle owned by Philip Green, successfully acquired Sears PLC (a large British retailer not related to Sears Roebuck) after raising its offer to 359 pence per share after Sears rejected a previous offer of 340 pence.[33] Holding out for a higher bid is a logical decision that may dramatically increase the value of a deal to target firm shareholders. Target firm managers, as agents for the shareholders, have a duty to act in their best interests. However, there is a risk that the potential acquirer may withdraw the bid. Consequently, the optimal decision is not always clear. Also, this particular decision involves much more than a simple relationship between suitor and target. Resistance often provides time for competitors or other stakeholders to enter the scene.

Auction-inducing resistance includes such tactics as public opposition, litigation, and bidder solicitation. Resisting a bid provides other potential suitors time to evaluate the effect an acquisition might have on the industry and their own companies. Competitors, in particular, will evaluate a potential acquisition with great interest. If top executives of a competing firm see the acquisition as a threat to the market position of their firm or if the target, after analysis, looks as though it might be a good fit with their own company, they may enter a competing bid or file a legal action in an attempt to block the merger or buy time to complete a more thorough evaluation.[34] Once again, there is potential advantage here for the target firm, but increased risk as well. A competing bid can raise the price received, but a legal suit could delay or block the acquisition. The risk paid off for the Canadian firm Wascana Energy Inc., which accepted a bid for 1.7 billion Canadian dollars (US$1.2 billion). This bid was C$200 million higher than a rejected bid from Talisman Energy Inc.[35] In another case, Conrail's shareholders received a bid of $10.5 billion from CSX Corp., nearly one-third more than a CSX bid four months earlier, as the result of a bidding contest with Norfolk Southern Corp.[36]

In some cases, mere speculation that there might be an auction can raise the value of a target. For instance, Great Britain's Zeneca Group PLC and Sweden's Astra AB announced a $35 billion merger deal in late 1998. However, speculation that a disgruntled suitor might still enter a higher bid for Astra drove the company's stock price up an additional 19.5 Swedish kronor, or 13 percent, in Stockholm.[37]

Competition-reducing Resistance

Auction-inducing resistance can result in a much higher return for target firm shareholders. Consequently, this form of resistance is typically considered in the best interests of the target firm shareholders. However, another type of resistance strategy, called competition-reducing resistance, tends to make a target less attractive in the market and therefore discourages auctions, thus reducing gains to target firm shareholders.[38] This type of resistance can take many forms, but all have a common goal of making the firm much more costly to a potential suitor.[39] A basic assumption underlying this form of resistance is that managers act to protect their own jobs and/or organizational autonomy.[40] Most high-level executives dread the thought of losing their independence by becoming a division of a larger company. In many cases, they lose their jobs or experience a reduction in compensation and/or authority.

Competition-reducing resistance is known by a number of names. To provide clarity to this discussion, we will use the term "poison pill" to represent any action taken by management of a potential target that makes a takeover so potentially costly that it is likely to discourage an auction. We will refer to "shark repellents" as a special class of poison pills that typically require approval by the shareholders.[41] Common forms of shark repellents include classified board provisions, superma-jority provisions, fair price provisions, elimination of cumulative voting rights, and establishment of unequal voting rights. A classified board provision divides directors into distinct classes (typically three), with only one class up for election each year. Consequently, a successful takeover does not mean that the new owner will assume control of the board of directors immediately. Such a provision prevents the acquiring firm from firing top managers immediately on acquisition. Supermajor-ity provisions increase the percentage of shareholder votes needed to approve a merger. For example, they may require approval represent-ing two-thirds or three-fourths of the outstanding shares.

The fair price provision requires a supermajority vote for approval unless the board of directors approves the merger and some minimum fair price is paid for remaining outstanding shares. Eliminating cumula-tive voting rights precludes shareholders from casting all their votes in favor of a particular nominee for director, thus restricting one large shareholder, such as a corporate raider, from electing its representative. Finally, unequal voting rights provisions reduce the voting power of a shareholder once a certain threshold percentage of ownership is attained. The majority of large United States corporations have instituted some form of shark repellent and such measures are also common in other countries.[42] The popularity of such measures seems closely tied to indus-try norms. For example, poison pills are moving like a wave through the real estate investment trust (REIT) industry. In 1998, thirty-one REITs instituted shareholder-rights plans, compared to only five in 1997.[43]

Not all poison pills require the approval of shareholders. A flipover provision gives current shareholders the right to purchase additional shares of stock at a deep discount in the event of a tender offer. This right transfers to the acquiring firm in the event the takeover is accom-plished. A back-end plan allows shareholders to sell their shares back to the target firm at very attractive prices. Each of these strategies makes a potential takeover very expensive.[44] In addition, managers of potential targets may sell off their "crown jewels," which are highly prized assets, take on huge financial obligations, or make acquisitions themselves that a would-be acquirer might find unattractive or could create antitrust concerns. Golden parachutes provide huge payments to target firm top executives if an acquisition leads to their dismissal. In the Pac-Man strategy, the target purchases a large block of shares in the suitor in an attempt to gain control.[45] ITT Corp., in an attempt to thwart a hostile acquisition attempt by Hilton Hotels, spun off its hotel and gambling operations and its technical schools, took on $2 billion in new debt, and repurchased a large block of its own stock.[46]

Shark repellents and poison pills increase the power of management in the event of a takeover attempt or make a takeover so unattractive that potential suitors either withdraw or are discouraged from even trying. Not only do they reduce the frequency of takeover bids, but they do not increase the expected value of shareholder gains when takeover contests do occur.[47] In fact, just adopting an antitakeover charter amendment leads investors to devalue a firm's stock, even if no deal is in sight.[48] The attempted takeover of Citation, a metal component manufacturer, by Drummond, a coal-mine operator and land developer, is an excellent example of the ill effects of poison pills. Drummond announced in November 1998 that it had acquired the right to own one-third of Citation's stock from two large Citation shareholders. Citation's board acted quickly to erect an antitakeover plan and also refused to provide detailed financial information to Drummond. By early 1999, Morris Hackney, chairman of Drummond, seemed to change his mind. He canceled the stock purchase option before its expiration date and said he doubted the company would pursue an acquisition.[49]

This kind of evidence naturally leads to the question of why managers are allowed to pursue actions that are not in the best interests of shareholders. This point has been debated for more than two decades. A popular view is that entrenched managers, acting in their own self-interests, are able to pursue strategies that offer protection to their own positions at the expense of the shareholders because (1) ownership is so widely distributed, (2) shareholders typically are not well organized, (3) some shareholders may not be aware of the negative implications of such provisions, and (4) boards of directors are tightly linked to managers through both formal and informal (social) ties and therefore are more likely to support managers in such cases. The entrenchment hypothesis has received great deal of support.[50] For one thing, firms that adopt poison pills are less profitable than other firms during the year before adoption, lending support to the idea that managers are trying to protect their jobs despite their incompetence. Managers in these firms also tend to own a smaller fraction of their firm's stock, which reduces their ability to influence the outcome of a takeover bid.[51]

An alternative view is that antitakeover amendments are in the shareholders' best interests because they strengthen the ability of managers to fend off hostile suitors desiring to acquire the firm at an unreasonably low price.[52] Poison pills provide strong motivation for acquiring firm executives to negotiate directly with target firm executives, as opposed to offering to buy shares directly from shareholders in a tender offer. Most poison pills become void if the top executives of the target firm approve of the merger. The charter amendment that contains the pill may have wording to this effect or, if not, the terms can be revoked by shareholder vote as a part of the deal. However, because auction-inducing actions are a ready alternative to competition-reducing actions and because they are likely to accomplish the same objective of a higher price, the stockholder interests argument is hard to support. Furthermore, there is no real evidence that target firm executives are able to negotiate a higher return for shareholders than they would receive in a tender offer. In fact, there is some evidence to the contrary.[53]

Acquiring-firm Perspective

From the perspective of the acquiring firm, all types of resistance are costly. The existence of multiple bidders leads to lower returns for the acquiring firm and poison pills are often prohibitively expensive.[54] Tender offers, which are considered hostile, are most often associated with higher final bid prices, probably because so many of them are resisted.[55] Two decades ago, finance researchers found evidence that tender offers led to higher returns to acquiring firms' shareholders in the post-merger period than friendly deals worked out between the two firms' principals (actually they found returns that were less negative, since the average return was negative or insignificant in either direction).[56] However, this effect was found to be a result of a few high-performing "glamour" firms expecting to be able to sustain their high performance even after they had made an acquisition. As we have demonstrated in other chapters, this is a difficult task. Furthermore, the effect disappeared by the 1980s.[57]

Hostile takeovers are associated with higher levels of management turnover and lower post-acquisition performance for the acquirer.[58] Also, hostility adversely affects post-merger integration.[59] Perhaps most important, unexpected tender offers deprive acquiring firm executives of the advantages of working together with target firm executives, thus eliminating many of the advantages of a friendly acquisition we outlined in the first half of this chapter.

As we reported earlier, most larger companies have adopted poison pills and auction-inducing resistance is common. Does this mean that a potential suitor should not consider any firm that has a poison pill in its charter or withdraw at the first sign of resistance? If this were the case, acquisitions would be rare indeed. However, when acquiring firm executives work out a friendly deal with target firm executives, the ill effects of competition-reducing resistance can be eliminated and the costs associated with auction-inducing resistance are likely to be minimized. Consequently, we advocate a position in which acquiring firm executives work with target firm executives to strike a deal that makes sense for both companies. Of course, private negotiations are even more advantageous for the acquiring firm.

Laws regarding takeover resistance can have a large effect on the attractiveness of a potential acquisition candidate. Government responses to the ongoing resistance debate have been mixed. In some cases, governments are strong advocates for potential targets. Other instances seem to reflect a position that competition-reducing tactics are not in the shareholders' best interests. We now discuss some of these varied responses.

Government Responses

Under Dutch law shareholders must approve poison pills, which can reduce the ability of target firm managers to protect their companies against unfavorable acquisitions. For example, the shareholders of the Gucci Group, registered in Amsterdam, rejected a poison pill proposal in 1997. As a result, LVMH Moet Hennessy Louis Vuitton was able to build a 34.4 percent stake in Gucci during January 1999 without launching a tender offer or paying the customary high premium typically associated with a takeover. In the United States, top executives would have quickly adopted a poison pill when threatened with the takeover, but Gucci's executives' hands were tied.[60]

The courts may also decide that certain types of poison pills are illegal. In the United States, a Delaware court struck down the "dead-hand" provision, "in which directors ousted in a proxy fight are the only directors with the power to rescind the pill and sell the company."[61] In an even more recent challenge to this action, Quickturn Design Systems Inc. argued that its version of a dead-hand poison pill used to fend off a takeover by Mentor Graphics Corp. was legal because it expired six months after the acquisition. The Delaware court ruled in favor of Mentor Graphics, stating that such plans interfere with the rights of a new board to manage the affairs of their corporation.

Pennsylvania law, on the other hand, is highly protective of targets of hostile suitors. A state law adopted in 1990 discourages potential raiders from buying large blocks of stock in a company to "put it in play," or forcing a company to accept a friendly bid. The law requires hostile bidders to pay back to the target firm any profits gained from the increase in value of the stock that was acquired, in some circumstances. For example, AlliedSignal bought a 9.9 percent stake in AMP in October of

1998 for $44.50 per share. Due to rival bids, the stock was worth at least $51.00 per share by January 1999. However, AlliedSignal's paper gain of $130 million may have to be paid back to AMP if a rival bidder successfully completes the acquisition.[62]

Because takeover laws vary substantially from country to country and state to state, acquiring firms should carefully study the applicable statutes during due diligence. Of course, most of the negative implications of even the most unfavorable laws can be avoided by a friendly deal.

In summary, auction-inducing resistance typically is advantageous to target firm shareholders because it allows time for other suitors to enter the bidding contest or may motivate the initial bidder to increase the offering price. The primary risk is that the original bidder may decide to withdraw. Competition-reducing resistance is detrimental to the shareholders of potential targets because it makes the company less attractive to suitors. The mere adoption of a shareholder rights amendment can lead to a reduction in shareholder value. Both types of resistance are detrimental to acquiring firms and laws may or may not be supportive.

Doing a Friendly Deal

In this chapter, we have provided a strong case for friendly acquisitions. Our analysis leads to the following guidelines for acquiring firm managers:

1. Actively pursue a friendly acquisition climate. Understand the mentality of target managers and avoid a "we win, you lose" attitude. Begin transition planning early. Include transition team managers in the final negotiations. Announce the new management team immediately. Ensure honest and frequent communications with customers and employees of the target firm.
2. Pursue business ventures with the target prior to acquisition negotiations. Get to know each other's cultures, management styles, resources, strengths, and weaknesses.
3. Try to avoid an auction by offering a fair price that is perhaps a little lower than what you think the final price will be, but is not so low that the target perceives the bid as potentially hostile. Find out what a typical premium is at the time in the industry, since premiums vary widely over time and by industry.
4. Try to keep negotiations private, if possible. Some companies begin meeting with the intention of pursuing a different kind of transaction, such as a joint venture, and then end up merging.
5. Avoid hostile takeovers, including tender offers. Work with target firm management. The popularity of poison pills almost makes this a necessity.

6. Know when to walk away from a deal. Auctions can lead to prices that are too high to recover through potential synergies. Federal Mogul Corp. cancelled its plans to buy the British firm LucasVarity PLC after TRW Inc. entered the competition, stating that a higher bid wouldn't be financially favorable.[63]
7. Carefully evaluate the prospect of being a white knight. Many of the advantages of working with a cooperative group of target firm executives can be realized in these situations, but the purchase price is still likely to be higher than other bids.
8. Study the applicable legal statutes concerning takeover resistance during the due diligence process.

The nature of acquisitions is such that there is no way to ensure a friendly deal. However, Mr. Kozlowski of Tyco International has taken a wise position by deciding that Tyco will never make a hostile bid.[64] Friendliness is one of many keys that help organizations achieve synergy through acquisitions. In the next chapter, we describe the synergy creation process in more detail and show how crucial it is to success in many mergers and acquisitions.

6

Achieving Integration and Synergy

Integration decisions are often justified by the synergies they create. Synergies exist when assets are worth more when used in conjunction with each other than separately. Synergies of some form are essential for integration to be successful. Integration offers little or no potential benefits when they do not exist.

—T. N. Hubbard

On the day Intel, the world's biggest semiconductor manufacturer kicked off the integration process of the semiconductors division of Digital, six thousand different deliverables were due to be executed by hundreds of employees in dozens of different countries.

—M. Zollo

Based in Paris, France, Alcatel is the world's fourth largest telecommunications manufacturer. Operating in over 130 countries, Alcatel provides "complete solutions and services to operators, service providers, enterprises and consumers, ranging from backbone networks to user terminals."[1] Until recently, the firm had a relatively small presence in the United States. Because of this market's growth potential, Alcatel executives chose to execute a corporate-level strategy that requires the company to develop a more prominent position in the United States. Acquisitions are a principal means through which this objective is to be reached. Analysts believe that this strategy demonstrates Alcatel's desire to leverage its current core competencies with closely controlled technologies and to be able to build products in its own facilitates that it had been purchasing from other networking companies.[2]

Announced in October 1998, Alcatel's acquisition of Packet Engines, a U.S.-based innovator of Gigabit Ethernet and routing switch technology, was completed on December 14, 1998. Integration of the firms' complementary product lines was thought to be one pathway through which synergy would be created. In particular, Packet Engines' products were expected to complement Alcatel's data and enterprise offerings with high-end routers and with Gigabit Ethernet LAN switches. Beyond this, Alcatel intended to integrate Packet Engines' technologies and technological skills with its own technological capabilities. Expected from these integration efforts was a strengthening of Alcatel's significant worldwide position in operator networks and its leading position in European enterprise data-networking integration.

Thus, the two firms' executives anticipated that Alcatel's acquisition of Packet Engines would create synergies through the melding of the two companies' core technological capabilities as well as the integration of their then current, complementary product lines. To enhance the probability of acquisition and integration success, several managerial decisions were announced at the time the transaction was completed. The establishment of a "technology development plan"—a plan through which employees would receive cash awards for meeting product development goals—is an example of the managerial intentions and actions that are to be a part of the post-merger implementation of this acquisition.

As is true with all acquisitions, however, this transaction was not considered risk free. Executives at the two firms noted that a number of factors could affect the acquisition's outcomes. Included among them were foreign and domestic product and price competition, the effectiveness at which the firms could reduce their costs through the melding of their operations, changes in governmental regulations, and unpredictable yet potentially dramatic changes in general economic and market conditions in the world's marketplaces.

As we noted previously, time is required to determine the level of success a firm earns through a merger or acquisition. Nonetheless, Alcatel executives were encouraged by the early evidence from this transaction. By combining Packet Engines' capabilities with those possessed by two other acquisitions (Internet Devices and Xylan), Alcatel argues that it has created an important new development in enterprise networking. Thus, the acquisition of Packet Engines appears to be an action through which Alcatel is able to create value for customers.[3]

In this chapter, we discuss the need to create synergy as one prerequisite to acquisition success. As we noted in Chapter 4, the use of complementary resources between an acquiring and an acquired firm can create synergies that, in turn, generate a competitive advantage for the firm over its competitors. Continuing our analysis of the importance of synergy in acquisition success in this chapter, we discuss the four foundations of synergy creation. These foundations must be present to enable the firm to create synergy through an acquisition.[4]

As we will see through a review of this chapter's contents, managerial efforts that are expended to integrate disparate operations into a new company or business unit are critical to the attempts to create synergy through an acquisition. Without effective integration of formerly independent companies or units, it is unlikely that the sought-after yet frequently elusive synergy will be created through an acquisition.

This discussion is preceded with commentary about the link between *value* and *synergy*. Drawing again from the focus of Chapter 4, we briefly define synergy and describe its attributes. Before discussing the four foundations of synergy creation, we highlight the need for firms to expend considerable efforts to actually create synergy. This is necessary because acquisitions can quickly fail when personnel believe that synergy's benefits will emerge simply as a result of completing a financial transaction through which formerly independent firms' operations are combined. Thus, synergy is merely a *possibility* of competitive advantage and value creation until appropriate and effective actions are taken. In fact, synergy cannot be created when personnel do not understand the nature of interrelationships that may exist through the combination of firms' operations. For example, understanding the exact nature of the interrelationships between Alcatel's and Packet Engines' product lines *and* their technological capabilities will influence the degree to which synergy is created through post-merger integration activities. As we noted in Chapter 4, the creation of synergy through an acquisition generates additional value for stakeholders. The chapter closes with recommendations regarding managerial actions that facilitate acquisition success by creating synergy.

Synergy and the Creation of Value

Mergers and acquisitions are completed to create value for stakeholders. More strictly, the synergy motive for acquisitions suggests that these transactions take place in anticipation of economic gains that can result from the merging of the resources of two units or firms.[5] Beyond this, the argument is that acquisitions should take place only when gains will accrue to acquirer firm shareholders. In free-market economies, the main interest of the firm's agents/decisions (i.e., top-level managers) should be to enhance the value of shareholders' (i.e., principals') ownership positions in the firm when seeking to create synergy through acquisitions.

Perhaps particularly in what is rapidly becoming a borderless business economy, effective merger and acquisition decisions are made in awareness of governmental regulators' philosophies regarding such transactions.[6] At the end of the twentieth century, for example, some believed that the then current head of the U. S. Justice Department's antitrust department was making policy-related decisions that were intended to establish the rules of competition through which high-technology firms (among others) would compete against each other during the twenty-first century.[7] Astute corporate-level strategists are aware of key regulators' actions and beliefs and at least partly frame their merger and acquisition decisions in light of them, realizing that these beliefs influence the actions the firm will take in efforts to create synergy.

As this discussion suggests, merger and acquisition decisions are an important part of the firm's overall corporate-level strategy and are believed by some to be a special case of strategy.[8] In terms of mergers and acquisitions, *value* is created when the benefits of the synergy that is gained through the combination and integration of formerly separate firms exceeds the costs (including the payment of any premium) that are incurred to create that synergy. A firm's share price is one indicator of the value that is generated by an acquisition. However, especially when a significant premium is paid to complete the transaction, acquisitions, as a corporate strategy, can be risky.[9] This risk is apparent when we consider the fact that the long-term effects of mergers on the firm's value and performance are frequently somewhat negative. Reasons for this negative outcome include inexperience of those involved in the transaction, lack of a strategic purpose for the acquisition, and poor postmerger integration. In slightly different terms, these reasons can be interpreted as an indication that synergy was not created through the completion of an acquisition.

Sometimes, the managerial decision to attempt to create value through the completion and integration of mergers and acquisitions is influenced by an industry's structural characteristics and the conditions resulting from them. For example, in 1999 Deutsche Bank of Germany allocated another DM6bn ($3.4 billion) to the fund it uses to complete acquisitions in Europe's rapidly consolidating banking industry as well as in the rapid consolidation of other nations' financial sectors. To become a more prominent competitor in the United States, Deutsche Bank paid approximately $10 billion to acquire Bankers Trust. Combined, these decisions demonstrated Deutsche Bank leaders' belief that the consolidation of the banking and financial industry occurring throughout the world mandated the need to attempt to create value through the synergies that can result from scale and scope economies.[10] Because of the consolidation in this industry, Italian banks are also beginning to consolidate. Seen as a revolution in the Italian banking industry, one of the intended transactions demonstrating this change was the launching of a bid by UniCredito Italian to purchase its Milan rival, Banca Commerciale Italiana (BCI).[11] Some analysts envision the pursuit of synergy through this type of merger and acquisition activity as the precursor to a "tumultuous upheaval in Italian banking and finance."[12]

In the oil industry, BP Amoco announced its intention to acquire

Atlantic Richfield Co. in 1999. Both companies agreed to complete the transaction. This transaction was identified by analysts as the eighth major merger or acquisition in the oil and gas business during a six-month period—a time in which the industry had been shaken for over a year by rapidly declining oil prices and increasing demand for cleaner fuels. The combination would create the world's second largest oil producer. Moreover, the newly formed firm would own 59 percent of the refining capacity in the United States and 28 percent in Europe.[13] An estimated stock deal valued at approximately $25.6 billion, this intended transaction "would be the latest integration in a rapidly consolidating oil industry and the second acquisition for the former British Petroleum Co., which completed its $57.6 billion merger with Chicago-based Amoco Corp." in December 1998.[14]

In a broader sense, it has been argued that the consolidation of industries through mergers and acquisitions (such as the ones we have briefly described) increases the competitiveness of weaker companies and makes it possible for smaller firms to combine to generate the critical mass that is required to create synergy and then exploit it as one means of achieving success in the global economy.[15] In each instance, though, the degree to which this success is achieved is influenced considerably by how effectively combined units' capabilities and processes are integrated and the amount of synergy that is created through that integration.

Pursuing Value by Creating Synergy

As we noted previously, synergy is derived from a Greek word meaning "working together."[16] As we have discussed in different contexts of what must take place for acquisitions to be completed successfully, creating significant amounts of synergy is inherently difficult. Moreover, managers should understand that creating synergy involves opportunity costs. Pursuing synergy through attempts to create a new unit by integrating formerly independent operations can "distract managers' attention from the nuts and bolts of their businesses, and it crowds out other initiatives that might generate real benefits."[17] In fact, in many instances, attempts to create synergy destroy rather than create value for stakeholders. An important reason for this, in addition to opportunity costs, is the "hidden" costs that can accompany acquisitions. Examples of these include culture clashes and misunderstandings, "turf" battles, and the lack of requisite knowledge to develop and use effective acquisition integration processes.

In financial terms, synergy can be thought of as the present value of all future profits that are directly attributable to a new combination that an acquisition has created. In operational terms, synergy reflects the ability of two or more firms or units to create more value working together than they were able to create operating separately. In managerial terms, synergy is created when the firm's decision-makers are dedicated to finding ways to integrate units so that their newly formed patterns of joint efforts generate a competitive advantage and, in turn, create additional value.[18] For shareholders, financial and/or operational synergy must yield gains (as represented by enhancements in their overall wealth) that they cannot obtain through their own investment decisions.[19]

As we have shown, actual synergies result in the creation of a competitive advantage for the firm over its rivals. Such value-enhancing synergies can be generated through several sources,[20] including: (1) improved operating efficiencies that are based on scale or scope economies, and (2) the sharing of knowledge or skills across units (it is possible, for example, that "value can be created simply by exposing one set of people to another who have a different way of getting things done").[21] Across industries and types of acquisitions, history shows that "strategic acquisitions," ones in which firms with overlapping businesses couple their operations, tend to generate more synergy than acquisitions that bring together firms competing in unrelated businesses.[22] It is because of this that the melding of complementary resources, as discussed and described before, can play a crucial role in efforts to create synergy and, ultimately, acquisition success.

Creating Synergy

In each case—that is, for every acquisition that is completed—synergy must be created to reach intended levels of success. Executives at U.S. Filter Corp. (the current ownership status of this firm is described later in the chapter) are recognized as individuals who devote a significant amount of their time and energies to integrate newly acquired units into the firm's existing corporate structure and culture. As pointed out, driving these integration efforts is the top-level managers' intention of melding their firm's expertise, resources, and product offerings into a single, seamless source for industrial and municipal water-treatment processes.[23]

The actual creation of synergy is an outcome that is expected from managers' work. Achieving this outcome demands effective integration of combined units' assets, operations, and personnel. Experience and history show that at the very least, creating synergy "requires a great deal of work on the part of managers at the corporate and business levels. The activities that create synergy include combining similar processes, coordinating business units that share common resources, centralizing support activities that apply to multiple units and resolving conflicts among business units."[24] It is not unusual for managers to underestimate the magnitude of issues and problems that can accompany integration efforts. One of the key problems concerns people and their acceptance of the actions that are required for the desired integration to be completed effectively and efficiently.[25]

Sometimes, job cuts are used as part of an integration process as the firm seeks to create synergy after completing an acquisition. For example, near the end of the 1990s Halliburton Co. reduced its worldwide workforce by approximately 8 percent. The firm's president noted that "job cuts were planned to obtain necessary merger synergies and react to continued market conditions."[26] This decision was one of the managerial actions taken following Halliburton's acquisition of Dresser Industries Inc. for $9.2 billion. Generally speaking, the synergies obtained through personnel reductions are short-lived and do not contribute to a long-term competitive advantage for the firm over its rivals.

Interested in achieving economies of scale primarily in distribution and marketing, RPM paid a premium (in excess of one-times sales) to acquire Rust-Oleum. A leading producer of protective coatings and other specialty chemicals for both consumer and industrial markets, Rust-Oleum's product lines were deemed highly compatible with RPM's. To create synergies, efforts were undertaken to integrate the selling of the newly created firm's products through multiple distribution channels, including distributors for industrial products and hardware stores, home centers, and other mass merchandisers for consumer products. Analysts concluded that the synergies being created through the sharing of strong distribution channels and strong brand names would result in competitive advantages and generate additional value for shareholders. It appears that these expectations are being reached since RPM remains a worldwide leader in protective paints and coatings for both home and industry. Additionally, publicly available information notes RPM's belief that customers for the firm's diverse set of consumer products are being served effectively and efficiently through the synergies generated by integrating Rust-Oleum with some of its other brands, including Painter's Touch and American Accents, for example.[27]

The failure to integrate firms' operations contributes to a lack of acquisition success. This is thought to account for AT&T's inability to add value to shareholders' ownership positions through its purchase of NCR, an acquisition that was eventually divested. Having paid $4.2 billion for NCR in 1991, AT&T endured losses of $720 million in 1995 alone. Rather than actively manage the acquisition to *create* synergies through the firms' combined operations, "AT&T voluntarily left NCR executives in place to conduct business as usual for two years after the acquisition. In fact, they were even put in charge of AT&T's old computer production and marketing business. NCR executives were merely asked by AT&T to look for synergy."[28] Beyond this, AT&T later split itself into several major units. This strategic action was interpreted by some as an indication that the firm simply was not able to create expected synergies across its business units.[29] The much-maligned acquisition of Snapple Beverages by

Quaker Oats (another acquisition that was divested) suffered from managerial inattention to integration processes. In fact, some analysts suggest that Quaker Oats virtually ignored sales and marketing efforts for Snapple rather than concentrating on finding ways to integrate such efforts with those being undertaken to sell and distribute its popular Gatorade drink.[30]

Integration Processes

It is necessary to properly integrate acquisitions into the firm's current operations if synergy is to be created and competitive advantage and additional shareholder value are to result. The importance of effective integration processes is highlighted by the argument that "improving the acquisition integration process ... may be one of the most urgent and compelling challenges facing businesses today."[31] In fact, some believe that merger and acquisition integration creates managerial challenges that are unlike any others.[32] One of the objectives of integration processes is to uncover potential problems that could prevent the newly formed firm from operating in ways that create competitive advantage and value and to determine actions to take that prevent other integration-related difficulties.[33] The probability of achieving integration success is improved by acting quickly. In this respect, two experienced integration consultants suggest that "failure to move quickly to put the companies together will destroy the value the company hoped to gain in the first place."[34]

The success GE Capital Services has achieved with respect to integration processes has resulted in a core competence. Executives have had practice with acquisition-integration processes, in that GE Capital is a financial conglomerate with 27 separate businesses, more than 50,000 employees worldwide, and businesses that range from private-label credit-card services to commercial real-estate financing to railcar and aircraft leasing. In recent times, the intention of GE Capital's managerial personnel has been to use its acquisition integration competitive advantage as an important means for the company's continuing growth. GE Capital has developed an acquisition-integration process that is divided into "four action stages, starting with the work that goes on before the acquisition is completed—that is, before the deal closes—and continuing all the way through assimilation."[35] However, because each acquisition is recognized for its uniqueness, modifications are made as to how the parts of each stage are used as well as to the timing of their use.

We pointed out that there are four foundations to the creation of synergy. These foundations are strategic fit, organizational fit, managerial actions, and value creation. Although we examine each foundation separately, it is only when all four of them exist that the probability of the firm being able to create synergy is increased substantially.

Strategic Fit

Strategic fit "refers to the effective matching of strategic organizational capabilities."[36] The manner in which capabilities can be matched through merger and acquisition activity is virtually endless. Generally speaking, however, the opportunity to create the type of synergy that leads to a competitive advantage and the enhancement of shareholder wealth is reduced when an acquisition combines firms or business units that are both strong and/or weak in the same business activities. In such instances, the newly created firm exhibits the same capabilities (or lack of capabilities), although the magnitude of the strength or weakness is greater.

The "merger of equals" between pharmaceutical giants Zeneca (of the United Kingdom) and Astra (a Swedish firm) is an example of a transaction that some analysts believed lacked strategic fit. In this instance, the argument was that the merger did not result in strategic fit in two key performance areas—research and development and managerial skills. Although the merger resulted in greater scale for the two companies, analysts did not believe that it solved problems with both firms' medium-term pipeline of products needed to replace big-selling drugs that were set to expire early in the twenty-first century.[37] Others observed that the two firms had a great deal in common including the aforementioned large number of soon-to-expire patents and "relatively parochial management in an international industry."[38] In the instance of this merger, it is possible that the type of strategic fit required for positive synergy to be created is absent. If this proves to be the case, shareholder value may not be enhanced as a result of this transaction.

As discussed next, there are four potential sources of strategic fit that can lead to synergy through merger and acquisition activity. These sources of strategic fit are operations synergy, R&D/technology synergy, marketing-based synergy, and management/managerial synergy. In each instance, synergy is created through the integration of value-enhancing activities between two or more units or businesses. In presenting these examples, it is important to note that it is not uncommon for synergies to be sought through more than one type of strategic fit. Thus, the ultimate success of perhaps many mergers or acquisitions is a product of how well synergy is created through efforts to link businesses' activities across multiple organizational functions. In each case, though, strategic fit must exist for synergy to be created.

Strategic Fit Through Operations Synergy

The focus of this source of strategic fit synergy is how the newly created firm will integrate functional activities. Operations synergy can be created through economies of scale and/or economies of scope. In the airplane construction industry, for example, discussions were held in the late 1990s among European manufacturers, including, among others, Daimler-Benz Aerospace of Germany, Aerospatiale/Matra of France, and British Aerospace PLC of the United Kingdom. Seeking both scale and scope economies through this potential merger and/or acquisition activity, one senior executive indicated that a key objective of these discussions and the decisions that may result from them is "to create one of the world's biggest aerospace/defense companies so that in a few years' time we could buy one of the U.S. giants."[39] Similarly, WorldCom Inc.'s acquisition of MCI Communications Corp. allowed the pairing of World-Com's local facilities with MCI's long-distance traffic. Synergies (based on both scale and scope economies) were anticipated through this combination by: (1) integrating the firms' long-distance and local businesses, (2) melding costly administrative functions, and (3) paring back MCI's ambitious plans for a local telephone network.[40] The business activities through which "operational" synergy can be created include purchasing, training programs, common parts, and the development of larger scale manufacturing facilities.

Based in the United Kingdom, Glynwed is now the world's leading plastic pipe systems business. This market position was solidified through Glynwed's acquisition of Friatec, a German company (this purchase was the firm's largest ever acquisition). Commenting favorably about this transaction, an analyst suggested that "in one step they (Glynwed) had become the world leader in an industry that's almost certainly growing faster than gross domestic product." In addition to a strong hold in the German market, this acquisition gave Glynwed entry into Eastern Europe, Brazil, and the United States as well as an opportunity to participate in other industries such as gas and fresh and wastewater. Combining the two firms' purchasing functions and integrating some manufacturing operations were highlighted as business activities in which operational synergies were expected.[41]

Founded originally only six weeks apart from each other, Bright Horizons Inc. and CorporateFamily Solutions had been spirited competitors until they agreed to merge. The new firm created through this transaction (called Bright Horizons Family Solutions) has more than 250 employer-sponsored care centers across the United States. This company offers a comprehensive array of work-life capabilities, including worksite schools and consulting services on how to make businesses more family-friendly. Operational synergies created by this transaction include relatively modest yet nonetheless symbolically important savings on insurance policies, accounting fees, and the preparation of public relations documents (including annual reports). More significant operational synergies were expected through the clustering of childcare centers. These clusters permit the sharing of full-time and substitute teachers. In terms of the development of personnel, the cluster approach allows the newly created firm to train clusters of staff from both companies' centers instead of training on a site-by-site basis.[42]

Vivendi SA is one of France's largest industrial conglomerates with businesses in media, telecommunications, and utilities such as water and waste management. To support its interest in gaining a dominant position in the management of municipal wastewater treatment facilities on a global scale, Vivendi acquired U.S. Filter Corp.[43] This acquisition gave Vivendi a foothold in the United States in its core water business. Analysts responded favorably to what they concluded was a strategic acquisition. Moreover, in the view of Vivendi's chairman, Jean-Marie Messier, "Vivendi and U.S. Filter have both been targeting the growing worldwide water market, but from different starting points and with an emphasis on different types of client. What we recognized [though], is that we share a vision of a full-service, global water enterprise."[44] Analysts and company personnel anticipated the creation of operational synergies through the combining of a number of different activities such as purchasing and treatment facilities in addition to the synergies earned by melding the two firms' product and service lines. Enhancing the probability of being able to create significant operational synergies is the scale and scope of what the acquisition would create—namely, the undisputed world leader in water-related businesses.

Strategic Fit Through R&D/Technology Synergies

To create synergies through this type of strategic fit, firms seek to link activities associated with research and development (R&D) processes and the technologies that often are critical to them. The sharing of R&D programs, the transfer of technologies across units, products, and programs, and the development of new core businesses through access to private innovative capabilities (i.e., innovation capabilities that are available in the newly created firm but unavailable to the general market and to competitors) are examples of activities firms trying to link to create synergy.

Rohm and Haas is a Philadelphia-based manufacturer of the chemicals that are found in products such as paints, shampoos, and semiconductors. This firm is pursuing an acquisition strategy to increase its revenue growth and improve its financial performance. At a cost of $4.6 billion, Morton International Inc. is one of Rohm and Haas' acquisitions. Known primarily for its salt business, Morton is also a producer of multiple specialty chemicals, including sodium borohydride, which is a bleaching agent used in the newspaper industry to make news pages whiter. In the main, Morton's chemicals are manufactured to increase the quality and performance of end products. According to Rohm and Haas' CEO, it is the addition of Morton's technologies and technological capabilities to those residing in his firm that drove this particular acquisition. In his words, "This deal will extend Rohm and Haas' technology platform beyond its premier position in acrylic chemistry and electronic materials. Morton's technology will add significant expertise in urethanes, powder coatings, plastic automotive coatings and inorganic chemistry."[45]

An indicator of the further consolidation of Europe's aerospace industry is the merger of units of two larger companies. GKN, a United Kingdom engineering group, and Finmeccanica, an Italian firm, intend to merge their helicopter manufacturing units (this transaction was to be completed immediately following anticipated regulatory approval). The combination of the two firms' business units will command approximately 20 percent of the world market for helicopters. According to officials from the two companies, the primary means through which synergies are to be created is by combining the units' technological skills and marketing capabilities. Some analysts, however, noted that in addition to synergies that were to be created by the melding of these particular types of skills and capabilities, operational synergies were also expected as a result of this transaction. In these analysts' view, the merged activities "will seek to make savings by bringing together the two partners' purchasing activities to win greater leverage with suppliers, and by a rationalisation of production processes."[46] United Kingdom's defense secretary spoke in favor of this transaction, noting that "there is an urgent need to restructure Europe's aerospace industry to ensure that it can compete effectively in global markets and contribute to the strengthening of European defence."[47]

Strategic Fit Through Marketing-Based Synergies

Synergy is created through this type of strategic fit when the firm successfully links various marketing-related activities including those related to the sharing of brand names as well as distribution channels and advertising and promotion campaigns. Decision-makers must recall, though, that in each instance customers should be their firm's focus when seeking to create synergies by linking marketing-related activities. In the financial services industry, for example, some executives believe that efforts to create synergy through marketing activities have failed because they have not been sufficiently client focused. This may be especially true when seeking to cross-sell products to customers. Commenting about this activity, a top-level manager at John Hancock suggested that firms in his industry are learning that "clients ... want to pick the best provider of each financial service." This manager further observed that "his own experience with cross-marketing was quite frustrating. Trying to get an insurance agent to refer a client to a stock broker just didn't work," he indicated.[48] Thus, seeking strategic fit through marketing-based synergies in the financial services industry challenges firms to determine how to share brand names, distribution channels, and products in ways that add value to clients/customers that exceeds the value customers can create through their own actions.

Marketing-based synergies can sometimes be created through the merging and subsequent sharing of a sales force. New England Business Service Inc. (NEBS), for example, is using acquisitions to transform itself from a direct-mail business forms supplier to a diversified provider of products and services to small businesses. NEBS suggests that the acquisition program is creating a company that is "the single source for quality imprinted business forms and checks—both manual and computer—as well as labels, greeting cards, stationery and promotional products."[49] The firm's market niche and the nature of its intended acquisitions are demonstrated by the following comments from NEBS' Investor Relations Officer: "We're not after the business of the General Electrics of the world. Our ability to handle small orders economically and efficiently, with the kinds of gross margins that we have, distinguishes us from many other companies." To enact this transformation, NEBS completed a number of acquisitions. A key attraction of McBee Systems Inc. and McBee Systems of Canada Inc., which NEBS acquired from ROMO Corp. in 1998, was the 350-person sales force. Combining the McBee personnel with its existing sales force was intended to create synergy by allowing NEBS to establish personal selling relationships with small businesses. Although it possessed a competitive advantage in terms of direct-mail customer relationships, NEBS believed that the synergy between this advantage and the McBee's personal selling relationships competitive advantage would create significant value.[50]

Gaining quick access to a market through an established brand name is another way marketing-based synergies can be created through acquisitions. In response to Internet retailers' growing successes, Bertelsmann, the German group that owns the world's largest book club and book publishing business, acquired a 50 percent stake in barnesandnoble.com. This Internet operation is a unit of Barnes & Noble, one of the largest book chains in the United States. A portion of Bertelsmann's investment was to be spent on marketing activities. Moreover, for Bertelsmann, this transaction allowed the firm to enter the U. S. online book business in partnership with an established brand name rather than starting on its own. According to a company official, "We can make use of a strong presence in the [U.S.] market from the start" through this purchase. Additional synergies were expected by using barnesandnoble.com's distribution capabilities to supply BooksOnline, the Internet bookselling operation that Bertelsmann had started in Europe before the transaction between the two firms was initiated. The CEO of barnesandnoble.com viewed this activity quite favorably, suggesting that "from a financial perspective, [this transaction] is a winner and from a strategic perspective, it's a blockbuster."[51]

Strategic Fit Through Management/Managerial Synergies

Strategic fit can also be obtained through management synergies. These synergies are typically gained when competitively relevant skills that were possessed by managers in the formerly independent companies or business units can be transferred successfully between units within the newly formed firm.

Founded in 1981 as an independent producer of electronic manufacturing services to original equipment manufacturers, EFTC Corp. has used strategies of both internal growth and targeted acquisitions to become a multistate leader in its chosen market niche.[52] Building complex circuitry devices that are used in products such as computers and navigation systems for airplanes, EFTC has positioned itself to provide superior service to customers requiring small-lot processing in the manufacture and repair of electronic products. When completing an acquisition, EFTC allocates a great deal of time and energy to build management teams. By describing and discussing in detail the vision and strategy it has in mind through an acquisition to those managing the target firm, EFTC executives believe that they are able to identify managerial skills that can be shared between units.[53] Similarly, before the merger was completed between paper producers Abitibi-Price and Stone-Consolidated, senior executives from the two firms spent a significant amount of time together. Among other discussion points, these upper-level managers held frank talks about the roles the combined executive team would play once the transaction was finalized and how their respective firms' managerial skills could be shared productively.[54]

Our two examples of management synergies have been concerned with linking the activities of upper-level managers. However, acquiring and acquired firms also seek to find ways to share the capabilities of managerial personnel at the middle and lower levels to achieve strategic fit through management synergies. In fact, given the growing importance of middle and lower-level managers to the formation and implementation of all types of strategies, these combinations are becoming increasingly critical to the creation of synergy and, ultimately, to acquisition success.

Organizational Fit

Organizational fit, the second foundation to the creation of synergy, "occurs when two organizations or business units have similar management processes, cultures, systems and structures."[55] As a foundation to synergy creation, organizational fit means that firms are characterized by a reasonably high degree of compatibility. From an operational perspective, the existence of compatibility suggests that the integration processes that are developed and used to meld the firms' or business units' operations can be expected to bring about desired results rather quickly, effectively, and efficiently. Thus, organizational compatibility facilitates resource sharing, enhances the effectiveness of communication patterns, and improves the company's capability to transfer knowledge and skills. The *absence* of organizational fit stifles and sometimes prevents the integration of an acquired unit.

Earlier, we described the merger of Bright Horizons Inc. and CorporateFamily Solutions. These two firms were founded on a similar principle—namely, to provide high-quality services in the workplace childcare market. Perhaps partly because the two firms began their operations within six weeks of each other, they developed similar operational procedures. Moreover, the proximity in strategic goals being pursued by the two companies caused them to target virtually the same customer base. The CEOs knew each other quite well and had established similar systems and structures to influence their firms' methods of operating. Awareness of the proximate nature of their companies' philosophies and operations eventually caused the CEOs to "decide that they could better achieve their goals if they started working together."[56] Thus, the significant degree of organizational fit that existed between these two companies can be expected to facilitate efforts on the part of Bright Horizons Family Solutions, the newly formed company, to create synergies through the compatibility of their management processes, cultures, systems, and structures. Similarly, Alcatel and Packet Engines, the firms discussed at the beginning of the chapter, were operated through the guidance of compatible management processes and organizational control systems. The respective firms' concentration on and control of technological capabilities demonstrate the compatibility that is expected to facilitate synergy creation in the newly formed firm.

The number of decisions that must be made regarding the integration of operations is not insignificant, even when the involved units or companies are judged to be compatible. In fact, one estimate is that to bring about a modest amount of integration through completion of a merger or acquisition demands the making of roughly 10,000 major, nonroutine decisions.[57] Generally, these decisions are to be made about actions to take to reach the promise of strategic fit. Conditions are evaluated in order to make decisions regarding multiple issues, including those of the launching of new products, the design of new systems that are capable of satisfying the financial and strategic control needs of the newly created firm, rationalization of existing sales forces, and the integration of R&D programs.

Organizational incompatibility can exist even when an analysis of firms involved in a merger or acquisition suggests that this should not be the case. For example, the merger of FedEx and Flying Tigers seemed to have great potential to create synergy, a competitive advantage, and value for stakeholders. This expectation appeared reasonable given that FedEx specialized in the delivery of small packages while Flying Tigers' focus was on large shipments. The intent of this transaction was to meld the two firms' operations to form a total package delivery company. Among other avenues, economies of scale that were expected through the combination of the firms were an anticipated source of synergy. Unfortunately, however, sufficient organizational fit did not exist between the two firms. In particular, their organizational cultures were quite different. Because of these differences, conflicts arose, communications become inefficient and ineffective, and the expected synergies, including those of scale economies, never materialized.[58] Similar to the experience of these two firms, history is showing that the failure of a number of mergers and acquisitions involving banks and brokerage houses can be attributed to clashes between organizational cultures.[59]

Organizational culture has been identified by some analysts as a key determinant of the outcomes achieved as a result of Daimler-Benz's acquisition of Chrysler Corporation. In speaking to risks associated with this acquisition, one analyst suggested that "when it comes to downside risks, the greatest is certainly culture. Beyond the fact of both being carmakers, the two companies differ in just about everything: language, markets, work traditions and governance. And in the executive suite, how will Chrysler's sky-high American salaries and stock options fit with the German structure of employee representation and a supervisory board?" However, a position articulated by Jurgen Schrempp, the chairman of Daimler-Benz, in a discussion of his firm's acquisition of Chrysler indicated an awareness of culture as a key component of organizational fit and the acquisition's success. In Schrempp's words, "We are set to build a truly global culture." Robert Eaton, Chrysler's former chairman, supported this intention by observing that "this is precisely one of the reasons we immediately agreed to run the business initially together. We both believe that integrating and merging cultures is possibly the greatest art of management."[60] Thus, there appears to be a commitment between the top executives of the acquiring and acquired firm to take definitive actions to prevent organizational culture from having a negative effect on the acquisition.

Firms sometimes cancel an intended merger or acquisition if the lack of organizational fit is recognized before the transaction is finalized. Interestingly, this is not an uncommon occurrence, as demonstrated by the fact that over 2,140 mergers that were planned to take place between 1992 and 1998 were called off.[61] Of course, these intended transactions were canceled for a variety of reasons. However, an example of a planned transaction that was not completed because of a perceived lack of organizational fit involves American Home Products Corp. and Monsanto Co. A review of the merger-related experiences between these two firms suggests that they called off their $33.6 billion merger "over what some analysts said was a disagreement among top executives on who would run the pharmaceutical-biotech company."[62] On paper, the possibility of forming a life sciences firm that would have $3 billion in anticipated annual profits and a market value of $96 billion was attractive to the firms' top-level managers. However, discussions among upper-level managers regarding the leadership patterns that were to be used to influence and control the merged company revealed incompatibilities with respect to managerial processes and operating objectives. Commenting about this incompatibility, an analyst observed that executives from the two firms "could not see eye to eye on a number of issues including staffing . . . and the direction of the company."[63] Because of the lack of cohesion regarding what would have been the merged firm's strategic direction and the incompatibilities of the independent companies' managerial processes, among other potential incompatibilities, deciding not to finalize the intended transaction best served shareholders' interests.

After a potential merger or acquisition is canceled, for whatever reason, troublesome issues may still surface. An example is the set of competitively sensitive information, data, and insights that firms share often during the negotiation stage. Exchanges of information, data, and so forth between the acquired firm and its target is understandable. In fact, these sharings are required to promote the completion of a transaction that is in the best interests of all parties. Moreover, we have contended in this chapter that open and detailed discussions permit firms to isolate areas in which synergy can be created. An outcome often associated with these deliberations is determination of the other firm's strengths and weaknesses, and vice versa.

Ernst & Young and KPMG Peat Marwick found themselves in a situation that could be interpreted positively in one sense but negatively in another following the termination of the firms' merger talks. This simultaneously positive and negative status is a function of the fact that strengths and weaknesses of each firm become "public" knowledge during the negotiation stage. One of the many issues examined during the merger discussion stage concerned the two firms' Internet Web sites. For KPMG, the swapping of information about the two firms' objectives and methods of operations with respect to web sites proved quite useful. According to one of the firm's partners, KPMG decided to "revamp both its Internet web site and its own intranet based on information it gathered about Ernst's sites during the five-month negotiations."[64] Even in light of the risks associated with symmetrical information flows between the acquiring firm and its target, upper-level managers remain convinced that full disclosure is required to determine if a proposed merger or acquisition can be expected to be successful.

Managerial Actions

The third foundation of the creation of synergy concerns actions and initiatives that managers take for their firms to actually realize the competitive benefits that are promised by the prospects of different types of synergy. In other words, creating synergy requires the active management of the acquisition process. When considering the need for proactive behavior on their part to create synergy, managers should recognize the magnitude of integration issues and the pervasiveness of human resource concerns that surface often when engaged in efforts to create synergy.[65]

Some of these actions should take place during the negotiation stage; others should occur once a transaction has been finalized. The reality driving the need for specific managerial actions to be taken is that even when strategic fit and organizational fit are associated with a merger or an acquisition, the prospective and desired synergy will not be realized until managers form and execute actions that facilitate the creation and exploitation of synergy. Thus, various managerial actions must be initiated to effectively match the strategic capabilities that are demonstrated by the "strategic fit" foundation of synergy *and* to gain the competitive benefits that are permitted by the similarities in managerial process, cultures, systems, and structures that are represented by the "organizational fit" foundation of synergy. As we stated previously, synergy does not create itself simply because a merger or acquisition has taken place. Rather than letting an acquired firm operate on its own, actions must be initiated by acquiring firm managers that will bring about the sought-after synergies.

In the main, history and experience show that the probability of synergy creation and eventual acquisition success are increased when managers engage in or display the following actions: (1) dedicating their time and energy to helping others in the firm create intended synergies, (2) forming a leadership team that is responsible for facilitating of actions linked with synergy creation, (3) creating and stating a sense of purpose and direction for the firm with each acquisition so all can understand how individual transactions will create synergy and enhance performance, and (4) modeling the behaviors that are expected of others in order to create synergy.[66] Examples of actions managers can take to engage in or display these behaviors include the holding of joint meetings between acquiring and acquired firm personnel and making decisions to achieve the scale and scope economies that result from using consolidated purchasing routines, combined manufacturing facilities, and the sharing of R&D knowledge and skills. As mentioned previously, customers should be prominent when evaluating actions to take to complete a merger or acquisition. Some observers of synergy creation and acquisition success suggest that managers should initiate courses of action that will inform customers of the value that a completed merger or acquisition will create for them. Scheduling meetings with customers to explain how additional value will be generated for them is a recommended action for managers to take as representatives of the newly formed firm.[67]

Mentioned earlier, EFTC Corp. seeks growth through both internal means and acquisitions. When completing an acquisition, EFTC officials seek management synergies. Beyond this, the firm allocates the amount of time that is required to form and develop a management team that demonstrates genuine and deep excitement about being responsible for the successful operation of the newly formed company or business unit. Often, this team is the one that is in place in the target firm. During frequent meetings that are held before completing an acquisition, EFTC managers provide detailed information about their vision and strategy if the acquired firm were to become a part of EFTC Corp. Open and free-flowing interchanges are the norm for these meetings. In the words of EFTC's CEO, "We want to have a team that is excited about our strategy and feels that it can contribute to that strategy. No matter how good a company may be, if the management team doesn't believe in our strategy, we would not buy the company."[68]

We have emphasized the importance of culture when seeking to create synergy through the organizational fit foundation. To increase the likelihood that parties would understand each other's culture, managers from two hospitals that had been merged met to describe and evaluate their respective culture. During the session, managers from the acquiring and acquired firm described their own culture, indicated what it thought about the other firm's culture and estimated how they believed their culture would be perceived and evaluated by their managerial counterparts. The session yielded unique opportunities for the managers to work on integrating the two firms by using the similarities and strengths of each organizational culture.[69]

In other instances, managerial personnel from an acquiring company can spend time in the offices of those leading the target firm while negotiations are under way. This time can be used to highlight how the merger or acquisition can create value for stakeholders. Moreover, such interactions allow parties from both companies to learn more about the mind-set driving their actions and the nature of each firm's procedures, processes, and control systems.[70]

Value Creation

Value creation is the last of the four synergy creation foundations. The point with this foundation is that, for synergy to be created, the benefits that can be derived from synergy must exceed the costs associated with developing and exploiting it.[71] The costs that should be less than the value of the synergy that is created include those associated with

(1) a purchasing premium, (2) the financing of the transaction, and (3) the set of implementation actions required to integrate the acquired unit into the existing organizational structure.

Premiums continue to be paid to acquire companies. For example, the 12-month moving average of purchase price premiums over stock prices edged upward in the first quarter of 1998 from late 1997 levels.[72] Premiums sometimes exceed the market value of the target firm by 100 percent or more. Moreover, in the last two decades, the premiums paid for acquired firms have averaged between 40 and 50 percent.[73]

In contrast to these percentages, Daimler-Benz estimated that it paid a 28 percent premium to acquire Chrysler Corporation. This premium cost Daimler-Benz approximately $8 billion. On the other side of the equation, officials from the two firms evaluated the synergies that were to be created through the acquisition at $1.4 billion in the first year and roughly $3 billion annually within three to five years. Among other sources, the synergies were to be a product of (1) additional sales of Mercedes-Benz models in the United States and Chrysler models in Europe, (2) the melding of purchasing operations on a global scale, (3) the combining of some R&D sites and administrative facilities, and (4) the sharing of manufacturing and engineering knowledge and skills. The sum of the synergies expected in the future suggests that their present value exceeds the $8 billion premium. However, some analysts concluded that the estimates were not a net figure in that the firms lacked reliable data that would be required to place a realistic value on various hidden acquisition costs, such as culture clashes and misunderstandings.[74] Thus, the degree to which this transaction will be judged a success remains open to debate.

The acquisition of U.S. Filter by Vivendi for approximately $6 billion involves the payment of a premium that some believe may be high. Although reducing Vivendi's reliance on Europe in the highly fragmented water services market through this acquisition was evaluated favorably, it may be that the price of reducing this dependency through an acquisition will prove to be excessive. Following study of this acquisition, one analyst observed that "against an average in the industry for [the acquisition of water services' firms] of around eight times earnings before interest, tax and depreciation, Vivendi is offering more than 11 times." On the other hand, expected operational synergies could possibly reduce the multiple to around nine times, "which does not seem unduly rich given the new entity's market position."[75] This example demonstrates the relationship between premiums and synergy. If the value of the synergy that can be created through strategic fit, organizational fit, and managerial actions is highly significant, what may appear to be "above average" premiums can be paid. However, the difficulty of achieving this objective should not be underestimated.

As we have noted previously, firms often increase their total debt to dangerous levels to complete an acquisition.[76] For example, Conseco Inc. has acquired a large number of companies to fuel its intention of growing rapidly. In fact, over a 16-year period, the firm acquired 40 insurance companies as well as other finance-related concerns. In 1998, this set of acquisitions was capped by the purchase of Green Tree Financial Corp. for more than $6 billion. As suggested by the following comments, it is possible that this string of acquisitions, coupled with premiums paid, has created a financial burden that will be difficult for Conseco to bear: "The acquisitions have put $5.32 billion in total debt on the company's books, compared with total capital of $7.37 billion. And 'goodwill,' the balance-sheet asset representing what Conseco paid above book value for its acquisitions, is $3.96 billion, or a large 75 percent of Conseco's book value."[77] Thus, as implied by this analyst's commentary, one reason Conseco's debt is so large is that the firm has perhaps paid too much in acquisition premiums. Again, the costs of premiums paid and the cost of debt cannot exceed the value of synergies that are created as a result of strategic fit, organizational fit, and managerial actions.

We have now discussed the four foundations to synergy creation. As noted earlier, these foundations must exist for the firm to be able to create desired levels of synergy through acquisitions. Once created, synergy contributes to the development of one or more competitive advantages for the firm over its rivals and to the generation of additional value for stakeholders.

In the next and final section, we offer recommendations for managers to consider when trying to create synergy through a merger or acquisition.

Recommendations for the Creation of Synergy

The purpose of this chapter has been to discuss the importance of creating synergy when seeking acquisition success. Our analysis of this topic leads to the following managerial guidelines:

1. Recognize the need to create synergy for an acquisition to be successful. When synergy is created, the probability is increased that an acquisition will facilitate the development of competitive advantages in the newly formed firm as well as the generation of value for stakeholders (and especially for stockholders).
2. Accept the fact that events occurring within the firm's industry can influence acquisition processes and acquisition success. However, this influence should be evaluated within the context of the firm's capabilities, core competencies, and opportunities. If an entire industry is active in terms of acquisition programs, firms should exercise even more caution and complete careful and detailed analyses before selecting target companies.

3. Pursuing wealth enhancements, for the firm and its owners, through synergy creation as permitted by acquisitions should be examined relative to other opportunities available to the firm. As a corporate-level strategic choice, acquisitions are but one means of competing in a complex global economy. Thus, the opportunity costs associated with an acquisition strategy should be evaluated in comparison to the costs associated with other feasible strategic options.

4. Be committed to the need to talk extensively and carefully about the synergy creation during the negotiation phase of a transaction. Before finalizing an acquisition, it is critical for all parties to be aware of the type of synergy that can be created and the actions that will be required for that to happen quickly and effectively.

5. Recognize that the most successful acquisitions are those in which all four foundations of synergy creation exist. Combining operational and marketing-based synergies through appropriate managerial actions is powerful, especially when the cost of doing so is less than the costs incurred to complete the transaction.

6. As we have cautioned in terms of multiple dimensions of acquisition success, acquiring firm managers must avoid hubris when evaluating possible sources of synergy between their firm and a target. Unlike its appearance might suggest, synergy is an elusive outcome. Moreover, for synergy to be created, managers must actively manage organizational processes. Synergy is created only through deliberate commitments and actions; it does not surface by chance.

7. Synergies can sometimes be created through personnel reductions. However, because knowledge is increasingly important as a pathway through which long-term synergies are created and used successfully, firms must be "prudent and wise" when evaluating the possibility of job reductions. Too many reductions in the short term may result in a lack of competitive knowledge that is required for long-term effectiveness and efficiency.

In this chapter we described what firms should do to create synergy. Increasingly, the insights and knowledge resulting from efforts to create synergy help the firm to *learn* more about what creates (as well as what hinders) merger and acquisition success. In the next chapter, we explore acquisitions as a particular type of experience through which firms learn.

7

Learning
from Experience

After a major event—a product failure, a downsizing crisis, or a merger—many companies stumble along, oblivious to the lessons of the past. Mistakes get repeated, but smart decisions do not. Most important, the old ways of thinking are never discussed, so they are still in place to spawn new mishaps. Individuals will often tell you that they understand what went wrong (or right). Yet their insights are rarely shared openly. And they are analyzed and internalized by the company even less frequently.

—Art Kleiner and George Roth

General Electric, through frequent acquisitions, has built a portfolio of businesses ranging from financial services to medical systems to aerospace. In 1998 alone, GE completed 47 acquisitions, making it the most active acquirer of the year.[1] Among the deals were the $599 million purchase of UIS, the $897 million acquisition of Marquette Medical Systems, and the $500 million deal for Kemper Reinsurance. This was not an unusual year for GE. In 1997, the company also made 47 acquisitions.[2] The relatively poor performance of conglomerates is well documented and understood. As we have detailed in this book, acquisitions also have the potential to reduce corporate performance. Defying these statistics, GE has an admirable financial performance record over several decades, thereby posing an important question: How can GE consistently enjoy high performance with a corporate strategy from which many others cannot derive positive results?

At least part of the answer is that GE makes so many acquisitions that its executives have the expertise to do them better than most others. For example, when Jack Welch, former CEO of GE, was asked how he created wealth for his shareholders, he responded, "I would say that our whole thrust here was to get into the right businesses, find businesses with growth, get an organization that could respond to change quickly, and get as much out of the capital we employed as we possibly could."[3] Although he makes it sound easy, skills associated with selecting businesses for acquisition and developing a responsive organization to manage them are not simple to develop and are highly valuable.

General Electric's skill and experience with acquisitions were aptly demonstrated in its acquisition and subsequent integration of reinsurers from Europe and the United States. GE bought the midwestern U.S. company Employers Re and added it to its GE Capital group. Employers was then transformed into a global player through several European acquisitions, including the European companies Frankona and Aachen (the European company Nordisk was also a part of Employers). Realizing that it would be difficult to assimilate these companies into an American parent, GE selected Kaj Ahlmann, a European, as CEO of Employers Re. Bernhard Fink was hired away from Gerling, where he was head of international operations, and put in charge of integrating the European operation. As some Germans tried to stir up negative feelings about the merger, Fink said, "People didn't take it too seriously. Many of our clients know that Employers Re does not have a record of being a company which moves in and out of markets. Also, many people know and appreciate that it is a U.S. company headed by a European."

The name given to the four consolidated European companies was ERC Frankona. This name was especially important because "the ERC in our name shows that we are part of a global player and the Frankona part shows that we have a strong European heritage. It is not a German group with some international outlets, it is a truly European group." Another challenge was to overcome internal divisions. After two years of work, Fink believes that this problem is largely resolved. "Our managers are no longer stuck in the past, thinking they are still Frankona or Aachen or Nordisk people. It's true that that used to be the case until the beginning of 1997 but that is gone now. We are now all looking forward. We have created a strong European identity, under the name of ERC Frankona."

General Electric appointed European managers and allowed them liberty to do what was necessary to make the combination a success; nevertheless, the GE influence was felt very strongly. Regular reviews were conducted by Gary Wendt, CEO of GE Capital and even Jack Welch himself. Other areas were also strongly influenced. Says Fink, "The first is control: they are very good about managing their figures. That has been very useful to us. The other thing is human resources [HR]: how you identify talent and how you make that talent perform much quicker.

This is what GE calls 'empowerment'—how do you get people to live up to their potential and not wait for years to grow into a senior position. That is an area where GE is extremely good."[4]

A company with the experience of GE has *learned* to complete acquisitions successfully. This chapter discusses how organizational learning from acquisitions and other large-scale change can be transferred to the execution of future acquisitions. We also outline steps firms can take to increase the likelihood that they will learn from their acquisition experiences.

Acquisitions as Learning Experiences

Organizational learning is critical to sustained success. Everyone can think of an organization that was once very successful and later failed because it did not change and develop. Many of these firms were unable to change because they did not learn (acquire new knowledge). For example, General Motors continues to struggle as a result of resisting the wide-scale changes that occurred in the automobile industry during the 1970s. Sears Roebuck lost significant market share as the upstart company Wal-Mart developed a superior way to deliver value to customers: namely, quality merchandise at lower cost.

Acquisitions offer an interesting paradox to managers with regard to organizational learning. Experience with acquisitions and other types of large-scale organizational changes such as management restructuring or divestiture can produce learning that can be used to enhance the performance of future acquisitions. However, acquisitions may appear to stifle other types of learning associated with R&D and innovation. They create conditions within the organization that make outsourcing organizational skills more attractive than building those skills internally.[5] They also provide executives with the option of "buying" the skills they need instead of developing them "in house." These negative implications of acquisitions are addressed more fully in the next two chapters. We now turn our attention to some skills that firms can develop as they experience acquisitions or other large-scale organizational changes.

Skills Gained from Experience
with Acquisitions and Large-Scale Changes

What can organizations learn as a result of experience with prior acquisitions? The skills to be mastered can be classified into the general categories of deal negotiation, financing, integration, and assimilation. Each of these areas holds the potential for substantial success or significant problems. Rodney Gott, a management researcher, described the acquisition process well when he said, "There is a legitimate analogy between a corporation with a new company acquisition and a family with a new baby. The new company, like the new child, does not simply represent the addition of one more member to the corporate family; it changes the relationships between everyone concerned. This requires patient adjustments of the new relationships and readjustments of the old."[6] In an acquisition, the parent must develop systems to communicate with and manage the newly acquired company. Promotion, compensation, and benefit systems must be integrated. People have to learn to work together. Sometimes significant differences between two cultures make these processes difficult. From the acquired firm perspective, much of what was understood with regard to administrative process is now changed. Fear and uncertainty are common among managers and employees. Many times integration means layoffs and restructurings, all of which create stress.

One of the most critical areas in which firms can develop expertise is management of employees during the merger process. Management turnover is, as expected, higher in a target firm during the acquisition period.[7] A middle manager of a large industrial engineering firm recently described his feelings of frustration, anguish, and despair subsequent to the acquisition of his firm by an even larger competitor. He had just received a letter of resignation from his marketing manager, one of many managers to quit. He also was considering leaving the firm. At the foundation of all these feelings was the sense that the new parent had no appreciation for the unique qualities that made the acquired company a success. The acquisition had made him rich (he owned a significant block of the stock in the acquired firm prior to acquisition), so he felt very little need to stay. He was tired of struggling to make a success out of what he saw as a very bad situation.

Employee tension is also high and morale low because so many acquisitions result in layoffs, plant closings, and relocations. For example, the acquisition of Amoco by British Petroleum resulted in the layoff of 10,000 employees.[8] As firms gain experience, their executives can learn how to manage employees effectively during each phase of an acquisition and can anticipate and plan for common employee reactions such as fear, anger, resentment, confusion, and survivor guilt. Continuous, open, and honest communication is important to effective management of employees. Respect for the existing culture of the newly acquired firm is also essential. In these areas, experience can help an organization master the techniques that help reduce employee tension through the transition period.

Unlocking synergy is another area in which experience makes a difference. As pointed out earlier, synergy creation requires not only relatedness (or complementarity) and fit between or among units, but also actions on the part of managers to make synergy happen. Operational resource sharing, the transfer of functional skills, and the transfer of general management skills all require actions such as coordinative meetings, employee and manager transfers across units, and crosstraining.[9] An organization can develop skills in these types of activities through acquisition experiences.

Experience with other types of large-scale organizational change may also help organizations prepare for a merger. For example, a major restructuring involving realignment of the management hierarchy can prepare a firm for the processes associated with merger integration. In one of the highly successful mergers we studied, the acquisition of Anderson Clayton by Quaker Oats, Anderson Clayton was in a period of restructuring and divestiture prior to acquisition. Anderson Clayton sold American Founder's Life Insurance and many of its Latin business assets during the previous year. The knowledge that was obtained by Anderson Clayton as a result of these changes was useful in making its integration into Quaker a success.[10]

Some of the skills mentioned here would be difficult, if not impossible, to master in a small number of acquisitions (or large-scale changes). A great deal of organizational knowledge is based on the discovery of patterns over time. For example, higher performance is found in unrelated acquisitions when managers are given more autonomy (this does not hold true for related acquisitions).[11] A pattern such as this one would be hard to discern after a small number of acquisitions. Consequently, organizations that are highly active in the acquisition market should be in a better position to master the necessary skills, if they make efforts to learn from their experiences.

Much has been written about the development of core competencies, defined by Prahalad and Hamel as the "collective learning in the organization, especially how to coordinate diverse production skills and integrate multiple teams of technologies."[12] Skill in making acquisitions is a core competence in companies such as General Electric. Thomas and Betts is another excellent example. This firm, an electronic and electrical products manufacturer, completed 30 acquisitions between 1992 and 1997. More than satisfied with the results of its acquisitions, the firm continues to seek additional companies to add to its portfolio. Unlike many companies, T&B has not established a merger and acquisition department. Because growth via acquisition is viewed as a company-wide responsibility, M&A activity is an integral part of the firm's daily operations. Thomas & Bett's CEO stated the following: "This is something we all do. It's a core competency of the entire company and everyone has a role to play."[13]

We believe that Thomas & Betts is an example of an organization that has learned how to successfully acquire target firms. Through the expectations and support of the firm's top-level manager, Thomas & Bett's personnel have learned and mastered the behaviors that are required to establish and use a successful acquisition strategy. Cohen and Levinthal suggested that an organization can absorb and exploit information more readily in activities that are closely related to what the firm does on a regular basis.[14] At Thomas & Betts, learning is facilitated by the fact that acquisitions are central to the activities of the firm. In fact, managers must include acquisition plans as a part of their regular planning processes.

Nevertheless, a relatively high frequency of acquisitions does not ensure that an organization will learn from its acquisition experiences. For example, investors reacted unfavorably to the announcement that Quintiles Transnational, a medical research firm, would buy Envoy Corp. for $1.4 billion in stock. This was the fifteenth deal announced by Quintiles in 1998. Investors could not understand the logic behind the combination. Quintiles specializes in clinical testing and medical devices. Envoy provides information systems for processing payment-claims information. News of the combination caused the share price of Quintiles to drop 18 percent. Analysts perceive the acquisition as out of Quintiles' core business area and they also expect the acquisition to dilute earnings. This is an excellent example of a company that did not learn from its past acquisitions, even though they were numerous.[15]

Acquisition Experience and Performance

Among the most successful transactions we examined was the acquisition of Signal Companies by Allied in 1985. Allied was a highly active acquirer prior to the Signal deal, purchasing Bendix in 1983 and Eustar in 1984. The Bendix acquisition, in particular, was successful from a financial perspective. In all, Allied had completed nearly 40 acquisitions in the six years prior to its acquisition of Signal, resulting in 400 percent growth in the firm. Signal also had significant acquisition experience, having recently acquired Wheelabrator. Both Signal and Allied had been involved in major restructuring as a result of their acquisitions. Consequently, all the executives involved in the merger of these two giant companies had meaningful experience with the kind of changes that would be necessary to make their acquisition a success.[16]

Most of what we have discussed in this chapter so far leads to the logical conclusion that prior acquisition experience should ensure higher financial performance in future acquisitions. However, the data demonstrate that few firms are able to transform this experience into successful performance.[17] Our own study of mergers and acquisitions clearly demonstrates that most highly successful mergers are between companies with a very strong base of experience with acquisitions and/or large-scale organizational change.[18] Also, researchers have discovered that higher performing acquisitions occur when the acquiring firm has a pattern of acquiring targets in its same industry. Apparently, industry familiarity facilitates learning from acquisitions.[19]

Our analysis of acquisition patterns in high and low performing mergers suggests that organizations would be more successful if they either enter the acquisition market on a very large scale and take advantage of learning effects, or on a very small scale, thus limiting organizational disruption and other costs associated with acquisitions. Also, as demonstrated with the Quintiles example, experience alone does not ensure that learning will occur. In the next section, we discuss actions firms can pursue to increase the likelihood that they will learn from prior acquisitions.

Learning Facilitators

The creation of new knowledge can be a source of organizational renewal and sustainable competitive advantage.[20] Related to acquisitions, knowledge creation is essential to helping organizations learn from past mistakes and develop processes that will lead to future acquisition success. Tyco International, a diversified manufacturer that has made over 100 acquisitions with an amazing success rate, has learned from years of experience how to do a deal with a minimum of problems.[21] Four important processes are related to how much organizational learning occurs. They are knowledge acquisition, information interpretation, information distribution, and organizational memory.[22] This section is organized around these processes.

Knowledge Acquisition

A worthwhile goal of firms involved in regular acquisition activity should be to learn as much as possible about how to do acquisitions in as little time as possible. In effect, firms want to rapidly move along the learning curve in which the monetary and nonmonetary costs of acquisitions are reduced as quickly as possible.[23] Tacit knowledge (learning by doing) is gained that can facilitate this movement along the curve. Obviously, organizations learn quicker if many acquisitions are pursued, but the more essential element is facilitation of learning regardless of the number of acquisitions.

Learning is facilitated if companies make the same type of acquisition repeatedly because they can learn from patterns of what does or does not work. Repetition of this sort represents a trend in acquisitions that has developed in the past years.[24] National City is a $50 billion bank holding company in the midwestern United States. It acquires a large company every three years and two or three small companies each year. This pattern has been successful. In fact, its acquisition of IFG, a $15 billion Pittsburgh bank holding company, was the first time the acquired firm did not experience a decline in revenues during the acquisition process. Since that merger, National City has made two other large acquistions, having become the eleventh largest bank in the United States and doubling its assets between 1995 and 1999. Profits remain very strong.[25] National City relies on open, honest communication with employees and also acknowledges the importance of speed in making successful bank mergers.[26] Excellent communication helps employees from becoming confused, fearful or frustrated. Speed can help minimize costs.

Companies actively using an acquisition strategy should also learn from the experiences of competitors and other companies pursuing similar types of deals. This reduces the need to learn from mistakes and therefore decreases learning time, as well as unnecessary costs.[27] Major consolidation is occurring in many industries, including banking and aerospace. The supermarket industry has experienced a wave of consolidating acquisitions as well. Albertson's agreed to acquire American Stores in August 1998. Shortly thereafter, in October that same year, Safeway agreed to buy Dominck's Supermarkets.[28] Consolidations offer a wealth of information to imitators—those companies that may want to follow the trend at a later date. For instance, imitators can learn what may be expected with regard to size of premium and the reaction from regulators and competitors. The popular business press follows acquisition activity closely and may actually contain articles about lessons learned from a particular acquisition. An imitator can also get a sense of how long integration will take place.

Several obstacles may prevent or slow learning from experience. Human beings are imperfect sensors of experience. Thus, as employees, they are limited in their abilities to absorb and interpret information.[29] Also, feedback of the results from an acquisition may be distorted, suppressed by management or too late to make a difference.[30] In larger multiunit organizations, one unit may obtain knowledge that would be useful to another one that is making an acquisition, but the knowledge is not conveyed because the systems through which such knowledge can be communicated are not in place or because the various units are unwilling to share information that may help another one that competes for vital resources.[31]

Another problem can occur when managers incorrectly associate either success or failure with factors that have nothing to do with the actual performance of an acquisition.[32] For example, a company may do well because its marketing program is working or because of newly created operating efficiencies. If these successes occur at the same time an acquisition takes place, executives in the acquiring firm may incorrectly associate at least a part of the corresponding increases in performance with the acquisition. Alternatively, an obsolete product or increased competition may be the real reason for a decline in performance. However, managers may attribute the reduction to an acquisition.

All these obstacles are common in organizations that make acquisitions. They partially explain why an organization such as Ecolab, a worldwide marketer of services with numerous recent acquisitions, could make such a huge mistake with its purchase of Chemlawn.[33]

Employee turnover was high in Chemlawn, and Ecolab managers were overconfident in their ability to turn around Chemlawn's performance. Furthermore, the excessive premium paid by Ecolab saddled the company with heavy debt. To exacerbate problems, there was a cultural mismatch between the companies.

Learning obstacles cannot be eliminated completely. However, their effects can be minimized when management visibly and tangibly promotes learning.[34] Information creation and sharing systems need to exist in the firm (e.g., meetings to discuss "lessons learned" during and after an acquisition). Conclusions should be documented and disseminated to decision-makers throughout the organization. Dan Patterson, president of Lockheed Martin Aircraft and Logistics Company, documents "lessons learned" after every major organizational change. In such an organization, learning from acquisitions is a natural extension of the learning that is already taking place.[35]

Many organizations create a special acquisitions unit that is involved in every transaction. Creating such a unit is a luxury that an infrequent acquirer may not be able to afford, providing further evidence that frequent acquirers have a potential advantage in the acquisitions market. Acquisitions units, if formed, should not work in isolation of other managers that will have responsibility for managing parts of the acquisition. Managers who will be involved in any way with negotiations or post-merger integration should be actively involved in every decision that is made. Acquisitions units have the responsibility to make sure that the organization is learning from prior acquisitions. An alternative to creating an acquisitions unit is to develop an organizational culture in which acquisitions are perceived as everyone's job, as in the case of Thomas & Betts Corp.

The key to knowledge creation is that managers should make conscious efforts to learn from experiences with acquisitions and large-scale organizational changes. Much of the effort that is expended to create knowledge within the firm will also help with two other learning processes, information interpretation and distribution.

Information Interpretation and Distribution

Organizations need to "make sense" out of their experiences for learning to take place. Often an organization does not realize what it knows because the information that would lead to the creation of new knowledge is divided into pieces and spread throughout the organization.[36] Consequently, a significant challenge associated with learning is discovering where relevant information is, combining it, and then making sense out of it.

Interpretation is a "process through which information is given meaning."[37] This process is facilitated by the encouragement and sharing of multiple perspectives. Braniff International Airlines collapsed largely because its CEO, Harding Lawrence, had a singular perspective (his own) on Braniff's route acquisition strategy. As negative information began to flow into the organization, Lawrence attributed it to mistakes made by his management team instead of realizing that the acquisition strategy was too aggressive. Had Lawrence been more open to other perspectives on how the acquisition program was working, the airline might have been saved.

A deliberate approach to learning was pursued in the merger of L'Alsacienne and Belin, both acquired by the French food group BSN Danone. The merger began in April 1993 as the company established a series of workshops to facilitate every stage of the process. Every workshop included between five and ten managers from each company. In all, 44 workshops were set up for the purposes of realizing maximum potential from each company, integrating the operational, managerial, and cultural aspects of the two acquired companies and deciding on the direction of the newly combined entity. Rules were developed to enhance learning processes. "The rules governing the workshops were very precise. Statements were testable and open to any possible reaction from the partner in the dialogue. People questioned each other, searched for all available information and worked with valid data. When a participant advanced an explanation, the other participants reacted, trying to disconfirm the argument. It was thus in everyone's best interest to debate without playing games of hiding or lying."[38]

Outcomes from the merger workshops were very positive. "The exchanges in the merger workshops were never a pure dialogue. They focused on task analysis, information exchange and joint problem solving. But they formed a learning environment characterized by a high level of confrontation and a high level of openness to discuss....As they proceeded, the workshops engendered a general atmosphere that induced a shift in opinions and judgements and directed old ways of thinking into new channels."[39] Committees were also formed to guide the merger process.

Such an enlightened approach to organizational learning assists in interpreting and disseminating information. Because so many managers were involved in the process, the probability of uncovering all relevant and valuable information was dramatically increased. Furthermore, their involvement provided rapid dissemination. However, there are three other aspects of effective dissemination. First, the information that is gained must be documented. In the merger of L'Alsacienne and Belin, lessons learned were recorded in detail. Second, knowledge must be conveyed to other parts of the organization that can make use of it. Managing knowledge about mergers and acquisitions is like managing other important strategic information. Personnel, systems, and processes should be put in place to make sure that knowledge is transferred where and when it is needed. Finally, new knowledge is only valuable to the extent that it is retained in the organization as a part of its memory.

Organizational Memory

Most executives have experienced information overload (i.e., they receive multiple reports but don't have the time or the energy to try to make sense out of them). Information about acquisitions and other large-scale changes is strategic. As such, it should be a part of an organization's management information systems, especially in the area of decision support. Of course, one of the functions of a well-designed MIS is to sort through information to discover what is most relevant, thereby reducing information overload. Information overload represents an obstacle to organizational learning.[40]

Many other factors reduce the ability of an organization to remember. Employee turnover can be problematic.[41] In the martial arts, there is a tradition that martial artists grieve the death of a master because of all the knowledge that is lost. Similarly, when an organizational member who has been involved in a significant amount of organizational learning leaves the organization, much organizational knowledge is lost. From this perspective, two recommendations are relevant. First, managers who have extensive experience with acquisitions should be treated as valuable resources by the organization in an effort to reduce turnover. Second, organizations should have many individuals involved in acquisitions, as opposed to a few, so that knowledge is widely shared. This is similar to succession planning.

Organizations may not store relevant information about acquisition experiences because they do not think it is necessary or will not be used frequently. In addition, information may exist but organizational members may not be aware of its existence or how to access it. These types of problems exist with regard to all strategically relevant information. We recommend that a top manager assign a key employee to manage acquisition information and make it available to managers and others as needs arise.[42]

Taking Advantage of Learning Opportunities

Learning from large-scale organizational changes such as past acquisitions greatly increases the likelihood of success in future acquisitions. However, learning processes need to be actively managed. We offer the following guidelines:

1. Corporate managers should make a deliberate decision to be active acquirers or casual acquirers, thus taking advantage of learning on the one hand or limiting disruptions and other costs on the other.[43]

2. If an organization is a casual acquirer, executives should consider only those acquisitions that represent highly positive opportunities. They should not actively pursue acquisitions, but instead turn their attention to other managerial issues such as innovation and internal operations. When an acquisition is highly desirable, they should make heavy use of advisors who are acquisition experts in order to limit the number of mistakes that are made.

3. Active acquirers should consider purchasing companies that are strategically similar to those that have already been acquired, so that knowledge gained from earlier acquisitions will be most relevant. In particular, industry familiarity facilitates learning.

4. Acquiring firms should actively study and learn from the acquisitions of other companies such as competitors. Trade and business magazines and personal contacts can provide a wealth of valuable information.

5. Acquiring firm managers should provide visible and tangible support of the acquisition process and take deliberate steps to promote learning. These may include insisting that learning be documented as "lessons learned," assigning someone responsibility for managing information about acquisitions and making it available as needed, and forming workshops and retreats in which learning occurs.

6. Active acquirers should assemble a team of acquisition experts who are involved in all the firm's acquisitions. In this way knowledge will be accumulated and transferred to future transactions. Alternatively, active acquirers can make acquisitions "everyone's responsibilty," as in the case of Thomas & Betts. To do so effectively, the organization should make acquiring companies a core competence.

7. Knowledge about acquisitions should be held by as many organizational members as possible. Many people should participate in each acquisition process, especially all managers who have some responsibility for the acquisition process or post-merger integration.

8. In firms with an active acquisition program, acquisition experts should be treated as a valuable organizational resource and encouraged to remain with the organization.

9. There obviously is no guarantee that following these suggestions will result in GE-type acquisitions performance; however, they are a step in the right direction.

One of the most commonly stated reasons for an acquisition is to diversify a firm's portfolio of businesses. How valid is this reason? We address that question in the next chapter.

8

Avoiding the Hazards of Diversification

Because of overdiversification, the merger and acquisition craze, and the use of extraordinary debt, many firms have had to restructure in the late 1980s and early 1990s.

—R. E. Hoskisson and M. A. Hitt

Roche intends to spin off its fragrances and flavours division, creating a separate company outside the Roche Group....The proposed spin-off of the fragrances and flavours division is in line with the strategy Roche has followed consistently for years of concentrating on its core business. Roche is positioning itself even more strongly as a research-based company in the healthcare sector.

—Roche Corporate Communications, December 6, 1999

In June 1999, AlliedSignal Inc. agreed to acquire Honeywell Inc. in an exchange of stock valued at slightly less than $15 billion. AlliedSignal's CEO, Lawrence A. Bossidy, described the acquisition in this way: "AlliedSignal's tie-up with Honeywell gives us diversity. It gives us reach." Furthermore, he stated that the acquisition would integrate AlliedSignal's "insatiable appetite for efficiency with the technological progress of Honeywell." Both firms are considered industrial conglomerates, but each had a business or businesses in the aerospace sector. While their aerospace businesses focused on different market segments, they also have the potential to complement one another. The combined firm is generating approximately 40 percent of its revenues from the integrated aerospace businesses. Therefore, the diversification move by AlliedSignal provides

opportunities for synergy by integrating the aerospace businesses, opportunities to share differing sets of capabilities (AlliedSignal's emphasis on
efficiency and Honeywell's prowess in new technology development),
along with gaining economies of scale in several support functions. For
example, analysts expect Honeywell's operations to become more efficient through application of AlliedSignal's productivity improvement and
cost reduction methods. Likewise, AlliedSignal's product line should
benefit from Honeywell's capabilities in system integration, industrial
controls, and service. Greater diversification can help balance revenues
across strong and weaker economic periods. Because of these opportunities, the stock market reacted favorably to the announced acquisition
as the price of both firms' stocks increased almost 6 percent after the
acquisition announcement.

As with any acquisition of this size, integration of the two firms may
not be achieved easily. Both firms have different and unique cultures
that could clash as integration is implemented. The intent of AlliedSignal and Honeywell was to integrate their operations rapidly (within a
six-month period). Furthermore, they intend to follow the "one plus
one equals one" rule whereby the number of staff in any two departments that are combined will equal no more than the size of the larger
pre-acquisition department. Achieving this objective will not be a simple
task. Therefore, while there is considerable optimism about the opportunities and potential benefits created by this acquisition, *The Economist*
stated the following caveat with regard to diversification transactions
such as this one: "Most institutional investors would prefer to choose
which industries they invest in themselves, rather than add another
layer of conglomerate managers to make that choice for them."[1]

Diversification is one of the primary reasons that firms acquire other
companies. Generally, firms seek growth through diversification of their
product lines. They use acquisitions to diversify their product lines
because it is faster and often cheaper than to develop new products internally. Furthermore, it is much more difficult to diversify into new
markets by developing products internally. Most of the in-house product development expertise is related to the current product lines. Companies also attempt to diversify their product line to enhance the value of
the firm through economies of scope, economies of scale, and market
power, among other goals.[2]

Firms also diversify for reasons other than those identified above. For
example, diversifying the company's product line spreads the risk as
implied in the discussion of AlliedSignal's acquisition of Honeywell.
Antitrust laws may also encourage executives to diversify the firm's
product line to meet goals for continued growth. However, there was a
major change in the interpretation and enforcement of antitrust laws in
the United States in the 1980s. Before this time, many acquisitions
involved product diversification because firms were disallowed from

acquiring competitors or firms in highly related industries. Since 1980, there have been a larger number of horizontal acquisitions (acquisition of competitors in the same industry). Diversification still remains an important motive for acquisitions, as suggested in the AlliedSignal acquisition of Honeywell.

An additional reason for product diversification involves top executives' personal motives. By diversifying the firm's product lines, top executives reduce the risk of losing their own jobs. Remaining in a single or highly focused product market(s) creates risk of loss of demand for the product line. If this occurs, a top executive is likely to lose his or her job. Therefore, the top executive may diversify the firm's product line to reduce personal employment or career risk. As noted in the quote from *The Economist*, some investors may prefer to diversify their own portfolio rather than invest in highly diversified firms. In other words, investors can more easily diversify their portfolios than firms can diversify their product lines. Furthermore, shareholders are more likely to gain value from diversifying their portfolios as opposed to the value they would receive from owning shares in a firm with diversified product lines.[3]

In this chapter, we explore the outcomes of acquisitions made to diversify the firm. Thereafter, we compare and contrast acquisitions of related and unrelated businesses. Next, the problems with acquisitive diversification are discussed followed by an examination of how firms can learn from diversification. Finally, we present managerial implications of diversification transactions.

Outcomes of Acquisitions for Diversification

As noted earlier, a primary reason for acquisitions and diversification moves is to increase the size of the organization. Many recent acquisitions to diversify the firm have substantially increased size. For example, the 1998 acquisition of Citicorp by the Travelers Group significantly increased the size of that organization. The value of the acquisition was approximately $70 billion.[4]

Studies showing the performance of diversifying acquisitions provide mixed results. For example, one analysis of mergers and acquisitions between 1986 and 1996 found no performance differences between those acquisitions completed for consolidation within the industry and those completed for diversifying the firm's product line. The stockholders' value three years after the acquisition was relatively the same regardless of the reason for the acquisition.[5] However, the type of diversification seems to make a difference in the performance outcomes. Most studies show that conglomerate acquisitions (i.e., acquiring firms outside the focal company's traditional industry and area of expertise) tend to produce negative performance outcomes. Evidence indicates that these types of acquisitions may increase net profits in the short term but tend to have a negative effect on shareholders' wealth over a longer period of time.[6] In contrast, another study showed that acquisition of firms operating in markets and industries related to the firm's core business increased shareholder value. This same study demonstrated that acquisitions of businesses operating in unrelated markets had negative effects on shareholder value.[7]

In the 1990s, Cablevision acquired several companies to develop a diversified telecommunications and entertainment company. Companies acquired include a consumer electronics retail chain, Nobody Beats the Wiz, Madison Square Garden Properties, and Radio City Productions. These can be classified as unrelated acquisitions. It is difficult to identify a common thread among Cable TV, the Radio City Rockets, and Walkmans at the Wiz. Executives at Cablevision argued that the intent was to create synergy between distribution and content of cable services and products and at the same time focus on three geographical areas. Further, executives argued that acquisition of the retail outlet created a means of distributing new technologies, such as cable modems and HDTV, important to Cablevision's future. However, at the time, Cablevision did not make computer or cable modems and did not broadcast Digital TV.[8] Cablevision argued that the intent was to create synergy between the distribution and content of cable services.

During 1995–97, Cablevision investors expressed displeasure because they felt that the firm was overleveraged and undervalued. They were not pleased with the acquisitions that had been made. However, the owners at the time, Charles and James Dolan, decided to allow greater influence by John Malone and Leo Hindery of TCI. By 1999, Cablevision was generally performing well. Its cable operations posted strong results, along with several of its other businesses, including American Movie Classics, Bravo, and Madison Square Garden. However, some of its other diverse businesses such as its retail electronics chain, The Wiz, were not performing well. Thus, it had achieved appropriate synergies among several of its businesses but not with the more unrelated ones such as The Wiz.[9]

Evidence shows that many acquisitions, between 33 and 50 percent, are later divested because of poor performance.[10] Between 1989 and 1998, the number of annual divestitures (whole and partial businesses) increased approximately 60 percent and the value of the completed divestitures more than tripled.[11] Many of the businesses divested have little or no relationship to the divesting firm's core business. In fact, the majority of unrelated acquisitions are divested a short time after their purchase.[12] Some refer to this divestiture process as downscoping.[13] Essentially, these firms are attempting to refocus on their core business to improve performance. In so doing, they redeploy other assets and create the flexibility to develop more and better product and process innnovations.[14]

Next, we examine the different values and opportunities of acquiring related and unrelated businesses.

Acquiring Related Versus Unrelated Businesses

In recent years, the large majority of diversifying acquisitions involved buying businesses related to the acquiring firm's core business. Many of the older more established conglomerate firms (unrelated businesses) experienced performance difficulties and had to restructure by downscoping the firm to refocus on more specific business areas. For example, Hanson PLC, a well-respected British conglomerate, experienced performance problems and restructured into four different businesses. Hanson was well known for acquiring poorly performing businesses, restructuring them and thereby improving their performance. The improvements were largely the result of the implementation of management efficiencies and financial controls. Most of the firms acquired were in mature, low-technology industries, allowing Hanson to avoid making risky investments in R&D.[15] However, Hanson had to implement changes as the global environment for business changed and became increasingly competitive. Thus, in 1995, Hanson managers began the change process by spinning off a set of unrelated businesses that were located in the United States. In the following year, three more sets of businesses in energy, tobacco, and chemicals, respectively, were spun off.[16]

Not all divestitures are of unrelated businesses, however. For example, another relatively famous divestiture was completed by AT&T. It undertook what some referred to as a trivestiture. In effect, the NCR Computer Business and Lucent Technologies were spun off, separating them from the core AT&T business. The primary reason for this change was because of the poor performance of the NCR Computer Business, acquired several years earlier. The NCR business was requiring substantial amounts of AT&T managerial time and efforts. The spin-offs allowed managers within each of the businesses to focus their efforts to improve performance.[17]

Acquiring Related Businesses

The primary value of acquiring related businesses is the potential to create synergy between the two businesses when they are combined. Essentially, synergy (described in Chapters 4 and 6) is created when competencies or resources can be shared across businesses. For example, if the products of the two businesses are similar enough, a combined sales force might sell the product lines of both. This is a form of economies of scope. For example, in the new company resulting from the AlliedSignal acquisition of Honeywell, the aerospace product lines of both businesses may be sold by a single sales force. Therefore, AlliedSignal's aircraft engines, brakes, environmental controls, and anti-collision systems can be marketed along with Honeywell's cockpit controls and navigation equipment. In fact, the company can offer integrated packages of these components in addition to individual components. Other forms of competencies can also be transferred. For example, Honeywell's expertise in system integration, industrial controls, and service can be applied across AlliedSignal's product lines, thereby improving their performance.[18]

One of the classic cases of transferring core competencies across businesses is the Philip Morris acquisition of Miller Brewing. Philip Morris had developed a core competence in marketing. It applied this competence in Miller Brewing after its acquisition to improve the marketing practices of this company in the brewing industry. These improvements, particularly in the advertising of Miller's products, allowed Miller Brewing to earn above-average returns, a substantial increase over its prior mediocre financial performance. One of the primary ways Philips Morris accomplished the transfer of these competencies was through the movement of key Philip Morris marketing managers into new management positions with Miller Brewing.[19]

Another example can be found in the 1998 acquisition of TCI by AT&T. This acquisition was accomplished with the intent of merging the technologies of the two companies to provide an all-encompassing set of communications to customers.[20] The chairman of AT&T, C. Michael Armstrong, stated that this acquisition combined the best brand in the industry (AT&T) with the best broad-band company in the industry (TCI). AT&T acquired most of TCI's cable and digital assets and its cable-backed Internet service. In fact, the Internet was the prime driving force for AT&T's acquisition of TCI. The acquisition gives AT&T access to TCI's 10.5 million customers to which it provides cable TV and telecommunications services. [21] It also allows AT&T to control Liberty Media Group, Inc., the programming arm of TCI. Liberty is a major player in cable programming. With the acquisition, Liberty will become a freestanding company and have access to capital from AT&T to finance new ventures.[22] Integrating the two firms and achieving the potential synergies will not be easy. The two companies were not direct competitors, but their technologies and capabilities are largely complementary. As such, they can bundle their services and sell them to the ultimate consumer.[23] Basically, AT&T has the goal of selling TCI's residential consumers local and long-distance telephone service along with high-speed Internet access and cable television using a highly efficient network based on Internet technology. To do so will require AT&T to integrate multiple varied local technological platforms. This will be a challenging task.[24]

A number of the acquisitions made in the latter part of the 1990s were horizontal acquisitions. In other words, firms were acquiring competitors with the purpose of consolidation within the industry. For the most part, these acquisitions did not represent diversification. However, they do constitute an increase in market power for the combined firm. The British Petroleum acquisition of Amoco and the acquisition of Mobil by Exxon are both horizontal as all companies are in the energy industry. Low prices for petroleum were a major incentive for these consolidating acquisitions, driven largely by the need for more economies to reduce costs. For example, the British Petroleum acquisition of Amoco reportedly would reduce the total combined employment of 93,000 employees by 6,000 jobs. This was expected to result in an annual cost savings of $2 billion.[25] In contrast, ExxonMobil planned to cut 14,000 to 16,000 jobs, approximately 15 percent of its total workforce, by 2002. This reduction will produce a cost savings of $3.8 billion annually.[26]

Similar practices are exemplified in the SBC acquisition of Ameritech Corporation and Bell Atlantic Corporation's acquisition of GTE. Although these acquisitions also provide significant market power, they create a degree of diversification through different geographic markets served by the separate companies and to some degree the separate sets of services provided by the companies. The combined companies offer both local and long-distance telephone services as well as a fiber-optic network that can provide easy Internet access.[27] An excellent example of a horizontal acquisition that added more services is seen in the Halliburton acquisition of Dresser Industries. It provided Halliburton the capability to offer a wider variety of oil field services and products to its customers. For example, the acquisition supplied Halliburton with the best capabilities in the industry in drilling fluids and directional drilling. Furthermore, the acquisition made Halliburton the largest competitor in the oil field service industry.[28]

Related acquisitions are often undertaken to spread the geographic diversification of a firm as well. This is evidenced in the acquisitions by the different telephone companies previously discussed. But it also is shown by firms entering new international markets exemplified by the Vodafone group acquisition of AirTouch. This acquisition provided Vodafone of Great Britain an entry into the U.S. market and created the largest global cellular phone company.[29] Vodafone also made the largest hostile takeover bid for Mannesmann AG of Germany. Mannesmann initially rejected the approximately $148 billion bid, but Vodafone moved forward with a takeover attempt and eventually acquired it.[30] Ford Motor Co.'s acquisition of Sweden's AB Volvo auto unit also exemplifies geographic diversification.[31]

Of course, achieving synergies to gain the benefits of related diversification acquisitions is challenging. It requires careful and thorough planning and coordination as well as effective integration of the two firms; acquiring unrelated businesses does not necessitate this coordination and integration. Next, we examine the acquisition of unrelated businesses.

Acquiring Unrelated Businesses

Unrelated diversification is based on the premise that financial synergies can be achieved in a firm with a widely diversified portfolio of businesses. The assumption is that a conglomerate firm will have more information about each of the companies in its portfolio than the external capital market does. The top executives in this firm can thus better allocate resources to the businesses that will provide the highest returns.[32] Of course, because the businesses are largely unrelated, there are no other opportunities for synergies (e.g., sharing resources or capabilities) as in the related diversified firms. However, there are problems created by having a highly diversified portfolio of businesses. Top executives in this firm do not have appropriate knowledge of each of those businesses and their markets to provide effective oversight. In other words, they can only identify problems after they are evidenced in the financial outcomes. This is referred to as a loss of strategic control; they do not have adequate knowledge to evaluate the appropriateness of strategies selected by the managers of each of the businesses. Therefore, corporate managers attempt to control these businesses by using financial targets that, in turn, frequently produce a short-term orientation on the part of the business-level managers. Business-level managers are less willing to invest in actions that may produce positive returns in the long term but could reduce returns in the short term (e.g., investment in R&D).[33] These potential problems frequently offset the financial synergies that can be obtained in widely diversified businesses. As a result, unrelated acquisitions are often the least successful ones.

Because of the change in interpretation of the antitrust laws and the discovery that many conglomerate firms do not perform as well as more focused firms, a considerable amount of restructuring (downscoping) occurred during the late 1980s and early 1990s. This downscoping produced more focused firms.[34] In general, the focused firms were managed more efficiently and effectively, thereby producing strong positive financial performance throughout the rest of the 1990s. Some refer to this process as *demergers*. Essentially, it is the process of ridding the firm of problematic acquisitions made in prior years.[35] For example, the United Kingdom's Sainsbury PLC experienced problems because of its lack of focus. By concentrating on diversification and making acquisitions, Sainsbury managers failed to effectively manage the firm's core business, food retailing. In so doing, some of its major competitors such as Tesco became more innovative and began to capture significant amounts of market share.[36] Sears Roebuck and Company faced the same problem with its retailing operations. After Sears diversified outside of its core business,(i.e., into financial services and real estate), it began to lose its focus on the retailing business and its competitors (e.g., Wal-Mart, Target) captured significant amounts of market share. Sears was no longer a top retailing firm and experienced poor financial performance. For example, in 1992 Sears Merchandise Group lost $1.3 billion.[37] However, Sears downscoped by selling its nonretail businesses and refocused on its core business. In addition, it closed its catalog business and laid off 50,000 employees. Shortly after these strategic moves, Sears returned to profitability. Its positive financial fortunes continued into 1999. Net profits exceeded $1 billion, a considerable increase over 1998.[38] Thus, we can conclude that while some potential benefits of diversification exist, it is a significant managerial challenge to realize them. Next, we consider some of the negative outcomes and problems related to diversification by acquisition.

Problems with Acquisitive Diversification

Unfortunately, some diversification efforts, even highly related ones, produce negative outcomes. For example, in 1997, Eli Lilly & Co. had to write off $2.4 billion of the $4.1 billion paid in 1994 for its drug distributor PCS Health Systems Inc. Thus, in the span of three years, it lost approximately 60 percent of its investment. Aetna Life & Casualty Co. continued to experience problems with its acquisition of U.S. Healthcare. It acquired U.S. Healthcare in 1996; in 1997, the poor performance of this business reduced Aetna's third-quarter profits by $103 million.[39] Similarly, a once famous company, Westinghouse, known for its acumen in electronic products, simply faded away after diversifying. All of its electronic businesses were eventually sold and it became the nation's largest radio operator.[40] The firm has changed its name to CBS to more accurately reflect the character of its businesses.

The primary reason for poor performances and changes such as those previously noted is the inability of the firms to achieve synergies either in the sharing of resources and capabilities or in financial resource allocations. Often, the negative effects of diversification overcome the positive benefits. For example, the short-term emphasis that can result from too much diversification may harm a firm's competitiveness because of its inability to introduce new products of the quality and timeliness of its competitors.[41] Often, this problem begins with conflicts and differences in styles and strategies between the two firms. For example, the merger of Exxon and Mobil could experience problems because of differences in styles and strategies between the CEOs of these firms. Lee Raymond, CEO of Exxon, has developed a reputation for being an independent and sometimes arrogant competitor. However, Lucio Noto, CEO of Mobil, has a reputation for operating in a wily New York manner. Both are low-profile company managers but each has a different style and strategy. Mobil has formed multiple joint ventures and conducted discussions with several companies about mergers prior to the negotiations with Exxon. In contrast, Mr. Raymond shunned acquisitions until being forced to do so because of demand and price problems in the industry. Only time will tell whether the merger between these two companies will be a success or how long it will take for it to be successful.[42]

Likewise, other proposed mergers failed because of problems between the top executives and/or the firms' cultures. Reportedly, the once-agreed-to merger between KPMG Peat Marwick and Ernst & Young collapsed because of differences in the cultures of the two companies and the problem of integrating their different sets of managers.[43] Additionally, the once-agreed-to merger between SmithKline Beecham PLC and Glaxo Wellcome PLC failed because the two firms could not agree over who would manage the combined company. In fact, top executives of SmithKline Beecham cited insurmountable differences in completing the merger between the two companies. Their discussions revealed a number of differences that included distinct management philosophies and corporate cultures.[44] Interestingly, the market was quite positive about the potential deal. The stock prices for both firms increased significantly after the proposed merger was announced.[45] In fact, Glaxo shares increased 18 percent over a relatively short period after the merger was announced.[46] The market obviously felt that there was a strong potential for synergy between these two firms. Thus, it may be unfortunate that differences precluded the merger. Alternatively, it is best to learn about these differences prior to the merger rather than after.

Unfortunately, not all firms experience a positive reaction from the market after announcing acquisitions and/or diversification moves. In 1999, Global Crossing announced a proposed acquisition of two firms, Frontier Corporation and U.S. West, a much larger baby Bell. Global Crossing entered the telecommunications industry by building an undersea cable between the United States and Europe. It sought to acquire U.S. West and Frontier to further diversify its service portfolio in the telecommunications industry. Unfortunately, analysts and investors were not certain of the strategic value of these acquisitions and thereby Global Crossing's stock price decreased after the announcement. Shortly thereafter, Qwest Communications International advanced a hostile bid to acquire both U.S. West and Frontier Corporation. Its offer was substantially larger than that of Global Crossing. In fact, Qwest's offer represented a 45.8 percent premium over the U.S. West's stock price at the time of the announcement and a 35.3 percent premium for Frontier Corporation. Unfortunately, investors and stock analysts also questioned Qwest's proposed acquisition. As a result, Qwest's stock price fell by approximately 25 percent after its proposed hostile bid was announced. The market obviously did not perceive a valuable synergy between these companies.[47] After considerable sparring between Global Crossing and Qwest, Qwest acquired U.S.West and Global Crossing acquired Frontier. The Qwest-U.S. West merger created a company of 64,000 employees with $65 billion market capitalization. The Global Crossing-Frontier created a company with 11,000 employees that was included in the S&P 500. Both are now global communications companies and believe that the acquisitions positioned them to be competitive in global markets. Time will tell if that assessment is accurate.[48]

These examples suggest that managers must take great care in deciding to acquire firms, particularly those for the purpose of diversifying the product line, even into highly related business markets. Acquisitions are highly complex strategies to design and implement and they are only further complicated by acquiring firms with product lines that differ from the firm's current core business(es). However, there are potential positive benefits of diversification moves. Some of these were identified earlier. Another is discussed in our next section on learning from diversification.

Learning from Diversification

If they are well managed, acquired businesses that operate in different product markets from the firm's core businesses can provide knowledge that may be useful to multiple businesses in the firm's portfolio. In Chapter 7, we emphasize the importance of learning from acquisitions. Here our focus is on diversifying acquisitions. If firms are able to learn new skills and competencies and develop knowledge from their diversifying acquisitions, it may help them make further acquisitions and/or operate more effectively in their current product markets. The most valuable diversifying acquisitions from a learning point of view are those that are more highly related to the firm's core business. This is because firms have the experience and knowledge on which to build and learn from the related businesses. Alternatively, it is much more difficult to learn from unrelated businesses that are acquired, because the knowledge bases have much less overlap, if any. Firms can also develop knowledge from their diversifying acquisitions over time. More often, the knowledge learned over the long term relates to developing new technological capabilities, a more complex form of learning.[49]

Firms can also learn when they combine acquisitions that create both product diversity and international diversity. They can learn new skills and competencies from the new business but also develop knowledge of new markets, customers, and cultures that may be valuable as they expand further into other international markets. The interaction effect of product diversification and international diversification exists in most large firms, as they often are not only product diversified but also internationally diversified (operating in multiple international markets). Therefore, both forms of diversification create the opportunity or potential for learning. However, the interaction of the two greatly complicates the learning process and thereby creates managerial challenges.[50]

Product diversification can help firms prepare for international diversification. Traditionally, firms are more likely to diversify their product lines before they move into international markets. In so doing, managers can develop competencies in managing internal diversity. For example, as firms diversify their product lines, they often change their structures to allow them to better manage the diversified product lines. Sometimes they implement multidivisional structures in which each division operates as a profit center for a particular product line.

Similarly, as firms move into international markets, particularly across different regions of the world, they need to develop structures that allow them to manage these dispersed operations. If they have developed structures for different product lines, the learning from that process should help them develop more effective structures and policies to implement international diversification. For example, if firms have separate divisions for different product lines and the divisions sell products to each other, the firm is likely to have developed a transfer pricing policy. As firms move internationally, it is common to transfer products from one operating unit to another in a separate region of the world. Consequently, they need some means of pricing the products that are transferred. Should the products be transferred at cost or at market rates? The selling unit would prefer transferring the products at market prices because it could obtain a market price for that item in its particular product markets. Alternatively, the buying unit would prefer to purchase it at cost so that it could resell the product in its markets at a profit. Without appropriate transfer pricing policies, conflict could ensue. However, the learning from past practices likely allows firms to develop appropriate policies and structures as they continue to diversify.[51]

There are multiple forms of learning that can occur from diversification moves and managers must often make conscious efforts to learn and thus develop and codify the new knowledge. Therefore, we conclude that there are several potential positive outcomes from diversifying acquisitions.

Conclusions and Managerial Implications

Acquisitions that diversify the firm may be completed for several reasons. There are multiple potential benefits but also some potential negative outcomes of diversifying acquisitions. Following are several managerial implications of diversification transactions.

1. Diversifying acquisitions do not necessarily lead to positive performance outcomes. Acquired businesses that are unrelated to the acquiring firm's core business are less likely to produce positive results. That is because they only have the opportunity to produce financial synergies. Often, the negative outcomes of unrelated acquisitions offset the positive outcomes of financial synergy.

2. Acquired firms that are related to the acquiring firm's core business have a higher probability of leading to positive outcomes. To produce higher returns for shareholders, related business acquisitions must be integrated so as to achieve synergies between the two firms. However, achieving this synergy is a managerial challenge. It requires significant coordination between the two businesses and effective integration of their operations. Often, the inability to achieve synergies, even when it is obvious that the potential for synergy exists, results from different management philosophies and culture. Therefore, management philosophy and culture should be taken into account when the acquisition decision is made. Furthermore, if managers decide to make an acquisition, they should undertake special efforts to overcome any potential differences in management philosophies and culture in order to achieve effective integration and positive synergy.
3. Firms can learn from diversifying acquisitions. This usually requires managerial emphasis on learning and special actions taken to ensure that new knowledge is created and codified. Learning from past diversification moves may facilitate future diversification. This is particularly true as firms learn from product diversification and move into international markets.

The bottom line, however, is that diversifying acquisitions should be undertaken with great care and only under selected conditions. In most cases, focus on a firm's core business is of critical importance. Even then, acquiring firms that are in the same business does not guarantee success. This suggests that acquisitions, whether or not to diversify, represent substantial managerial challenges.

In the twenty-first-century competitive landscape, innovation is critical for firms in many industries to be successful. In fact, less diversified (focused) firms are more innovative. In general, firms following an aggressive acquisition strategy often invest less in R&D to produce innovation and instead acquire companies with new products. The next chapter explores the effects of mergers and acquisitions on firm innovation.

9

Deciding If Innovation
Can Be Acquired
Successfully

An innovation is different from an invention. An innovation brings
something into new use, whereas an invention brings something
new into being. The criteria for success of an invention are technical, whereas for an innovation the criteria are commercial.

—P. Sharma and J. J. Chrisman

The rapid change and diffusion of new technology, along with
substantial competition in domestic and international markets, has
placed increasing importance on firms' ability to innovate and to
introduce new innovations into the marketplace. In fact, innovation may be required to maintain or achieve competitive parity,
much less a competitive advantage in many global markets.

—M. A. Hitt, R. D. Nixon, R. E. Hoskisson, and R. Kochhar

Founded as the Newell Manufacturing Company, but known now as
Newell Rubbermaid, Inc. , this firm manufactures and markets multiple
lines of high-volume staple consumer products. Employing over 32,000
globally, the company's products are sold through a variety of retail and
wholesale distribution channels.

Widely diversified, Newell Rubbermaid's business segments
include Amerock cabinet hardware, Bulldog home hardware, Eberhard
Faber and Rotring writing instruments, and Anchor Hocking glassware,
among others. In total, Newell Rubbermaid owns leading brand names
in housewares, hardware and home furnishings, office, infant/juve-
nile, and commercial products. As suggested by the diversity of this list

of consumer product categories, Newell Rubbermaid's basic strategy is to market a multiproduct array of brand-name consumer products to mass retailers and wholesalers and to provide superior service to its customers while doing so.

Although internal product development is one path to growth that the firm follows, Newell Rubbermaid's acquisition strategy is the primary driver of its growth and the principal source of its financial success. The closing of the firm's 1997 fiscal period showed that on an annual basis over the most recent ten-year period, sales had grown an average of 20 percent and earnings per share had increased an average of 17 percent. As the twenty-first century begins, the company remains committed to meeting or exceeding its aggressive yearly financial goals, which are to: (1) maintain return on beginning equity at 20 percent or above, (2) achieve earnings per share growth averaging 15 percent, (3) increase dividends in a manner that is consistent with earnings growth, and (4) maintain a prudent degree of leverage.

This chapter begins with an additional and brief commentary about innovation's importance for firms competing in the global economy. This section is followed with definitions of the different types of innovation. Flowing from this discussion is an explanation of factors that influence executives to acquire other companies to gain access to their innovation skills and products rather than allocate limited resources to internally develop innovation skills and the products that result from their use. This discussion shows that, under the right circumstances, firms can successfully use an acquisition strategy to acquire innovation. The chapter closes with a presentation of managerial guidelines regarding actions to take when using an acquisition strategy to acquire the innovation skills and innovative products that are necessary to achieve competitive success in the twenty-first century's global economy.

Creating Value
Through the Acquisition Strategy at Newell

To promote growth and improve earnings, Newell Manufacturing Company started actively acquiring firms in the early 1960s. Daniel Ferguson formalized the primacy of Newell's acquisition strategy as a pathway to growth and competitive success when he became the company's president in 1965. Since then, Newell has acquired more than 80 companies. At least 18 major acquisitions were completed in the 1990s alone. These major transactions resulted in over $2 billion in additional sales revenue. Over time, Newell has evolved from a small drapery manufacturer with revenue of approximately $30 million in 1974 into a $6 billion-plus multiproduct consumer goods company. The vast majority of this growth has been achieved through the firm's often used, effective acquisition strategy.[1]

In November 1998, Rubbermaid Inc. stated publicly that it had agreed to merge with Newell. Through a stock swap valued at roughly $5.8 billion, the transaction was finalized on March 24, 1999. Announced as a merger, the operational reality of the transaction was that Newell had acquired Rubbermaid. In the words of a business writer, "Newell will be calling the management shots. The merged board will include nine people from the current Newell board and six from Rubbermaid's board. Newell's chairman, William P. Sovey, will be the chairman of the new company."[2] Moreover, when the transaction was completed, the future role and responsibilities after the first year of life for the newly created firm for Rubbermaid's CEO, Wolfgang R. Schmitt, were unclear.

At the time of this transaction, Rubbermaid had an impressive stock of well-known brand-name product lines. In addition, the firm continued to be recognized for its ability to consistently develop innovative products and for the powerful brand franchises that resulted from its stream of product innovations.[3] One of its recent innovations is a series of insulated filtered water bottles. Offered in an assortment of sizes and different configurations (e.g., bottles and pitchers), these personal sized bottles of filtered water are designed for "people on the go." With each filter lasting for 284 refills of treated or potable water, these products give consumers what the firm believes is "better tasting water" at a cost below that of the per-glass cost of bottled water.

Although known for its innovativeness and the high quality of its goods, Rubbermaid had not been able to earn a consistent stream of profits from its product innovations in recent years. Describing this situation, one analyst noted that "Rubbermaid has excellent product-development skills but has had trouble bringing that to the bottom line."[4] A key reason for this is that Rubbermaid remained a high-cost producer while manufacturing its innovative products. Operating as a high cost producer in an increasingly complex and dynamic global economy and dealing with major global and powerful customers such as Wal-Mart created pressures for Rubbermaid. For example, with its strong power base as a large purchaser, Wal-Mart, which at one point accounted for approximately 15 percent of Rubbermaid's sales revenue, exerted constant pressure on Rubbermaid (and its other suppliers as well) to reduce its prices. As a high-cost producer, Rubbermaid experienced serious problems as a result of the lower profit margins that it earned when selling to Wal-Mart and other major customers at prices yielding margins that were insufficient to cover the firm's high operating costs. In contrast to Rubbermaid, Newell has earned a reputation for its ability to enhance productivity and profits in the companies it acquires. The company uses a process called "Newellization" to achieve these outcomes. Newellization is oriented to creating operating efficiencies and margins in companies Newell believes are managed poorly and ineffectively. However, less of a commitment to innovation and a reduction in innovative output can result from the Newellization process. Newell must continue to acquire firms to have access to innovation across time.

Newell executives were convinced that the combination of their firm's execution skills with Rubbermaid's product innovation capabilities was an excellent strategic fit. In highlighting the acquired firm's skills, Newell's CEO observed that "the Rubbermaid brands are universally recognized and synonymous with value for consumers. Their reputation for innovation and new product development is legendary."[5] Joining Newell's ability to restrain costs and provide superior customer service with Rubbermaid's product innovation skills was the key to value creation in the new company. In fact, Newell expected to create revenue and operating synergies by leveraging Rubbermaid's product innovation skills and brand names across some of the product lines manufactured of its other units. Executives anticipated that "by 2000, these efforts (to create synergies) would produce increases over anticipated 1998 results of $300 million to $350 million in operating income for the combined company."[6] Thus, Newell acquired Rubbermaid's innovation skills to stimulate further growth and profitability.[7]

As suggested by this description of Newell Rubbermaid, innovation can result from using skills and capabilities that are inside the firm (called internal innovation) or by acquiring innovation skills or innovative products through purchasing other firms. Regardless of the path taken, achieving innovation success is critical to organizational competitiveness in the global economy. In the twenty-first century, innovation facilitates firms' efforts to deal flexibly with rapidly changing conditions and distinguish themselves from rivals.[8] Thus, an increasing number of businesspeople and academics believe that competitive success in global markets accrues to firms able to take entrepreneurial risks when seeking to develop innovation skills and innovative products.[9] As shown by the following comments, writer Rosabeth Moss Kanter supports the need for consistent innovation: "Winning in business today demands innovation. Companies that innovate reap all the advantages of a first mover. They acquire a deep knowledge of new markets and develop strong relationships within them. Innovators also build a reputation of being able to solve the most challenging problems."[10]

Innovation's Importance and Its Relationship with Firm Success

Years ago, Peter Drucker suggested that, along with marketing, innovation is one of two factors crucial to a firm's economic health.[11] Evidence from studies in several disciplines (e.g. , finance, marketing, economics, and management) shows that a positive relationship exists between innovation and firm performance, lending support to Drucker's proposition.[12] This evidence is interpreted frequently as an indication that innovation (whether developed internally or acquired) is a source of value creation and competitive advantage for individual firms.[13] However, learning how to manage the research and development activities that permit innovation on a global scale is challenging.[14]

Thus, in both domestic and international economies, innovation increasingly is recognized as a key link to the firm's strategic competitiveness.[15] Moreover, because it challenges the firm to be continuously devoted to strong product lines and taking actions that will cause the goods in those lines to be improved constantly, innovation is a factor that differentiates companies from competitors.[16] As a differentiating factor, innovation helps companies satisfy their customers' needs. Sybron Laboratory Products Corporation's acquisition of Molecular BioProducts, Inc. was completed in part to fill gaps in Sybron's product lines. By acquiring BioProducts' well-known product innovation abilities, Sybron hoped to satisfy its customers' needs for particular molecular biology products.[17]

Definitions and Types of Innovation

Innovation is a complex construct or phenomenon that may be especially difficult to achieve in large organizations.[18] In fact, some believe that effective organizational innovation may be relatively rare, certainly as compared to the frequency with which normal administrative routines are established and used. In addition to innovation's complex nature, other reasons for the possible rarity of effective innovation include the uncertainty and controversy it can create within the firm and the coordination across units that implementing it demands.[19] For example, greater organizational power might accrue to those involved with successful innovations. When not managed properly, this type of change in the firm's power structure may result in a lack of harmony among employees. Without harmony and the consistency of focus that it can provide, some employees may not take the actions necessary for the firm to derive full benefits from its innovations.[20]

Despite potential controversies as well as the difficulty of developing and implementing innovation, companies interested in achieving and maintaining competitiveness in the global economy commit to actions required to innovate. In this context, competitiveness can be thought of as a marathon to achieve excellence.[21] Thus, although difficult and challenging, effective innovation is a critical part of the skill set that firms need to participate successfully in the "excellence" marathon. Evidence of a relationship between high innovative propensity and sustained superior profitability for U.S. pharmaceutical companies can be interpreted as fairly strong support of the decision to allocate resources to innovation.[22]

Because it is influenced by an array of organizational, individual, and environmental factors, businesspeople and researchers define innovation differently.[23] A comprehensive definition suggests that innovation is "any action that either puts the organization into new strategic domains or significantly alters the way the organization attempts to serve existing customers or constituents."[24] This definition suggests a strategic role for innovation by affecting choices made about the individuals and groups the firm is serving and intends to serve and how their needs are to be satisfied. Innovation has long been thought to have a strategic role at GE. For those who are a part of the firm's corporate research and development function, it has been suggested that "every technical contributor at the corporate-level Research and Development Center is working on a program essential to current business plans, or to strategic growth initiatives."[25]

A concise yet still "strategic" definition suggests that an organizational innovation is a novelty that is useful.[26] A key indicator of usefulness is the degree to which the innovation helps the firm improve its effectiveness as it responds to changes in its internal and external environments.[27] A final definition views innovation as a means of changing an organization. When thought of in this context, innovation is defined as the adoption of an idea or behavior new to the adopting organization.[28] Regardless of its precise definition, innovation is concerned with the seeking of creative, unusual, or novel solutions to issues or expressed or latent needs.[29]

There are different types of organizational innovation, including new products or services, new manufacturing processes or technologies, and new administrative processes and systems. Each type of organizational innovation can be developed internally or obtained through acquisitions.

Product innovations are new products or services that are introduced to satisfy an external user or market need. These innovations help the firm adapt to changes in markets, technology, and competition.[30] Developing new products finds the firm (1) forming a compelling new product concept, (2) assessing the concept's technological and commercial feasibility, (3) demonstrating the product's performance capabilities and benefits, and (4) validating the business plan through which the product is to become a marketplace reality.[31] *Process innovations* "are new elements introduced into an organization's production or service operations—input materials, task specifications, work and information flow mechanisms, and equipment used to produce a product or render a service."[32] Study of results achieved through effective use of process innovations suggests that firms can affect productivity significantly (especially in manufacturing companies).[33] Internally focused, *administrative innovations* are related indirectly to the firm's basic work activities and directly to its management systems and routines. These innovations are usually concerned with the organization's structure and its administrative processes.[34]

APCOA, Inc. merged recently with Standard Parking. The combined firm manages airport, urban, and hospital parking facilities across the United States and Canada. Driving this transaction was the objective of combining the firms' complementary innovation abilities. APCOA is recognized as the industry leader in terms of developing and selling administrative innovations to clients. APCOA's innovation skills are used to develop highly sophisticated financial reporting and management systems for use by parking facilities. In contrast, Standard is known for its product innovations, including its "patented musical reminder system to help patrons locate their cars, ParkNet® traffic reports, Midas® CarCare Service, Books-To-Go® audiocassettes, loaner umbrellas and effective facility security measures." Thus, the transaction between these companies results in access for each firm to a set of innovation skills that it lacked. In addition to being of value in the marketplace, Standard now has opportunities to use APCOA's skills to develop internal administrative innovations while APCOA has access to a set of skills through which it may learn how to develop innovative products that complement those resulting from its administrative innovations.[35]

Innovating Through Internal Development and External Acquisitions

As we pointed out previously, firms can pursue product, process, and administrative innovations through two approaches—internal development and external acquisitions.[36] Each approach has advantages and disadvantages.

Innovation Through Internal Development

Firms using their resources to develop innovations internally attempt to successfully introduce multiple innovations across time. Hewlett-Packard (H-P) promotes a close relationship between those involved with the firm's research and development and product development functions as a key means to its ability to continuously introduce a host of successful product innovations.[37]

Firms able to achieve what H-P does through its internal innovation efforts increase the probability of developing a sustainable competitive advantage based on innovation-related capabilities. With rapidly changing product portfolios, these firms seek first-mover advantages while relying on their internal innovation capabilities as the foundation for continuous and successful product introductions. Linked with successful internal innovation efforts is the development of a culture that "evokes incredible energy, enthusiasm, initiative, and responsibility-taking connected to achievement of extraordinarily high goals."[38]

An electronics innovator, Sony seeks first-mover advantages through internal innovation. However, at the level of individual products (e.g.,

Walkman), Sony often enjoys only short-lived competitive advantages. Reducing the duration of an individual product's ability to earn above-average returns is the relative ease with which it can be reversed engineered. "However, by looking at the total returns earned by Sony across all of its products over time, the source of Sony's sustained competitive advantage becomes clear.... Sony is able to constantly introduce new and exciting personal electronics products.... Over time, across multiple product introductions, Sony's capability advantages do lead to a sustained competitive advantage."[39] To achieve these advantages, the firm relying on internal innovation capabilities as a source of lasting competitive advantage must allocate the resources required to continuously support, nurture, and upgrade those capabilities.

A German company, Seidenader makes image analysis systems that are used to check the quality of pharmaceutical products (e.g., quality control of pills at the end of the production line). Under the leadership of the founder's great grandson, innovation is sought inside this successful company. To support these efforts, the company split into two divisions. One uses internal innovation skills to concentrate on product innovations in the pharmaceutical industry; the other attempts to "spin out" some of the firm's innovative abilities to develop product innovations in other industries such as confectionary and orthopedics.[40]

Car manufacturer PSA Peugeot Citroen is committed to internal innovations in both technology and automobile styling and design. Unlike many of its competitors, this firm does not engage in merger or acquisition activity to achieve its growth and profitability objective. Instead, the company relies on internal innovations to grow organically.[41]

Despite the support for internal innovations demonstrated by many firms such as GE, Hewlett-Packard, Sony, PSA Peugeot Citroen, and Seidenader, internal innovation is not risk free nor is it achieved easily. Beyond this, companies' experiences show that developing innovations internally and introducing them into the marketplace can be expensive.[42] Moreover, significant amounts of time are often required for product innovations to earn a profitable return on the firm's investment. Even with proper support in terms of resources and time, the knowledge that eight of 10 new products fail commercially demonstrates that internal innovation is risky.[43]

In the global economy, other realities complicate the actions firms take to pursue successful internal innovations. Increasingly, for example, speed to the marketplace is recognized as a significant source of competitive advantage. In the view of executives in the automobile industry, innovation alone is insufficient. Instead, it is the speed of innovation that is the true source of competitive advantage.[44] When speaking about the pattern of competitive dynamics in the telecommunications industry, Nokia's executive vice president stated that "time to market is crucial to success in this business."[45] Driving the importance of dramatically improving the firm's "time-to-market" capability is the ease with which competitors are able to quickly imitate successful product innovations.[46] Time-based competition means that a firm attempts to increase profits by rapidly introducing innovative products while simultaneously containing costs and market risks.[47] In the context of our discussion, "Innovation speed is defined as the time elapsed between (a) initial development, including the conception and development of an innovation, and (b) ultimate commercialization, which is the introduction of a new product into the marketplace."[48] Being able to innovate quickly requires that all parts of the organization's operations are oriented to speed. This orientation, which may be unfamiliar in many parts of a large number of organizations, can be difficult to develop. Organizational experiences suggest that to successfully introduce a speed orientation in a company often requires changes to the firm's culture.

Innovation Through External Acquisitions

The difficulties surrounding internal innovation influence some firms to use external acquisitions as their primary innovation approach. The inability of eight out of every 10 new products to reach commercial success denotes the high level of risk that is a part of internal innovation efforts. In contrast, buying or merging with a company that already has innovative skills and successful products as well as process and administrative routines that are new to the acquiring firm can be appealing. In these cases, the target firm has a track record that can be evaluated. Careful study of the track record allows estimates of future revenue streams and cost structures. Developing these figures for unproven internal innovations is difficult and uncertain. Beyond this, an acquisition permits immediate access to the market with products that have established sales volumes with existing customer bases.[49]

The pharmaceutical industry is one in which innovation is linked strongly to competitive success. Recognizing this need is influencing companies to use innovation as the foundation on which two or more firms' operations can be combined. An analyst has described the actions being taken in light of this influence as follows: "From St. Louis to Basle, from Wilmington to Frankfurt, pharmaceutical and agro-chemical companies are joining forces and recreating themselves as enterprises based on biological innovation."[50]

Executives at Warner-Lambert are aware of innovation's importance and the increasing use of mergers and acquisitions in the pharmaceutical industry. At least partly because its product pipeline is not filled with anticipated blockbuster drugs, the firm acquired Agouron Pharmaceuticals Inc. in a $2.1 billion stock transaction. Particularly attractive to Warner-Lambert was Agouron's research and development expertise in areas such as cancer. Because of the paucity of major "hits" in its own pipeline, analysts expected the firm to seek other acquisitions to gain immediate access to both product innovations and innovative skills.[51]

In the same industry, Johnson & Johnson acquired Centocor, one of the top U.S. biotech firms, at a cost of $4.9 billion in stock. Influencing this transaction was the pressure J&J felt "to find new blockbuster drugs after several products fell short of sales expectations in recent years." Through the acquisition, J&J gained ownership of several new products. Among the most promising was Remicade, a drug that was approved to treat the bowel disorder Crohn's disease.[52]

Also competing in the pharmaceutical industry, Baxter International Inc. acquired Somatogen. The acquisition was intended to enhance Baxter's position in oxygen-carrying therapeutics. Baxter wanted to capitalize on Somatogen's innovation skills with respect to recombinant hemoglobin technology to develop next-generation products.[53]

An acquisition of an innovation skill can be person specific. This was the case when Inex Pharmaceuticals purchased a leading portfolio of drug products, patents, and manufacturing facilities from Lynx Therapeutics, Inc. The real value of this acquisition was thought to be the group of innovative Lynx employees who had been working to develop antisense drug products. In fact, INEX's CEO and president suggested that through this acquisition, his firm had "access to considerable antisense expertise in Drs. Geiser and Zon and their team to develop new antisense drugs and produce them to FDA-standards at the lowest possible cost."[54]

Many other acquisitions have been completed across multiple industry types in the pursuit of innovation or innovation capabilities. Nokia, for instance, bought Vienna Systems, a small Canadian firm specializing in IP (Internet Protocol) telephony. In addition to providing quick access to a new market, Nokia acquired what it determined was Vienna's technology-based innovation expertise in the IP network markets. With the innovation of packet-switching technologies for IP networks as its core capability, Vienna was thought by analysts to be an innovative and complementary acquisition for Nokia.[55] In the same industry, Telecom Analysis Systems Inc. (TAS) acquired the wireless and satellite communications testing product lines of NoiseCom Inc. Driving this transaction was the acquisition of the product innovation capabilities of the acquired entity.[56]

As our discussion of external acquisitions has shown, executives in Nokia, TAS, and those managing the pharmaceutical acquirers mentioned above seem to have decided that acquiring innovation and/or innovative abilities is preferred to attempting internal innovation. In other words, their actions seem to reflect a belief that acquiring innovations would allow their firms to enter markets quickly with proven innovations at a lower cost to their company and with lower risk for managers. We should also assume that executives believe that external acquisitions will contribute to levels of improvements in the firm's financial performance that are either equal to or greater than the improvements that would result from internal innovations.

What Is the Effect of Acquisitions on Innovation?

As we have seen, because of the low probability of success and the length of time required for innovations to satisfy hurdle return rates, some managers decide that internal innovation is a high-risk activity.[57] In these instances, acquisitions may be an attractive alternative because they offer immediate entrance to a market that is new for the acquiring firm and/or a larger share of a market the company is serving already. As with internal innovation, external acquisitions are not risk free; however, the outcomes from acquisitions are more certain and can be estimated more accurately compared to internally developed innovations.

Acquisitions can become a substitute for innovation in companies actively using an acquisition strategy.[58] When this happens, firms should expect a negative effect on their ability to innovate. There is some evidence supporting this expectation. For example, it has been reported that acquisitions have a negative effect on both R&D intensity (a measure of R&D inputs) and patent intensity (a measure of R&D outputs). Thus, fewer inputs to innovation efforts yield fewer innovations.[59] Relatedly, other evidence shows that firms making acquisitions introduce fewer new products into the marketplace.[60]

Companies are advised to think carefully about the possibility of experiencing such an outcome when acquiring a firm. For example, Hasbro Interactive Inc. acquired the rights to Atari arcade games. The intent was to repackage the games for use on various media, including Sony PlayStations, personal computers, and eventually Nintendo 64s. According to a company official, this "acquisition fit into Hasbro Interactive's three-pronged strategy of taking proven game brands with familiar play patterns and republishing them in a gussied-up form that includes 3-D graphics and other innovations."[61] One might wonder if this strategy could reduce Hasbro Interactive's ability to develop new, innovative products over time.

Given its importance, why would a manager allow acquisitions to substitute for innovation? In part, the reason for this is that most if not all companies lack the resources required to support multiple strategic emphases. In general, firm growth is achieved primarily through either acquisitions or innovations.[62] It is unusual for a company to have a resource base that can simultaneously sustain a focus on internal innovation and external acquisitions as the engines of firm growth. Moreover, the resources required to support use of the acquisition strategy (to engage in due diligence, avoid excessive debt burdens, etc.) reduce the amount of resources that can be used to promote other activities such as innovation.

A preference for financial controls that result from an active acquisition strategy further stifles efforts to devote resources to innovation. Financial controls are objective criteria (e.g., ROI) that are used to evaluate returns being earned by individual business units and the managers who have the responsibility for their performance. The net result is that managers and their firms continue to acquire other companies to gain access to innovation because of the reduced commitment to internal innovation efforts.[63]

Thus, as we have explained, there is a set of factors that explains why managers sometimes allow acquisitions to substitute for internal innovation activities. When this happens, managers have a tendency to become less committed to innovation. Because of its positive relationship with firm performance, reduced commitments to innovation can be expected to contribute to decreases in the firm's financial performance.[64]

Interestingly, however, we have not found that an active acquisition strategy reduces managerial commitment to innovation, subsequently causing fewer resources to be allocated to research and development (a key indicator of the firm's interest in internal innovation) in the newly created company.[65] In contrast, two-thirds of the successfully created new firms in our sample continued to emphasize innovation, often through healthy R&D investments. Beyond this, a small subset of our sample (the firms we have used as examples throughout) took great care to emphasize innovation following the merger or acquisition. General Dynamics, for example, had a significant commitment to R&D prior to its acquisition of Cessna. Remaining committed to the strategic importance of R&D and the innovation resulting from it, the amount GD allocated to R&D in Cessna after the transaction was finalized was an increase over the pre-acquisition allocation in Cessna. In fact, the synergies anticipated from this acquisition were based on an expectation of developing new technologies as the foundation for building innovative aircraft and related aviation products. Even though it does not compete in a high-technology industry, Fred Meyer (a discount merchandiser) continued to use resources to develop new stores and modernize existing ones following acquisition of Grand Central. Investments for these purposes have objectives that are consistent with those manufacturing firms seek through process innovations. Thus, it seems that Fred Meyer executives believed that innovation is the source of market leadership and competitive advantage even in an industry that at that time at least was not thought to be innovative.

Given the experiences of the companies we have talked about in this chapter, we offer three major conclusions. First and foremost, it is important to again highlight that innovation (e.g., product, process, and administrative innovations) is related to the firm's financial performance and, at the extreme, to its survival. In the twenty-first century's global economy, the "innovate or die" mantra that a growing number of executives cite will be a reality. Stated simply, the firm must be able to innovate if it is to be successful across time. The need for continuous and successful innovation exists for firms developing innovation internally and for companies acquiring innovation through an acquisition strategy. Second, when acquiring innovation, managers in the combined firm must focus on maintaining if not enhancing innovation activity during the integration process and thereafter. This commitment can be demonstrated through resources allocated to research and development and by helping to develop an organizational culture that supports innovative activity. Third, firms investing heavily in internal innovation and with an organizational culture supporting and encouraging those innovation efforts can be expected to outperform (with performance measured as return on invested capital) companies demonstrating less of a commitment (in terms of resources and culture) to internal innovation.[66] Thus, when pursuing internal innovation, the firm must be bold and aggressive. No one in the firm should be able to question the company's interest in internal innovation because of how available resources are used.

We are not suggesting that innovation is impossible when an acquisition strategy is used. However, we do mean to say that firms should be careful and cautious when trying to become innovative by acquiring other companies.

As always, we close this chapter with recommendations.

Recommendations Regarding the Acquisition of Innovation

As this chapter's discussion shows, using an acquisition strategy as an effective approach to innovation is challenging. To improve the likelihood that the firm can successfully acquire innovation, we offer the following guidelines.

1. Accept the difficulty of acquiring innovation. In addition to the challenges of successfully completing any merger or acquisition (e.g., achieving effective due diligence, integrating complementary resources, and maintaining relatively low debt levels), a premium is placed on being able to position innovative people properly in the newly created firm. Company experiences suggest that placing the right people in the right positions in the combined company is especially important when dealing with individuals who are developing product, process, and/or administrative innovations. In addition to their technical skills as an assignment criterion, the "behavior set" that the innovation-related job demands,

such as the ability to handle customer relations, act as a team leader, or manage a project, should be considered as well.

2. Have a specific objective in mind when acquiring innovation. Without specific objectives as a driving force, innovation and innovative skills can be used inefficiently in the combined firm.

3. Focus on speed when acquiring innovation. Quick innovators are more likely to earn above-average returns from their innovations, especially product and process innovations. Obviously critical in high-technology industries, innovation speed is increasingly a significant competitive weapon in other industries as well, even ones we typically do not think of as being fast-paced and dynamic (e.g., utilities).

4. Determine if innovation is to be a source of competitive advantage for the firm. To yield maximum benefit, sources of competitive advantage must be emphasized in the firm's daily operations and supported through constant reinvestments. It is only through bold, aggressive, and consistent allocations of resources to competitive advantages that they can remain dynamic in nature and capable of contributing to the firm's success. Identifying innovative technology as an intended source of advantage influences resource allocations across the firm as efforts are made to wisely use available resources.

5. Build a supportive culture. The importance of culture to merger and acquisition success has been emphasized in other parts of the book (e.g., complementary resources, synergy creation, and organizational learning). It is equally critical to being successful when acquiring innovation. Principles that help develop a culture that supports innovation include: (1) having people recognize that helping others to be innovative is part of their job, (2) encouraging people to share ideas to create innovation-related synergy, (3) expecting experimentation to be prized by everyone, and (4) viewing mistakes as valuable learning lessons.[67]

A key purpose of this chapter has been to demonstrate that innovation is linked to competitive success. In fact, a failure to innovate puts most firms on a path of failure. Typically, when thinking of innovation, we remember products that firms developed internally. Sony is a company that introduced an array of innovative products (e.g., the Walkman) by relying mainly on its own skills and capabilities. However, as we have talked about in this chapter, it is possible for companies to buy innovation and innovative capabilities. In the next chapter, we speak to the increasing growth of cross-border mergers and acquisitions. Occasionally, these transactions are completed to acquire innovation. But, as we shall see, merging with or acquiring companies from other nations adds a layer of complexity that challenges even the best decision-makers.

10

Acquiring or Merging Across Borders

There are many people who think 2000 will herald Europe's first major crossborder banking merger. Unicredito SpA of Italy and Banco Bilbao Vizcaya Argentaria, the recently merged Spanish bank, are at the top of the list, having declared an intention to ultimately consummate their already tight relationship. Moves underway for a pan-European stock exchange in 2000 should help this along by making all-stock mergers between banks in different countries more attractive to investors.

—E. Portanger

The revolution in the telecommunications industry created a surge of mergers and acquisitions in 1999 that is changing the way people live and work. Some of the deals were friendly, some were hostile, some were global—but together telecom takeovers accounted for 17 percent of the record $3.4 trillion in mergers and acquisitions in 1999.

—N. Know

The announcement that Germany's Daimler-Benz AG and United States' Chrysler Corporation intended to merge stunned the automobile industry. At the time, this cross-border transaction was the world's largest industrial merger. The merger between two of the automobile industry's most profitable manufacturers created a company that ranked third globally in sales revenue and fifth in vehicle unit sales. The official primary goal of this cross-border merger was to create the world's preeminent automotive, transportation, and services company.[1]

This merger was driven by the formerly independent companies' needs. Although profitable, Chrysler lacked the infrastructure and depth of management required to become a truly global corporation. Furthermore, executives concluded that Chrysler CEO Robert Eaton's goal to increase the firm's sales revenue by at least 20 percent annually could be reached only by substantially enhancing the company's presence in markets outside the United States. For Daimler-Benz, Chairman Juergen E. Schrempp interpreted the increasing competition in the luxury car market as an indication that his firm had to diversify its product line and distribution channels. In essence, Daimler-Benz had to sell its products in a larger number of national markets on a global basis to achieve its growth goals.

Given their respective needs, "Chrysler and Daimler were a perfect fit. Geographically, their core activities were in different areas: Chrysler was dominant in the U.S., while Daimler's strongholds were Europe and South America." The complementarity between the two companies encompassed product lines as well. The majority of Chrysler's profitable output consisted of sport utility vehicles and multipurpose minivans. In contrast, luxury automobiles were the source of Daimler-Benz's profitable car operations. A diversified corporation, Daimler-Benz also competed in other industries (e.g., aerospace and defense).[2]

As with transactions completed in single countries, synergies are sought through cross-border mergers and acquisitions. A desire for synergies clearly characterized the merger between Daimler-Benz and Chrysler Corporation. By integrating operations, for example, executives expected to save approximately $1.3 billion in 1999 alone. Twelve major integration projects were initiated almost immediately following the merger in an effort to achieve these cost savings and other potential synergies. Among these projects were the building of Mercedes M-Class cars and the Jeep Grand Cherokee on the same production line in Graz, Austria. Although built in the same facility, a decision was made initially to retain distinct platforms for the two vehicles. The company intended for the Graz facility to be its showcase of synergy creation. Simultaneously, though, the possibility of introducing common manufacturing and component sharing at what were then separate Mercedes-Benz and Chrysler manufacturing plants was being evaluated. Describing the reason for this possibility, a senior Chrysler executive observed that "we have discussed common production systems and started to talk to suppliers. There are additional financial benefits to be gained from common assembly."[3]

In addition to cost-based efficiencies, DaimlerChrysler sought cross-selling synergies through the merger.[4] For the most part, these synergies were to result from a melding of firm-specific assets and capabilities, such as the ability to consistently develop high-technology advances (Daimler-Benz) and rapidly introduce new products to the marketplace (Chrysler).

Some analysts believe that this combination of two prosperous companies has changed the nature of competition in the global automobile industry. At the time of the merger, Daimler-Benz Chairman Schrempp and Chrysler Corporation CEO Eaton shared this perspective. Speaking on their behalf, Eaton suggested that the merger was the first of a new trend of strategic actions that would change the automobile industry's future and its competitive characteristics.[5] However, the commitment to create DaimlerChrysler so that it will represent a new model for the global automobile industry is a daunting challenge. Among other tasks, "DaimlerChrysler has key product development decisions to sort out, complex computer systems to integrate, and thousands of managers who must get acclimated to new jobs and a new culture."[6] Complicating these tasks were questions about whether this transaction was a cross-border merger or acquisition. As the months unfolded following the joining of the two companies, evidence continued to mount suggesting that Daimler-Benz had acquired Chrysler Corporation and that this transaction was not a merger of equals as originally announced. Among other issues, if the transaction was indeed an acquisition, some analysts felt that U.S. mutual fund investors would be less willing to invest in what they saw as a German company.[7]

To discuss the increasing frequency and importance of cross-border mergers and acquisitions, such as the Daimler-Benz and Chrysler Corporation transaction, we examine several topics in this chapter. First, we note the difference between a cross-border merger and a cross-border acquisition. Next, we examine the influence of opportunities and threats in the firm's external environment on the decision to engage in cross-border mergers and acquisitions. The relationship between adopting a global mindset and successfully completing cross-border mergers and acquisitions is then examined. In the following section, we speak to the number of cross-border mergers and acquisitions taking place in the global economy. The description of the growing number of cross-border mergers and acquisitions is extended through the discussion of a set of reasons that influences firms to complete these transactions.[8] Each of the individual reasons denotes the source or nature of the value the newly formed firm intends to create through the cross-border merger or acquisition. We examine five reasons firms engage in this particular type of merger and acquisition. To fully consider the specifics of these reasons, our discussion of each one includes company-specific examples. Consistent with all chapters in this book, this one closes with a list of managerial guidelines regarding the use of cross-border mergers and acquisitions.

Definitions of a Cross-Border Merger and Acquisition

As the previous discussion implies, cross-border merger and acquisition activity has become a major strategic tool for corporate growth, especially for multinational corporations.[9] Although similar in nature, a cross-border merger differs from a cross-border acquisition. A cross-border *merger* is a transaction in which two firms with their home operations in different countries agree to an integration of the companies on a relatively equal basis. Driving the decision to blend operations on a relatively equal basis is the fact that the two companies have capabilities that, when combined, are expected to create competitive advantages that will contribute to success in the global marketplace. A cross-border *acquisition* is a transaction in which an expanding firm buys either a controlling interest or all of an existing company in a foreign country. Often, the acquired firm becomes a business unit within the acquiring firm's portfolio of businesses. Typically, managers in the acquired firm then report to the acquiring firm's management team.[10] As with mergers and acquisitions, the general purpose of a cross-border merger or acquisition is to create more value through the newly formed firm than could be generated by the involved companies' operating as independent entities.

Environmental Opportunities and Threats

Several factors influence a decision to complete cross-border mergers and acquisitions, including environmental threats and opportunities. In the case of Daimler-Benz and Chrysler Corporation, for example, threats in the firms' external environments affected executives' perspectives about what should be done if their companies were to remain successful. Overcapacity and constant and severe downward pressures on their products' selling prices (price pressures were especially severe for Chrysler's cars and trucks) were two of these threats.

In 1999, it was estimated that the global automobile manufacturing industry had more than 20 million units of overcapacity. For firms with a strong financial standing, either a merger with or an acquisition of a competitor might be an attractive course of action when the industry has too much capacity. Volkswagen, for example, used its financial position as the foundation for its acquisitions of Rolls Royce and Lamborghini. Overcapacity also engenders frequent rumors of impending cross-border mergers and acquisitions. With a 1999 cash balance of approximately $23 billion, Ford Motor Company was often rumored to be in an acquisitive mode. Among the suggested targets of Ford's possible intentions at the time were Honda Motor Company and Nissan. Rumors about Ford became especially prominent following its acquisition of Volvo's car division for $5.8 billion.[11] During the time of these speculations, Daimler-Chrysler considered and then abandoned the possibility of acquiring Nissan.[12] Later, Renault did form a relationship with Nissan.

Cross-border mergers and acquisitions have the potential to increase the efficiency and effectiveness of the world's automobile manufacturing industry in addition to affecting individual companies' competitive ability. This is so because these transactions are helping to consolidate the industry on a global level. Jack Smith, former CEO and Chairman of General Motors, believes that consolidation will continue until only six to 10 firms remain on a global basis.[13] Toyota's former president, Hiroshi Okuda, and Ford Motor Company's former CEO, Alex Trotman, are even more persuaded of the consolidation trend, believing that the world will soon have only five or six global car companies.[14] However, without consolidation (and the synergistic benefits that can accrue from it), overcapacity, and the cost pressures and cutthroat pricing tactics that accompany it, may well continue unabated.

An opportunity identified by executives at Daimler-Benz and Chrysler Corporation is the decline in nationalism in Europe. An essential factor stimulating this decline is the emergence of a single currency across Europe.[15] As nationalism declines, it becomes easier for European companies to participate actively and more fully in the emerging global economy. The ability to operate jointly with a cost structure that was less than the combined costs of the independent entities was a significant opportunity for the two firms, in that reduced operating costs increased DaimlerChrysler's ability to deal successfully with price pressures.

As our discussion about the global auto business suggests, cross-border mergers and acquisitions can increase the competitiveness of individual firms, industry sectors, and potentially even national economies. At the firm level (the focus of this book), cross-border mergers and acquisitions can help firms develop competitive advantages.[16] In fact, integrating Daimler-Benz and Chrysler Corporation is expected to create competitive advantages that would not be available to the firms had they decided to continue operating independently. Organizations that are particularly effective in completing cross-border transactions use a set of valuable, wealth-creating, firm-specific resources and capabilities that cannot be easily imitated or substituted.[17] Developed across time and through repeated use, these resources and capabilities are the foundation for successful cross-border mergers and acquisitions.

A Global Mindset

A global mindset affects the success of cross-border mergers and acquisitions. This mindset has several distinct components, including "multicultural values, basing status on merit rather than nationality, being open to ideas from other cultures, being excited rather than fearful in new cultural settings, and being sensitive to cultural differences without being intimidated by them."[18] Operationally, especially regarding actions taken to integrate firms into a single new entity, thinking globally means "taking the best (that) other cultures have to offer and blending that into a third culture."[19]

The importance of a global mindset also extends to government officials. Speaking about the European media and audiovisual industries, Jean-Marie Messier, chairman of Vivendi, the French utilities and communications group and active acquirer, suggested that it was "urgent that the European notion of competition in the media sector should not be an intra-eurozone vision but really a global vision." Thus, in Messier's view, the ability of European companies in these two industries to compete successfully in the global economy is affected by the degree to which "European bureaucracy" utilizes policies that encourage the emergence of a few strong players. Furthermore, Messier believes that cross-border mergers and acquisitions can help European companies in efforts to become stronger and more agile.[20]

Actions suggest that DaimlerChrysler executives use a global mindset. Beyond this, it is possible that this transaction is helping to create capabilities that will allow other units of DaimlerChrysler to complete successful cross-border mergers and acquisitions. Recently, for example, the firm's Dasa subsidiary, a competitor in the aerospace and defense industries, acquired Spain's state-owned aircraft company Construcciones Aeronauticas (Casa). Dasa's Chief Executive, Manfred Bischoff, noted that this acquisition marked Europe's first real cross-border linkup in the sector. Furthermore, Bischoff implied that this transaction was the first of several others to follow, including at least two with firms based in the United States.[21] Thus, DaimlerChrysler's experiences over the first 18 months or so of its life helped build a competitive advantage for the firm in terms of knowing how to complete successful cross-border transactions.

The Rapidly Expanding Pace of Cross-Border Mergers and Acquisitions

The number of cross-border mergers and acquisitions is growing quickly. Consider that by the end of 1999's first half, the year-to-date total of global merger and acquisition activity reached $1.5 trillion.[22] This was the largest amount expended for global merger and acquisition activity on record. Of this total, cross-border mergers and acquisitions accounted for slightly over 40 percent. On a year-to-year comparison, the percentage of cross-border mergers and acquisitions doubled between mid-year 1998 and 1999. Stimulating this increased activity were several conditions, including the worldwide phenomenon of industry consolidations (such as discussed for the automobile industry) and, in Europe, currency consolidation.[23] In the world's electricity industry, the privatization and liberalization of global power markets continue to spur cross-border transactions. In the first five months of 1999, for example, 41 cross-border mergers and acquisitions had been announced as compared to 35 announcements in 1998's first five months. The majority of these transactions are taking place in Asia Pacific and Europe.[24]

Viewed originally as primarily an activity of U.S. firms, cross-border mergers and acquisitions are becoming almost equally prominent among European companies.[25] Influenced by a number of realities, including global competition, deregulation, and the integration of the Euro throughout the European community, the volume of cross-border transactions completed by European firms alone reached a new record in 1998. The transaction total of $261 billion exceeded 1997's volume by some 37 percent. The largest two transactions of the 1998 cross-border European activity were British Petroleum's $48.2 billion acquisition of Amoco and Daimler-Benz's acquisition of Chrysler Corporation.[26] At the end of 1999's first quarter, the volume of cross-border mergers and acquisitions involving European target companies by a firm in a different country exceeded $100 billion. Over 2,100 transactions were completed during this three-month period. This number of transactions eclipsed the previous record of 1,925 deals that were recorded in the fourth quarter of 1998.[27] The number and size of cross-border acquisitions continue to grow as the twenty-first century unfolds.

Thus, the number of firms interested in merging with or acquiring companies outside their home country is increasing. Some believe that the growth in these transactions demonstrates the importance of globalization and the opportunities it creates for firms to pursue geographic or product diversification or both.[28] The opportunity to compete in multiple countries that geographic diversification permits exposes the firm to a rich array of environments. For example, HSBC Holdings, the London-headquartered international banking group, acquired the private banking empire of Edmond Safra at a price of $10.3 billion. This acquisition contributed positively to the firm's commitment to maintain a balance between relatively less stable markets (e.g., Russia) and more stable markets (e.g., Europe and North America).[29] Product diversification resulting from cross-border mergers or acquisitions allows firms to compete in multiple businesses (product markets) and encounter a richer set of demand characteristics for their expanded set of product lines.[30]

Based in Japan, Denso is the world's fourth largest global car components manufacturer. To fill gaps in its product line (e.g., meters and filters), the firm is interested in acquiring other companies. An initial acquisition involved the purchase of a division of Italy's Magnetti Marelli.[31] To increase its line of luxury cars, General Motors exercised an option to take full ownership of Swedish automaker Saab Automobile AB. Commenting about the benefits for both companies, an analyst observed that "Lord knows, they need some luxury brands. It's as simple as that. Everyone agrees that Saab is probably best-served by being 100 percent owned by General Motors."[32] Thus, in general, cross-border mergers and acquisitions are a quick pathway to enter a new market, permit the acquiring firm to achieve critical mass (presence) in a market rapidly, and result in more control as compared to other market entry modes (e.g., joint ventures and strategic alliances).[33]

Although occurring across industry sectors, cross-border mergers and acquisitions have been especially prevalent in the telecommunications and related high-technology industries as well as the pharmaceutical industry. For example, the pharmaceuticals industry was one of the most active sectors in terms of cross-border merger and acquisition activity in 1998. The consolidation of the highly fragmented global pharmaceutical industry that is occurring at least partly through cross-border transactions is being driven primarily by the need to consolidate operations in order to have the mass of resources required to fund large research and development budgets.[34] As we discuss later, the *costs required to develop new products* (a cost that is borne principally through the firm's research and development budget) is one of the five reasons companies choose to engage in cross-border merger and acquisition activity.

An interesting aspect of the growth in European cross-border merger and acquisition activity is the increase in the use of hostile takeovers.[35] In fact, the monetary value of European hostile takeover activity in 1999's first quarter exceeded the value of this activity in any previous full year.[36] Historically, analysts have considered hostile takeovers to be associated most commonly with American merger and acquisition activity.[37]

Two other 1998 developments (in addition to the increase in hostile takeover activity) contributed to the increase in cross-border merger and acquisition activity in that particular year and are continuing to do so today. First, some European companies have been able to persuade foreign shareholders to accept stock in their firm to complete a transaction. This differed from the previous practice in cross-border deals of using cash payments. Second, some United States acquirers were able to qualify their European acquisitions as a "pooling of interests" under newly developed tax laws. This made it unnecessary for the United States firm to capitalize and then amortize the goodwill amount associated with a cross-border merger or acquisition against future profits.[38]

Reasons to Complete Cross-Border Mergers and Acquisitions

Clearly, more than one reason exists for firms to complete cross-border mergers and acquisitions; five (increased market power, overcoming entry barriers, the cost of new product development, increased speed to market, and increased diversification) are described here. It is important to note, however, that the decision to merge with or acquire a firm in another country is rarely made because of a single issue. Thus, although the following reasons are discussed as independent influences, in many instances more than one reason accounts for the cross-border transaction decision. Nonetheless, individual descriptions allow us to emphasize the significant characteristics of each reason. Of the five reasons, the one that most commonly drives the decision to engage in cross-border mergers and acquisitions is the desire for increased market power. In part, this frequency indicates the significance of the relationship between firm size and competitive success in the global economy.

Increased Market Power

Market power exists when the firm can sell its products above the existing competitive market price or when its manufacturing, distribution, and service costs are lower than competitors'. Sometimes, the effectiveness of decisions made and actions taken result in the firm developing market power in terms of both revenues (i.e., the competitive market price) and costs (i.e., firms' costs structures).[39] Market power is a product of the firm's size, the degree of sustainability of its current competitive advantages, and its ability to make decisions today that will yield new competitive advantages for tomorrow.

Firms can increase their market power through either cross-border mergers or acquisitions. Of these two transactions, cross-border acquisitions are completed more frequently than cross-border mergers to gain market power. Because of this, our discussion of market power emphasizes acquisitions.

In general, cross-border acquisitions are used to increase market power when the firm acquires: (1) a company competing in the same industry and often in the same segments of the primary industry (a horizontal acquisition), (2) a supplier or distributor (a vertical acquisition), or (3) a business in a highly related industry (a related acquisition). An analysis of outcomes suggests that horizontal acquisitions of firms with similar characteristics result in higher performance than when a firm with dissimilar characteristics is acquired. Examples of important similar characteristics include managerial styles, strategies being implemented, and resource allocation patterns.[40]

In the following sections, we provide company-specific examples of horizontal, vertical, and related cross-border transactions.

Horizontal Acquisitions

To enhance its global competitiveness, the French electronics company Thomson-CSF has near-term plans to engage in both cross-border acquisitions and strategic alliances. The firm's chairman indicated that these strategic actions were to be taken to fulfill a desire to enhance the company's position as one of several prominent European defense manufacturers. In the chairman's words, "The plan is to make cross-border moves in our field, which is defense systems. Our vision is to build a transnational defense company." To achieve this objective, Thomson-CSF's executives decided that horizontal acquisitions would account for a significant portion of the intended transactions. Furthermore, a decision was made that the firm's targets would be companies in the United States as well as the rest of the world, including the remaining European countries.[41]

Based in Pennsylvania, York International is the largest independent supplier of heating, ventilation, and air-conditioning products in the United States. Executives at York decided that a significant portion of the firm's future growth should come through product and geographic diversification. By acquiring Sabore of Denmark in 1999, an emerging competitor, York became the largest industrial refrigeration company in the world. Consistent with its growth intentions, this acquisition allowed York to strengthen its position in several emerging markets (e.g., Latin America, Asia, and Eastern Europe). The two companies were believed to complement each other well, with the geographic areas of strength for one matching an area of weakness for the other. Additionally, Ole Andersen, Sabroe's CEO, noted that his company's industrial and marine contracting services, which became part of York's refrigeration division, balanced York's product offerings. Thus, combining these firms was expected to create significant market power for the newly formed company in multiple global markets.[42]

In the computer industry, Via Technologies is recognized as a leading Taiwanese chipset producer. Chipsets act as central nervous systems that link processors to memory and graphics chips and other parts. Via Technologies is one of the few companies to survive competition with Intel in the chipset market. To increase its size and thereby to have the critical mass required to compete more effectively against Intel, Via decided to acquire from United States-based National Semiconductor the unit in Cyrix that manufactures chipsets. To enhance its competitiveness, National retained the Cyrix unit that produces the integrated processors that are used to build complete systems on a single chip. Although challenging Intel seems a daunting task, Via Technologies' executives believed that their firm's cross-border acquisition of the Cyrix unit would result in increased market power. A comment from Via Technologies' sales director reflects the firm's globally competitive mindset: "We are not afraid to compete directly with Intel. We have had many fights with Intel before."[43] Preliminary results from this transaction seem encouraging. In January 2000, Via Technologies started volume shipments of the Via Apollo KX133 chipset to more than 20 leading motherboard manufacturers. According to company officials, these shipments greatly expanded the availability of high-performance mainboards that are optimized for the AMD Athlon processor.[44]

Although the majority of cross-border transactions are acquisitions, cross-border mergers are completed as well. In the steel industry, for example, British Steel and Dutch steelmaker Koninklijke Hoogovens agreed to merge their operations. This transaction created the world's third largest steel manufacturer behind Nippon Steel of Japan and Posco of South Korea.[45] The market power sought through this transaction was related to cost reductions. Speaking to this issue, one analyst noted that "British Steel is very efficient but a merger would help them cut costs in terms of economies of scale and combining manpower and different sites."[46]

Competing in the same industry, Australian steel manufacturer Voest Alpine Stahl (a medium-sized company) avoids mergers to increase market power. As mergers occur between some of the global industry's large firms (e.g., British Steel and Hoogovens), Voest Alpine Stahl's CEO argues that "the larger the blocks, the bigger the niches between them." Instead of mergers, this firm prefers to target selected cross-border acquisitions (including competitors) to gain market power. To continue its expansion into the finishing segment of the global steel market, the firm seeks to acquire companies in east central Europe.[47]

In a different industry, Safeway, the third largest food and drug retailer in the United States, has decided that, at least for the time being, it will not engage in cross-border mergers and acquisitions. The reason, according to Safeway's CEO and chairman, is that to increase the geographic scope of its acquisition program would spread the company's management team too thin. Thus, for this firm, only domestic acquisitions were being completed (at a point in time) to gain market power in the highly fragmented United States grocery industry. In the first half of 1999 alone, Safeway acquired three regional supermarket chains—Randall's Food Markets, Dominick's, and Carr-Gottstein.[48] The challenge for management teams is to recognize when their firms have the unique set of resources and skills required to successfully complete cross-border transactions. In the future, Safeway's executives may conclude that their firm is properly prepared to complete successful cross-border transactions.

Vertical Acquisitions

Through vertical acquisitions, firms seek to control additional parts of the value-added chain. Acquiring either a supplier (a backward vertical acquisition) or a distributor (a forward vertical acquisition) or an organization that already controls more parts of the value chain than does the acquiring firm can result in additional market power.

In a recent communication with shareholders through TXU's annual report, top-level managers indicated that the company's strategy was to "achieve excellent operations of significant scale in selected regions, which integrate capabilities across multiple products and services." Known formerly as TU Electric, this firm changed its name to describe more accurately what the company had become and to reflect its global acquisitions and aspirations.[49]

Decisions made by TXU executives and the company-wide actions resulting from them were influenced by changes occurring in the world-wide energy sectors. One of the important indicators of these changes is the continuing trend toward privatization of a large portion of the world's energy sectors. TXU believes that it is now well positioned to compete in the twenty-first century as a multiregional, integrated company. The firm has a significant presence in three major energy markets—Texas, the United Kingdom and continental Europe, and Australia. Each of these markets is in a different stage of a deregulation process that may eventually occur in virtually all of the world's energy markets.

TXU's presence in markets across the world's economies has been achieved through cross-border acquisitions. The acquisition of The Energy Group and its operating entity Eastern Group was completed in May 1998. This firm was recognized as one of the United Kingdom's preeminent energy companies. Moreover, at the time of its acquisition, Eastern was fully integrated across the value chain, from electricity production through retail sales. Thus, this acquisition gave TXU full ownership of suppliers and distributors with respect to the energy sector's value chain. In addition, TXU viewed Eastern's acquisition as a foundation through which further expansion in the United Kingdom and continental Europe could occur. To date, cross-border acquisitions have resulted in TXU owning market positions in Australia, the United Kingdom, Finland, the Netherlands, Norway, China, Mexico, Spain, and the Czech Republic.[50] Denoting his intentions, the firm's CEO and chairman indicated recently that TXU will continue to scan the world's energy markets and countries to identify acquisition candidates as the privatization trend continues to alter the once-staid world of electricity and natural gas.

Related Acquisitions

Market power can also be gained when the firm acquires a company competing in an industry that is highly related to the acquiring firm's industry. To reinforce a core business, France's Suez Lyonnaise des Eaux S.A. paid $4.5 billion, including the cost of assuming some debt, to acquire U.S.-based Nalco Chemical Company. A diversified company, Suez has core businesses in power, waste services, and communications.[51] The value of this related acquisition, according to Suez's chief executive, is Nalco's client base. Although powerful in municipal water treatment and energy systems, Suez had been a laggard in the industrial market, particularly in the critical United States market. The ability to use Nalco's client base to establish Suez as an outsourcing partner in the United States to industrial firms was highly valued by Suez decision-makers.[52] Analysts' responses to this acquisition were positive, noting that Suez gained Nalco's experienced management team and a strong position in the critical United States market while paying no more for the company than 11 times earnings before interest, tax, depreciation, and amortization.[53]

Overcoming Entry Barriers

Barriers to entry are factors associated with a market and/or companies operating currently in the market that increase the difficulty and expense another firm would incur to enter the market.[54] Examples of entry barriers include a well-established position by an incumbent in the segment of the industry targeted by the potential entrant and customer loyalty to existing brands. Evidence and company actions across time reveal that the higher entry barriers are, the greater the likelihood that a firm will seek to overcome them through an acquisition.[55]

Unilever, the AngloDutch consumer products' giant, is the world's largest tea company. Recently the firm spent approximately $15 million to acquire the state-owned Beijing Tea Processing Factory. Employing 235 people, Beijing Tea's primary product is Jing Hua jasmine tea. One of Beijing's leading tea brands, Jing Hua is sold in both packaged and loose form.

This acquisition demonstrates Unilever's commitment to its strategy of expanding into China through acquisitions. Already selling its Lipton brand of black tea in China, Unilever intended to marry the Lipton and Jing Hua brands. Although Lipton's branded tea was being sold in Beijing, Unilever officials believed that acquiring a prominent local brand would allow the company to overcome the problems of brand loyalty that were encountered in selling their product in China. Combining the brands would also allow more effective use of Unilever's distribution capabilities in China.[56]

Telecommunication companies also seek to overcome entry barriers by completing cross-border mergers and acquisitions. Founded in the United Kingdom in 1984, Vodafone AirTouch is the world's largest mobile phone group. One of the 10 largest companies in the United Kingdom, Vodafone has a market valuation in excess of 20 billion pounds.[57]

Vodafone purchased CommNet Cellular for $764 million in cash. CommNet was a United States-based cellular phone operator with networks covering a significant portion of rural western America. By giving Vodafone immediate access to over 360,000 customers in nine

western United States states, this acquisition allowed the firm to overcome entry barriers quickly. According to analysts, "The deal is further
evidence that Vodafone AirTouch is anxious to achieve national coverage in the U.S."[58] Late in 1999, Vodafone made a $125.3 billion hostile
takeover bid for Mannesmann AG, "an old-line industrial company that
reinvented itself as a telecommunications powerhouse."[59] At the time,
this was the largest hostile takeover bid on record. After its completion,
this transaction dramatically extended Vodafone's global reach.

Based in the United States, Enron is one of the world's premier
energy corporations. One of the firm's recent interests is to move to the
front rank of global water suppliers. Projected demand influenced
Enron's conclusion that the global water business was a significant
market opportunity. According to the World Bank, developing nations
need to invest $70 billion annually in new water facilities over the
1998–2007 decade. Combining this expectation with the predicted
investments of $30 billion per year in developed countries over the same
time period shows the market's potential.

Enron's acquisition of Wessex Water was completed to enter this
market quickly and overcome entry barriers. A UK company, Wessex
was a supplier of water and/or sewerage to 2.5 million people in south-
west England. Some observers believed that "Enron views the purchase
as a way of buying the operating and management skills it needs to break
into the global water market."[60] Evolving from this initial acquisition in
1998 is Enron's formation of Azuirx, a new subsidiary company. A global
water company, Azurix is committed to acquiring, owning, operating,
and managing water assets around the world. For its global customers,
Azurix provides water and wastewater related services and develops and
manages water resources. Thus, a cross-border acquisition, completed in
part to overcome entry barriers, is the foundation on which Enron has
built a new business enterprise.[61]

Cost of New Product Development

Developing new products and new businesses internally can be expensive and time intensive. Because of these realities, some managers
believe that internal development efforts are risky. In contrast, acquiring an existing company, one with an established sales volume, customer
base, and successful financial performance, is thought to be less risky.[62]
Reduced costs, compared to those incurred to develop products or businesses internally, along with the ability of an acquisition to yield an
immediate presence in a market combine to persuade managers to
acquire new products and new businesses instead of developing them
internally.[63]

Samsung Group's experience with automobile manufacturing
demonstrates the risk of internal product development. Through an

investment of approximately $4.5 billion, this South Korean conglomerate expected great success through its foray into the global car industry. Company executives even suggested that Samsung Motors would quickly become one of the world's top ten automobile firms. This goal was the basis for the firm's investments, even though the global automobile industry (including South Korea's car industry) was characterized by significant overcapacity problems at the time.[64] In fact, according to a business writer, "Analysts ... questioned the launch of Samsung Motors at a time when Korea was suffering from excess capacity in the car industry. It started production as domestic car sales fell by 50 percent due to the nation's economic crisis."[65]

At mid-year 1999, Samsung Motors' debts totaled $3.7 billion. Having failed in efforts to sell it, the firm's car business was to be placed into receivership. Beyond this, Lee Kun-hee, the Samsung "chairman who pushed for the car project, will help pay Samsung Motors' debts ... by donating $2.4 billion of his shares in unlisted Samsung Life Insurance to take 'moral and social responsibility' for the car company's failure."[66] Although clearly not descriptive of all firms' outcomes, Samsung's experience with an internally developed automobile manufacturing business reflects the risk managers and their firms accept when trying to develop new products or businesses through internal capabilities.

To expand its product capabilities, U.S.-based Texas Instruments acquired Libit Signals Processing, an Israeli high-tech company. Libit manufactures silicon chips that permit high-speed Internet and telephone communications via cable networks. This acquisition, at a price of $329 million, allowed TI to immediately add important capabilities to its core products without incurring the risks of developing those capabilities internally.[67]

In the pharmaceutical industry, Bio-Rad Laboratories Inc. (with headquarters in California) acquired Pasteur Sanofi Diagnostics, a unit of the French drug maker Sanofi-Synthelabo S.A. at a cost of $210 million.[68] According to Bio-Rad's President and CEO, the acquisition placed his firm "in a more favorable position in the diagnostics market. It gives us a significant presence in all key geographic areas, including the emerging economies, as well as a substantial product offering in market segments showing strong long-term growth."[69]

Increased Speed to Market

As compared to internally generated product developments and new businesses, acquisitions allow the firm to enter a new market more rapidly.[70] Thus, for companies seeking to compete in nations outside their home base, acquiring a firm is a much faster way to reach this objective as compared to the time required to establish a new facility and new relationships with stakeholders in a different country.

In the world's financial services sector, Merrill Lynch paid $5.3 billion to buy Mercury Asset Management, a London-based money manager. At the time, this was the largest international acquisition by a U.S.-based securities firm. This transaction made Merrill the fourth largest asset manager in the world. Thus, the acquisition of Mercury resulted in a significant global presence for Merrill that would have required many years to develop through internally generated efforts.[71]

The Polish government took actions to privatize that nation's banking sector in the late 1990s. Cross-border transactions have resulted from the government's privatization commitment. For example, UniCredito, an Italian bank, and Allianz, the German insurer, paid $1.1 billion for a controlling share of Pekao, one of Poland's largest banking entities. At a price of $582 million, Allied Irish Banks acquired an 80 percent ownership position in Bank Zachodni, a Polish bank with major interests in the nation's two regions with the strongest economies and growth capabilities. For UniCredito, Allianz, and Allied Irish Banks, these transactions permitted rapid entry into financial markets with significant growth potential.[72]

Heineken, the Dutch brewing group, acquired an 88 percent stake in Cruzcampo, Spain's largest brewer. With its current ownership of the El Aguila brewing operation, this cross-border acquisition resulted in Heineken's having 37 percent of Spain's beer market (the third largest in Europe). Heineken's intention was to integrate Cruzcampo with El Aguila and increase the distribution of its own premium lager beer through the combined firm's channels. Executives at Heineken believed that its acquisition and subsequent integration of the assets it owned in Spain would result in much faster market penetration by its own premium product than would be possible using only Heineken-specific distribution channels.[73]

Increased Diversification

Because organizations have a viable understanding of their current markets, it is typically easier for them to develop new products and new businesses in these markets. In contrast, it is more difficult for a firm to develop new products that differ significantly from existing ones and to enter new markets. Contributing to this difficulty is the fact that the company has little understanding of new markets, and the requirements to achieve competitive success in them, as compared to the knowledge possessed about the competitive dynamics of markets in which it competes currently. Thus, firms tend to complete acquisitions, rather than engage in internal development efforts, to diversify their product lines and operations. These actions are understandable, in that evidence about corporate experiences suggests that acquisitions provide the fastest and perhaps easiest way for the firm to change its port-folio of businesses.[74]

Weyerhaeuser, the U.S. paper and wood products group, is the world's largest producer of softwood lumber and market pulp. Paying a premium of approximately 40 percent, the firm completed a friendly takeover of Canada's MacMillan Bloedel for $2.45 billion in stock. According to an analyst, "The takeover of one of Canada's most promi-nent corporate names (is) the latest in a series of cross-border mergers and acquisitions by North American forest products groups responding to a global consolidation wave led by Scandinavian producers." Weyer-haeuser officials believe that MacMillan Bloedel is a perfect fit with their firm. An example of related diversification, Weyerhaeuser intended to use its acquired firm's assets to expand its packaging, lumber, and engi-neered wood products operations. The integration of these related assets would result in Weyerhaeuser's becoming one of the world's top three makers of packaging products, increasing its annual sales by over $13 billion in the process of doing so.[75]

We have now discussed several reasons causing firms to complete cross-border mergers and acquisitions. The increasing importance of this means of competing in the global economy suggests that additional key reasons to engage in cross-border transactions will surface during the twenty-first century. In the final analysis, firms can create synergy through a cross-border merger or acquisition and create additional value as a result of doing so.

In the next and final section, we present recommendations for managers to consider when evaluating cross-border mergers and acquisitions.

Recommendations for Effective Cross-Border Transactions

The purpose of this chapter has been to discuss the use of cross-border transactions in the pursuit of competitive success. As with domestic mergers and acquisitions, the decision to merge with or acquire a company outside the firm's host country should be a product of careful and detailed analyses.

1. Understand the firm's status with respect to geographic and prod-uct diversification. If it is concluded that the firm can increase its value through either or both types of diversification, the possi-bility that merging with or acquiring companies in other nations can create even more value than domestic mergers and acquisi-tions should be examined carefully.
2. Pinpoint the synergies that can be expected by completing a cross-border merger or acquisition before the transaction is finalized.

Simply believing that synergies will exist once two firms become a single entity rarely leads to increases in the value of the newly created firm.

3. Study the experiences with cross-border transactions of others in the firm's primary industry. By studying the results competitors have achieved through cross-border mergers and acquisitions, it is possible to gain valuable insights regarding actions that are linked with transaction success.

4. Seek to develop a global mindset among the firm's employees. Working with people committed to the importance of understanding business practices in other nations enhances the firm's overall ability to identify companies with whom an integration can be expected to increase the acquiring firm's value.

5. Try to identify exact reasons for the firm to either merge with or acquire a company in another nation. Can the firm increase its market power through a cross-border transaction? If so, is the cost of gaining the additional market power less than the value that is created by the merger or the acquisition? Identically, the firm should challenge itself to carefully evaluate strategic alternatives in terms of all other reasons for engaging in cross-border mergers and acquisitions. For example, is this cross-border transaction being considered the most effective way to over entry barriers? Through careful examinations of the reasons to complete a cross-border transaction, the firm increases the probability that decisions made to engage in these strategic actions will result in the firm's being more successful.

As we have seen, cross-border merger and acquisition activity is increasing. With stock market evaluations for some firms, relaxation of some nation-based legal constraints, and a generally favorable global economic climate, we can expect still more growth in the number of these transactions during at least the first part of the twenty-first century. But whether a merger or an acquisition is completed domestically or across country borders, firms encounter an array of ethical concerns when engaging in such transactions. In the next chapter, we talk about these concerns and what firms can do to deal with them successfully.

11

Taking an Ethical Approach to Mergers and Acquisitions

Lies, damned lies and managed earnings: The crackdown is here.
The nation's top-earnings cop has put corporate America on notice.
Quit cooking the books; cross the line, you may do time.

—*Fortune*, August 2, 1999

In July 1996, Al Dunlap, sometimes referred to as "chainsaw Al" because of his penchant for drastically downsizing firms and selling off assets, was hired as CEO to help turn around Sunbeam Corporation. True to his nickname, actions by Dunlap included laying off almost 50 percent of Sunbeam's 12,000 employees and reducing the firm's product offerings. In 1996, he took extremely large write-offs against profits amounting to $338 million, including $100 million of inventory. Wall Street continued to wait for a miracle and, in 1997, it seemed that one indeed had occurred. Dunlap announced that Sunbeam had increased its sales by 22 percent over 1996 and recorded an earnings per share of $1.41, a significant improvement over the $2.37 loss per share in 1996. In fact, in October 1997, Dunlap issued a press release declaring that the turnaround was complete and that he was searching for another firm to acquire Sunbeam. Unfortunately, he was unable to find a buyer and in March 1998, Dunlap announced acquisitions of three separate companies, Coleman Corporation, Signature Brands, and First Alert. These acquisitions were costly and many argued that Sunbeam paid too high a premium for these poorly performing firms. When Dunlap came to Sunbeam, the firm had only $200 million in debt. However, after the acquisitions, the company had over $2 billion in debt and a negative cash flow. Sunbeam's net worth dropped from a positive $500 million to a negative $600 million. Not surprisingly, Dunlap came under increased pressure from shareholders and debtholders to reverse Sunbeam's fortunes.

To the disappointment of shareholders and others, it was reported that Sunbeam experienced a $44.6 million loss in its first quarter of 1998. Further analysis of this loss suggested that it stemmed from "cooking the books" to create a false turnaround in 1997. A large number of sales were reported, but were not to be shipped until 1998. This made the 1997 sales look exceptionally good, but the revenues weren't actually received in 1997. This procedure is referred to as "bill and hold" scam and is unacceptable. While the intentions are not clear, one could speculate that the desire was to make it appear as though the turnaround was positive, allowing Sunbeam to be sold. When a sale seemed unlikely, Dunlap started searching for other ways to accelerate the growth and change the performance outlook for Sunbeam, and thus the three acquisitions. Unfortunately, the acquisitions only made Sunbeam's situation worse. The only positive outcome of this debacle was that no firm or investors acquired Sunbeam based on the bogus information. One analyst suggested that someone should have been skeptical given that a CEO was promising a 20 percent annual sales increase in an industry that was growing by only 3 percent. In fact, auditors afterwards uncovered several inappropriate accounting actions. First, they suggested that the financial statements overstated the loss for 1996, overstated the profits for 1997, and understated the loss for the first quarter of 1998. Therefore, new statements accurately depicting the firm's performance had to be issued; the results had to be restated. Instead of the significant positive net income previously reported for 1997, the restatement showed that Sunbeam actually suffered an operating loss of $6.4 million.[1]

Al Dunlap was fired because of his actions. Unfortunately, many others were also harmed by those actions. Investors lost significant value for their investment in Sunbeam and employees and other stakeholders were also losers because of unethical actions taken by the top executives of this corporation. For example, the acquisitions remain a significant problem, as losses continued. Although total sales have more than doubled, because of the acquisitions, losses reported in 1999 were greater than the restated losses per quarter in 1998. Sales of Sunbeam's products prior to the acquisitions fell by 24 percent relative to the previous year. Many of these problems stem from the improper "bill and hold" sales reported during Al Dunlap's term as CEO.[2]

Herein, we examine ethical issues in the merger and acquisition process. The ethical issues include managerial conflicts of interest with the owners (often referred to as agency problems), governance, and hostile takeovers. Each of these topics is considered in order. We end the chapter with several ethical implications of mergers and acquisitions.

Ethical Issues in the Merger
and Acquisition Process

There are several issues related to the negotiation and implementation of mergers and acquisitions in which a potential exists for ethical concerns to arise. These issues include lies and deception in negotiations, coercion, maximization of value without consideration of other parties' needs, and termination of employees.

It is difficult to justify lies or deceptions at any time during the merger and acquisition process. However, they are most likely to occur during a negotiations process in an attempt to make the acquisition more attractive to the other party. For example, the actions taken by executives at Sunbeam Corporation to enhance financial results in hopes of attracting a buyer represent deception. Even though no buyer for Sunbeam was found, the deception still affected others. For example, in the three acquisitions completed, Al Dunlap offered Sunbeam stock as payment for the other company. In one case, the investor accepted partial payment of stock. Of course, the stock value was based on the inaccurate results reported to investors. After the performance was restated and accurate results provided to the investors and stock market, the value of the stock drastically declined. Therefore, the value that investors obtained for selling the company to Sunbeam was much lower than anticipated. In other cases that we discuss later in the chapter, such as at Cendant Corporation and McKesson HBOC Inc., accounting improprieties overstated results and these improprieties were hidden from the acquiring firm prior to completing the acquisition. In these cases, both lies and deception occurred.[3]

It is not necessarily unethical to pursue one's own benefits at another's expense, but the manner in which the gain is pursued and obtained affects the degree to which the actions are considered unethical. Both parties may have different goals and desire to benefit from the merger or acquisition. Perhaps one of the most effective ways to deal with this concern is for the negotiators to place themselves in the "opponent's" position. Would they want to be treated in the same manner by the other party? Undoubtedly, the negotiators have a responsibility to their own constituencies and stakeholders. They should try to obtain high value for their shareholders' investment and the firm's other stakeholders. However, negotiation with the intent of maximizing value at all costs can lead to actions that create long-term problems, not only for the other party but also for some of the firm's stakeholders. For example, it could damage relationships between the two management teams, therefore making integration of the two firms much more difficult. Moreover, the negative outcomes may affect the reputation of the negotiating parties and investors such that they would have a more difficult time in future negotiations involving other acquisitions or sales of assets.

Such actions may result in lost opportunities, not only in the current acquisition, but also in future acquisitions or divestitures.[4] Thus, negotiations should entail a concern for the benefits of both parties. Ideally, win–win solutions can be found rather than win–lose solutions.

Coercion can occur at several points in the merger and acquisition process. Statements made by both parties prior to the completion of a merger or acquisition process often emphasize participation by both parties in implementing appropriate organizational change, yet the process of such change can be tightly controlled by the managers of the acquiring firm. Sometimes the acquirers can act like "victors" and simply demand that the acquired firm's employees make the necessary changes. In these cases, they are coercing a change in culture and procedures along with other types of changes being implemented. Although such changes may not be unethical, coercive changes often lead to ineffective integration. In these cases, employees frequently resist the changes, sometimes in subtle or tacit ways. Consequently, the changes may be less effective than they would be otherwise. Furthermore, if employees feel they are being coerced, the best ones are likely to leave, causing the newly merged firm to lose valuable human capital. These outcomes represent voluntary but undesired turnover and the inadvertent loss of human capital.

Of course, many mergers and acquisitions also produce involuntary turnover or terminations of employees. When units from the two firms performing the same or similar tasks are combined, economies of scale are often created. In these instances, some employees become expendable after the two firms are integrated. These terminations should be handled in a sensitive and humane manner. As mergers and acquisitions are announced and implemented, employees can feel stress, anger, disorientation, frustration, confusion, and sometimes fright. When this occurs, employees may reduce their commitment to the organization and lower their productivity as well. The employees' psychological states can produce potentially dysfunctional behaviors. The integration process in mergers and acquisitions is difficult enough without including questionable management tactics and decisions. Mergers and acquisitions often involve long waiting times with high uncertainty, frenzied activity, minor and major changes, and tensions and conflicts in the best of circumstances. These conditions create uncertainty and stress. If, prior to mergers and acquisitions (i.e., during their negotiation process), promises are made for both parties to participate in the implementation process, changes should not be forced on the other party after the merger or acquisition contract has been completed and signed.[5]

Probably the major concerns of mergers and acquisitions are agency problems related to managerial opportunistic actions. These are discussed next.

Managerial Conflicts of Interest
in Mergers and Acquisitions

Many of the potential ethical issues related to mergers and acquisitions stem from managerial conflicts of interest (agency problems). First, engaging in mergers and acquisitions may be designed to provide managers with more discretion in their jobs as well as reducing risk to their careers. If these are the primary reasons for engaging in a merger or acquisition as opposed to maximizing shareholder value and satisfying other constituencies' needs, decisions to engage in this activity could be considered unethical.[6] In this case, the manager is acting to satisfy self-interest. Such self-interested managerial behavior is considered an agency problem, because managers are supposed to operate as agents of the owners. Studies have shown that many of the poorly performing acquisitions were completed by managers acting in their own self-interest.[7] Often these firms were performing poorly prior to making the acquisition, suggesting that managers were failing to effectively manage the company. The acquisition only exacerbated the problems. Because of the poor performance, such acquisitions often require the use of risky debt to finance them (because of a lack of capital and/or appropriate financial slack in the poorly performing firm prior to the acquisition). The use of risky debt, in turn, may lead to underinvestment in the newly merged firm that creates the conditions for continuing poor performance.[8]

One frequent outcome of mergers and acquisitions based on managerial self-interest is targeting unrelated businesses to acquire. There is less potential synergy in the acquisition of an unrelated business and therefore a lower potential to enhance shareholder value with such an acquisition. Managers sometimes favor acquiring unrelated businesses because it reduces their career risks.[9] Buying an unrelated business should balance the risk of loss of demand in the firm's current businesses due to economic recessions or competitors' actions. Studies show that unrelated acquisitions often fail and are divested within a few years of the completion of the acquisition.[10] Investors generally react more positively to acquisitions of related businesses than unrelated businesses. Furthermore, investors generally favor firms that have track records of acquiring only related assets.[11] Firms with such track records focus on achieving synergies between their existing businesses and the acquired assets and have either avoided or found ways to reduce the seriousness of typical managerial conflicts of interest. Although investors generally favor firms that acquire related assets, some institutional investors will purchase large blocks of shares in highly diversified firms with the intent of forcing divestitures of the unrelated assets and improving firm performance and shareholder value.[12] However, in general, investors favor firms in which conflicts of interest are not evident with the current management team.

Managerial conflicts of interest clearly existed in the case of the merger between CUC and HFS to form the firm Cendant. Arthur Levitt, chairman of the Securities and Exchange Commission, made a speech in September 1998 in which he committed the SEC to a serious crack-down on managing earnings in corporations. A number of highly publicized cases of managed earnings such as at Cendant Corporation have occured. Cendant is the product of a "merger of equals" between HFS, a franchising company, and CUC International, a membership club organization. The merger was valued at $14 billion and completed in late 1997. The CEOs of each firm were highly regarded by investors and the merger was positively received by Wall Street. Unfortunately, after the merger was completed, it was revealed that CUC had been overstating its profits to meet Wall Street's expectations. In fact, an audit revealed that its operating income before taxes had been inflated by approximately $511 million over the 1995–97 time period. As a result of the announcement, Cendant's stock price fell from $41 to less than $10 per share, reducing the firm's value by approximately $29 billion.[13]

The profit padding that occurred was approximately one-third of the total reported pretax income for the three-year period. CUC employ-ees who were interviewed stated that the purpose of the inflated earn-ings was to meet analysts' expectations. Officially, in the first three quarters of each of the years noted, CUC communicated unaudited financial statements that the corporate office deliberately falsified by adjusting the organization's revenues upward and its expenses down-ward. The amount of the adjustment grew in each of the three years. In each year, before the external auditors from Ernst & Young began their annual audit, the company changed the process and inserted reserves for the "adjustments made." Even this process seemed inappropriate, but the explanations provided by CUC executives satisfied the accounting firm. It seems that Ernst & Young did not conduct highly thorough audits or these improprieties (several have referred to them as fraud) would have been discovered. Ernst & Young claimed that the adjustments from the reserves were immaterial. However, Cendant shareholders filed a lawsuit against Ernst & Young accusing the firm of negligence for failing to detect the accounting fraud. Ernst & Young settled the suit for $335 million, one of the largest shareholder settlements in history.[14]

Clearly, these accounting improprieties were not immaterial to HFS executives because they have caused the company considerable headaches, from which it has not been able to recover. HFS executives were not given full access to the accounting records and accounting activities of CUC prior to the merger. Thus, not only was fraud commit-ted in reports to investors, these improprieties were also hidden from the partner firm with which CUC was merging. As a result, even more improprieties were undertaken to cover up the activities of CUC management. Clearly, had these activities come to light prior to the merger, the merger would likely never have been completed. Furthermore, the price paid in the merger was likely too large because of the inflated profits. CUC was not as healthy financially as its financial reports suggested. These actions have created a miserable outcome for the merged company and resulted in millions of dollars of lost value for investors. This situation also represents a quest to please the market or Wall Street. Thus, it is a story of corporate greed and a willingness to take unethical or potentially illegal actions to satisfy and meet external constituents' expectations. Of course, it also shows the likely results of these unethical, if not illegal, actions.[15]

One area in which managerial actions can be considered highly ethical or questionable (as the result of conflicts of interest) is the use of "shark repellents" to prevent others from acquiring their firm. Shark repellents are devices used by managers to prevent unsolicited takeover attempts. If shark repellents are employed to promote shareholder value by protecting the firm against takeovers that would harm shareholder value, such actions are appropriate. Alternatively, if shark repellents are used to protect managerial jobs and perquisites, they portend serious ethical concerns.[16] Among some of the more popular anti-takeover provisions are "change of control covenants" and "golden parachutes." Change of control covenants are often used supposedly to protect shareholders, bondholders, and managers, yet they are generally designed to protect bondholders. Specifically, they provide bondholders the right to put their bonds back to the company or increase the interest rate if a takeover occurs. While these may protect the bondholder, they also make the firm less attractive for a takeover, thereby furthering the interests of the managers. Although these covenants can be in the best interest of the shareholders and bondholders, managers generally have substantial control over their terms and can promote their own self-interests in such covenants. For example, they may omit potential management buyouts from those covenants. Managers could use such covenants to avoid hostile takeovers that might increase firm value.[17] Likewise, golden parachutes can be used to promote shareholder interest, but also can be implemented to benefit managers. While they are sometimes controversial, it is not uncommon for boards of directors to grant managers golden parachutes in which they obtain substantial compensation if the firm is acquired. Such parachutes may provide incentives for managers to allow takeovers to occur that increase shareholder value. Alternatively, if golden parachutes are so large that they make the firm a less desirable takeover candidate, they may not be in the shareholders' best interests.[18]

Interestingly, managers of the firm targeted for acquisition are more likely to cooperate if they belong to a social network that includes managers of the firm making the offer to acquire (e.g., if they received their degrees from the same university). The managers of the firm targeted for acquisition are thus more likely to trust the intentions of the managers of the offering firm. Alternatively, the managers of the firm targeted for acquisition are more likely to resist the takeover attempts if they do not belong to the same social networks of the acquiring firm managers, particularly if the managers of the bidding firm are not members of a prestigious/elite social network. This suggests that the target firms' managers are acting more in their own self-interest rather than the interests of the shareholders and other constituencies. Otherwise, the social network to which the managers of the bidder firm belong would not affect the target firm managers' reaction to a takeover attempt.[19]

Perhaps this is what occurred in the case of Air Canada's adoption of a poison pill (shark repellent) to forestall the effort of Onex Corporation's hostile takeover attempt of Air Canada. Onex wanted to merge Air Canada with the financially troubled Canadian Airlines. In fact, Onex attempted to acquire both Air Canada and Canadian Airlines simultaneously and then merge them into one air carrier. The CEO of Air Canada, Robert Milton, argued that the poison pill is actually a shareholder rights plan designed to ensure that shareholders have a reasonable time to consider valid proposals that come forward. Furthermore, he stated that restructuring the airline industry in Canada should not be attempted in haste. The plan adopted gives shareholders the right to acquire additional shares if any individual or group acquires 10 percent or more of the company's common shares outstanding in a transaction not approved by Air Canada's board of directors. It is designed to make an unsolicited hostile takeover attempt prohibitively expensive. Because AMR, the parent of American Airlines, owns one-third of the stock of Canadian Airlines, it agreed to help finance the Onex deal. If the takeover had been successful, AMR would have owned approximately 15 percent of the merged carrier. AMR's participation also complicated the deal as Air Canada's alliance partners, particularly United Airlines and Lufthansa, expressed concerned about the takeover attempt. It is unclear, however, whether the poison pill was an appropriate action or one designed by managers to forestall losing their own jobs.[20] Alternatively, the issue became mute after Onex withdrew its offer because a Quebec court ruled that the transaction would violate Canadian regulations regarding foreign ownership of domestic air carriers.[21]

Concerns about managerial actions place increasing importance on governance in the organization and oversight of managerial actions. These topics are explored next.

Governance

The board of directors is intended to operate as a governance mechanism overseeing managerial actions and to ensure that managers operate in the best interests of the shareholders who elect members of the board of directors. Unfortunately, in companies in which top managers have engaged in unethical activities, board members are prominent largely by their absent voice. For example, one might wonder about the inaction of the members of the board of directors while executives at CUC and Columbia HCA were engaging in activities that were clearly unethical and, in some cases, possibly illegal. Governance in these cases may be more problematic when the CEO engages in such activities and also serves as chairman of the board of directors. For example, in the 1990s, Archer-Daniels-Midland (ADM) was investigated for conspiring to fix prices and paying under-the-table bonuses to executives, thereby allowing them to avoid federal taxes on this income. At a shareholder meeting after these problems surfaced in the media, the CEO and chairman of the board of directors, Wayne Andreas, allowed one critical shareholder to speak his mind. However, after others asked to have the floor to make statements, he turned off the microphone and announced that he was the chairman and was making the rules as he went along. Interestingly, in this case, 80 percent of the shareholders voted to reelect the current board of directors. In effect, the boards taking these actions fail to provide effective governance and oversight of managerial activities.[22]

Because of close personal relationships with the executives and a lack of time or interest, members of boards of directors may cede too much power to the firm's top executives. In a landmark case, *Smith v. Van Gorkom*, the Delaware Supreme Court held that directors of the Transunion Corporation breached their fiduciary duty by approving a merger at the price of $55 a share without obtaining information on the fairness of that offer. The directors relied solely on the chairman's evaluation of the transaction. Therefore, they did not follow a practice of obtaining an expert opinion on the appropriateness of that offer from a qualified investment banker.[23] This is an example of relying too heavily on the top executives of the firm, when it is the board's responsibility to oversee and govern those managers' actions.

There have even been cases in which boards of directors have acted unethically in taking specific actions. For example, some boards of large banks with financial problems adopted golden parachutes for the managers with the intention of exploiting the guarantees provided to banking institutions by the Federal Deposit Insurance Corporation (FDIC). The FDIC had to help subsidize takeovers of financially troubled banks by more healthy ones and had to pay extra costs because of the boards' adoption of golden parachutes. The FDIC (and as agents of taxpayers) thus had to subsidize rewards for managers who undertook overly risky projects leading to the failure of their banks.[24]

Of course, there are examples of boards of directors that act appropriately. In fact, the firing of Al Dunlap by Sunbeam's board of directors is such an example. The board of directors for Sunbeam had five outsiders, four of whom thought of Dunlap as a friend. However, when they discovered that Dunlap and one or more of the members of his top management team likely "cooked the books" to falsely portray Sunbeam as experiencing a turnaround, they took immediate action. Interestingly, Dunlap created a relatively independent board, even though its members were largely friends of his. Analysts speculate that his requirement that they buy company stock was one of the primary reasons. Each of the directors experienced financial pain directly because of Dunlap's actions.[25]

Therefore, ownership in a company may enhance the governance and/or prevent inappropriate managerial actions. For example, some studies have shown that when the ownership in a particular company is concentrated and outside members of the board of directors own equity in the company, firms are more likely to sell unrelated businesses in order to enhance firm performance.[26]

Evidence shows that the more equity owned by managers of target firms, the more they act in the best interest of the shareholders in situations in which their firm is acquired.[27] When they own less equity, they often are more concerned about their own perquisites. But as they own more, they tend to ensure that the acquiring firm pays an appropriate premium to buy their firm. Consequently, the shareholders of the acquired firm receive greater financial benefits. For example, when managers of the firm targeted for takeover have greater equity in the firm, there tend to be fewer antitakeover provisions that discourage or prevent takeovers.[28] Others believe that when managers own equity in their firm, it strengthens the relationship within the top management team and between the managers and major shareholders. It also tends to reduce the internal corporate politics and improve the effectiveness of the decision-making processes in the firm.[29] Thus, managerial equity ownership may have a number of positive benefits in addition to the reduction of opportunistic actions on the part of managers and the potential for unethical managerial behavior.

Of course, managers' equity ownership in a firm does not necessarily preclude their taking inappropriate actions. This is exemplified in the example of McKesson's acquisition of HBO and Co. There was intentional deception on the part of executives in the acquired healthcare information business, HBO. Reports suggest that a number of HBO's executives engaged in highly unethical accounting practices. Furthermore, the executives concealed these practices from McKesson during a financial review prior to the completion of the acquisition. Therefore, not only did they engage in improper accounting practices to inflate the earnings, they also engaged in intentional deception to hide those practices prior to the completion of the acquisition. As a result, McKesson likely paid too high a premium to acquire HBO. Furthermore, had

McKesson executives known about the improper accounting practices, they may not have completed the acquisition. The McKesson board fired five former HBO managers immediately on learning of their previous practices. Because of these practices, McKesson had to restate fiscal 1999 earnings. After announcement of the restatement, McKesson's stock price dropped by 48 percent.[30]

Actions such as those described in the McKesson scandal are similar to those discussed previously in the case of Cendant. These types of actions may have a long-term negative effect on the acquiring/merged company. Cendant's CEO, Henry Silverman, took several steps to overcome the problems caused by accounting improprieties. These include changing the management team, settling a lawsuit filed by bond buyers, selling noncore assets, and improving the firm's earnings. But Cendant's stock price has only increased slightly from its lowest level following the announcement of the scandal. One of the largest problems is the potential liability stemming from the fraud in which approximately $500 million in fictitious revenue was reported by executives of the acquired CUC firm. The biggest problem facing Cendant is one of the potentially largest securities-fraud suits ever filed against a public company. Because of the significant potential liability, a number of investors avoided buying Cendant's stock, thereby keeping its stock price in the doldrums.[31]

When internal governance fails, many believe that the market for corporate control becomes the governance mechanism of last resort. Thus, when governance fails, hostile takeovers may be the result. However, hostile takeovers are also controversial. In the next section, we discuss the pros and cons of hostile takeovers.

Hostile Takeovers

Hostile takeovers are assumed to be a governance mechanism in the market for corporate control. They are designed to focus on firms' assets that are undervalued by the market and the management of the firm is either unable or unwilling to make the changes necessary to ensure that the market properly values those assets.[32] However, evidence shows that not all hostile takeover bids are designed to accomplish these purposes. For example, in some cases, after the hostile takeover is completed, the managers of the acquired firm continue to operate the firm as they did previously. As such, the hostile takeover does not discipline poorly performing managers as assumed in these cases. Also, in some instances, hostile takeover bids have been made for firms that were performing well above their industry counterparts. The managers of these firms likely do not need to be disciplined.[33]

Dominant means of improving the market value of firms that are acquired in hostile actions include employee layoffs and asset sales. If the firm acquired is widely diversified, unrelated businesses are frequently sold in an attempt to downscope or refocus the firm on its core businesses.[34] Of course, the layoffs and asset sales can be controversial because of their effect on people and communities. Clearly, if managers of the targeted firm are operating in their own best interests and not in the interests of the shareholders, it seems that hostile takeover actions are justified. Alternatively, if the firm is performing well and stakeholders are satisfied, some believe that there should be protections against third parties who seek to take over companies by using inappropriate tactics.[35] Some argue that stakeholders other than shareholders must be considered to evaluate the appropriateness of hostile takeovers. For example, some workers and communities have suffered greatly from the layoffs and the sale of assets that accompanied hostile takeovers. In other cases, the hostile takeovers were unsuccessful because of actions taken by the firm. However, those actions sometimes entailed the use of significant amounts of debt or other steps that required a substantial reduction in expenses, often accomplished through employee layoffs or asset sales.[36] In these cases, takeover defenses may be appropriate except when they have major negative effects on other stakeholders such as the employees and communities in which the firm operates.[37]

The hostile takeover attempt launched in 1999 by Delta Gold to acquire its competitor Acacia Resources, both gold mining firms in Australia, exemplifies the primary goals of some hostile takeover attempts. The managers of Delta Gold believed that by merging the assets of the two firms, the costs of operation could be reduced by at least $20 million. This was to be accomplished by combining some mining teams, thereby allowing employee layoffs. Managers also argued that consolidation would provide a stronger base for future growth. In particular, the managers of Delta Gold believed that the merger of the two firms would offer greater market power for the combined firms and thereby attract more international investors and increase the market value of the firm.[38]

Interestingly, there are institutional deterrents to hostile takeovers in Japan and therefore very few occur. These deterrents reduce the risks to Japanese managers of potential takeovers. Some argue that this allows Japanese managers to take greater risks and invest in the development of more firm-specific skills. Alternatively, it also buffers these managers from external actions in a market for corporate control if they perform poorly and take inappropriate strategic actions.[39]

Although hostile takeovers have been primarily a U.S. phenomenon, they have been growing increasingly popular in western Europe.[40] This is exemplified by the hostile takeover by Olivetti of Telecom Italia in 1999. This takeover is also an interesting example because of the highly ethical approach of Telecom Italia's CEO. He largely refused to take actions that would benefit him personally or, in his opinion, harm Telecom Italia's shareholders. The CEO, Franco Bernabe, refused to acquire significant amounts of debt, making his firm more costly to take over, even though he opposed the takeover attempt. Others external to the firm (and some internal as well) criticized his actions that eventually led to Olivetti's successful takeover of Telecom Italia. Mr. Bernabe largely spurned ideas to approach other firms to avert Olivetti's takeover or to implement any type of shark repellent to avoid this outcome. In fact, he suggested that Telecom Italia could have bought Olivetti because its shares were so cheap, but he could not justify buying out a main competitor because he felt such action would be unethical.[41]

We conclude that hostile takeovers are not necessarily unethical, particularly if they target firms that are underperforming their industry. Such underperformance is often exemplified through assets that are undervalued by the market. However, when firms that are performing well are targeted, one could question the ethical status of such actions. Furthermore, we applaud the ethical stance taken by Mr. Bernabe, CEO of Telecom Italia. However, there may be times when it is appropriate for the CEO to take actions to forestall a hostile takeover, especially when the reasons for such a takeover are not in the best interests of the firm's stakeholders. Boards of directors should be encouraged to consider not only the stockholders' interests but also those of other stakeholders, such as employees, customers, and communities in which the firm operates.[42] Perhaps the quote from a long-term employee of a firm acquired during a hostile takeover summarizes some of the ethical dilemmas of such activities: "Look how I ended up, just like a run-over flat can in the street."[43] As evidenced by this quote, employees experience considerable stress during mergers and acquisitions, whether hostile or not.[44]

Conclusions and Ethical Implications

Perhaps the largest potential ethical problem related to mergers and acquisitions is the use of inappropriate accounting practices that inflate sales or earnings followed by deceptive practices on the part of the acquiring firm to cover up such actions. As noted earlier, this is often referred to as managers "cooking the books." A more positive term is often used by professional accountants and some managers, that of "earnings management." Unfortunately, in a number of cases, the managers have incentives to take such actions based on the manner in which they are rewarded for firm performance.[45] Still, there can be no justification for falsifying performance records and practicing deception to keep the falsification processes secret from those who may be purchasing the firm. Such actions lead to inappropriate premiums being paid

for firms and, as suggested in the case of Cendant, possible highly negative long-term consequences for shareholders and other stakeholders of
the firm.

Although not all agree, it would be helpful for CEOs to take into
account the effects of mergers and acquisitions on all stakeholders. This
may not require a change in the decision of whether to acquire or allow
the firm to be acquired, but it could affect the way that a merger or acquisition is implemented. Sensitivity to employees, customers, and other
stakeholders is critical to the long-term effectiveness of the combined
firm. Therefore, such sensitivity simply reflects effective management.[46]

It should also be recognized that auditing firms have responsibility
to more effectively review firms' accounting practices and not to support
inappropriate "earnings management," or other practices that could be
considered unethical. While there are differences in codes of professional
conduct globally, some standards must be maintained throughout the
firm (e.g., activities in the audit process, along with hiring and promotion criteria).[47]

Finally, it should be recognized that not all mergers and acquisitions
are likely to end in efficient outcomes or increases to the combined firm's
value. Therefore, it is incumbent on top managers who seek to acquire
other firms to thoroughly investigate the target firms and the potential
synergies between them.[48] Some have recommended that special periods be established for review of the potential acquisition and to make
appropriate decisions regarding such actions. The intent is to ensure that
such important decisions are not made in haste and without appropriate evaluation and information.[49] These conclusions have specific
managerial implications.

While most mergers and acquisitions are completed by managers
who operate from a strong value base and act ethically, there are potentially substantial negative outcomes for many stakeholders when ethical practices are not used. This is exemplified in the problems
experienced by Cendant and Sunbeam. Our analyses of the ethical issues
regarding mergers and acquisitions lead to the following managerial
implications.

1. Managers of acquiring firms should use the due diligence process
   to thoroughly investigate the financial records of firms targeted
   for acquisition. If full access to the target firm's financial records
   is denied, the acquiring firm's managers should either insist that
   the records be open or withdraw their acquisition offer. Furthermore, acquiring firm managers should thoroughly query the
   primary auditing firm that substantiated the financial records of
   the target firm.
2. Firms should provide incentives to managers who support actions
   taken in the best interest of the shareholders and other stake-

holders. Thus, incentive systems must overcome the potential agency problems that exist. These incentives may range from incentive cash compensation for particular actions to stock options and equity ownership for managers.

3. Governance is a critical issue in providing the appropriate oversight of managerial actions and avoiding ethical problems. The primary responsibility for this oversight falls on the board of directors. Thus, boards of directors should be vigilant in overseeing managerial actions and ensuring that no inappropriate actions are taken (e.g., earnings management). One recommendation that has merit is to ensure that board members, as well as managers, have an equity stake in the firm. The importance of equity ownership on the part of board members is exemplified in the Sunbeam case. The board members, even though they were friends of the CEO, took action to relieve the CEO of his responsibilities when unethical actions were discovered. Although these board members may have taken that action without ownership, they suffered financially because of their equity in the firm when it was announced that the earnings would have to be restated. As a result they were motivated to take action to prevent further reductions in the stock's value. Thus, equity ownership provides a security mechanism that better ensures that the board will take appropriate governance actions

4. The ethical status of hostile takeovers is not clear. Hostile takeovers may be appropriate as a governance mechanism in the market for corporate control when managers are unable or unwilling to take actions to increase the value of assets that are undervalued by the market. Alternatively, not all hostile takeover attempts target firms that have undervalued assets or are performing poorly. When hostile takeover bidders target firms that are highly valued in the market or are performing well relative to competitors, target firm managers should take actions to avoid the hostile takeover.

5. Both acquiring and target managers should consider the full range of stakeholders when making a decision to complete a merger or acquisition. While the stockholders are the most important stakeholder, managers should also be sensitive to the concerns and problems of other important stakeholders, such as employees. Acquisition integration problems are likely to ensue and customers and important employees may be lost. These outcomes could doom to failure a merger or acquisition with synergy potential. Furthermore, employees and other important stakeholders could be seriously harmed by mergers and acquisitions. This potential harm should be considered when making the final acquisition decision.

In this chapter we have focused on the importance of ethical practices in mergers and acquisitions. In the following chapter, the concluding one, we highlight the main ideas emphasized throughout the book. Furthermore, we identify important trends in mergers and acquisitions for the twenty-first century.

12

Beating the Odds
in the M&A Game

Once a potential target company comes on the market, or the board
has approved plans to expand into new businesses or markets, time
is short. The ensuing pressure to "do a deal," emanating from within
the corporation—senior executives, directors—and from external
sources—investment bankers who stand to gain from any deal and
shareholder groups or competitors bidding against the firm—can
become so intense that shortcuts are often made. Valuations rise as
companies become overconfident in their ability to add value to the
prospect company and as expectations regarding synergies reach
unrealistic levels; due diligence is done more quickly than is desirable and is almost exclusively confined to financial considerations;
integration planning takes a back seat; and differences in corporate
culture are often ignored. In this climate, even the best-laid strategies cannot guarantee a successful outcome as many companies or,
more precisely, their shareholders have learned.

—Cornelis A. de Kluyver

Mergers and acquisitions continue to set new records in both volume
and size. Acquisitions are a relatively quick way to grow compared to
other options and, from the perspective of top managers, they are exciting and often financially rewarding. However, by most accounts, acquisitions are prone to failure, with some having disastrous consequences.
The insights this book provides, based on many years of research by
numerous investigators and illustrated with hundreds of examples, can
help executives and their firms make successful acquisitions. Alterna-

tively, this book can help executives know when an acquisition should be avoided.

In this final chapter, we review some of the most important ideas from the preceding chapters. We also discuss why many of the ingredients that lead to success in acquisitions must be combined with other attributes for an acquisition to work. This final point may be one of the book's most important messages. Rarely will any one attribute, on its own, lead to success. Finally, we close by highlighting a few recent trends that are likely to influence acquisition activity well into the twenty-first century.

Seizing Success and Shunning Failure

Mergers and acquisitions are difficult under the best of circumstances. They are comparable to gambling in a casino in which the odds dramatically favor the house. However, some acquisitions are successful. In Chapters 2 through 11, we highlighted some of the important attributes that lead to success or failure in mergers and acquisitions. These attributes are summarized in this section.

Due Diligence

Inadequate due diligence has been the cause of many failed mergers and acquisitions, including the highly problematic merger of HFS and CUC International to form Cendant Corp., as described in Chapters 2 and 11. Managerial hubris can lead firms to do a poor job of due diligence or to ignore relevant information that might otherwise unravel a deal. Inadequate due diligence also can lead to the payment of excessive premiums to acquire a firm. Top executives should avoid managerial hubris through ensuring a dynamic due diligence process. Due diligence involves a comprehensive analysis of all important target firm characteristics, including its financial condition, management capabilities, physical assets, and other intangible assets relevant to the acquisition. As a part of the process, acquiring firms should carefully select organizations and individuals from whom to seek advice. Also, fees paid to investment bankers and other advisors by the acquiring firm should not be tied to acquisition price, because it might provide the wrong set of incentives.

Financing

Chapter 3 identified trends with regard to acquisition financing. At present, nearly half the mergers and acquisitions are cash purchases and this percentage is likely to increase after the turn of the century when pooling-of-interests accounting is eliminated (pooling of interests requires that a deal be financed primarily through stock). Cash transactions are popular, at least in part, because financial markets tend to reward these types of deals with more favorable stock price evaluations. Of course, higher than normal stock price adjustments are not common in acquiring firms, so market response really has the effect of punishing cash transactions less than stock deals. From one perspective, the market reaction is unfortunate, because stock deals can help acquiring firms avoid excessive debt. Manageable debt levels are a strong determinant of success or failure in acquisitions. The unsuccessful acquisition of Chemlawn by Ecolab, for example, was associated with a 265 percent increase in total debt. A company with high debt levels should usually avoid acquisitions. Even stock deals are associated with high transaction costs and fees.

Complementary Resources

A number of reasons may account for the less-than-enthusiastic response of the market to acquisition announcements. Clearly, acquisitions are expensive for the acquiring firm. However, R&D and many other types of corporate activities are also expensive. The key is whether the benefits from an acquisition will offset the costs. When benefits outweigh costs, economic value is created.

In Chapter 4, we explained why the melding of complementary resources is more likely to create economic value in merging firms than the combination of identical or unrelated resources. Complementary resources exist when the primary resources of the acquiring and target firms are somewhat different, yet simultaneously supportive of one another. We observed this kind of fit in the acquisition of Anderson Clayton by Quaker Oats. Efficiencies were made possible by combining the complementary resources of the two companies' pet foods businesses. Resource complementarity can enhance sharing of skills, facilitate organizational learning, and increase the probability that uniquely valuable synergy will be created.

Friendly/Hostile Acquisitions

Friendliness is another key to the creation of economic value. Target firm resistance or animosity between acquiring and target firm executives can destroy value for the acquiring firm by increasing the premium paid, reducing the transfer of important information during due diligence and merger integration, and increasing turnover of key target firm executives. Consequently, it is important to avoid the "we win, you lose" mentality that is so common in acquisitions.

Other important strategies outlined in Chapter 5 included announcing the new management team early, ensuring honest and frequent communications with customers and employees of the target firm, offering a fair price from the outset, keeping negotiations private if possible, and avoiding hostile takeovers, including tender offers. Pursuing business ventures together prior to acquisition negotiations allows firms to become aware of each other's cultures, management styles, resources, strengths, and weaknesses. For example, engineers from General Dynamics and Cessna began sharing technology three years before they merged.

Synergy Creation

Complementary resources and friendliness do not ensure that synergy will be created, but they greatly increase that likelihood. In Chapter 6, we explored in greater detail how synergy can be created. The four foundations to the creation of synergy are strategic fit, organizational fit, managerial actions, and value creation. Strategic fit refers to effectively matching organizational capabilities. Resource complementarity is an important type of strategic fit, which can lead to synergy through combining operations, R&D, marketing, or management. In general, economies of scale alone are not enough to justify an acquisition.

Organizational fit occurs when two organizations have similar management processes, cultures, systems, and structures. Obviously, no two firms are exactly the same on any of these dimensions; however, a reasonably high degree of compatibility can facilitate communication, learning and sharing activities, resources, and skills. Even when both types of fit are evident, managerial actions are needed to facilitate synergy creation. Knowledge is shared through organizational communication mechanisms such as meetings, memos, e-mail, and reports. Executive transfers across companies also create opportunities for knowledge transfer. Benefits from tangible relatedness in areas such as production or purchasing can only be gained as these activities are combined. Finally, value is only created if the benefits that can be derived from synergy exceed the costs associated with developing and exploiting it.

Organizational Learning

In Chapter 7, we described acquisitions as learning experiences. Successful acquirers learn from prior acquisitions. Similarity of targets facilitates this learning process. For instance, higher financial performance is found in acquisitions in which the acquiring firm has repeatedly made acquisitions of targets in the same industry in which it operates.

For learning to take place, the learning process should be managed. Active acquirers should take deliberate steps to study and learn from their own acquisitions as well as the acquisitions of other companies, including competitors. Some of these steps include documenting learning, assigning someone to make information about past transactions available as needed, and forming workshops and retreats in which learning is facilitated. Knowledge about acquisitions should be widely shared in an organization so that the turnover of a key executive does not "erase" the learning that has occurred. Consequently, many people should participate in each acquisition process. Although these activities are useful and important for frequent acquirers, they are not reasonable for less active acquirers. Casual acquirers probably should consider only the most attractive acquisitions because they are not as experienced with acquisition processes and are therefore less likely to learn and benefit from organizational learning.

Focus on Core Business

A consistent theme in Chapters 4 through 7 is that gaining economic value from acquisitions requires meshing of resources to create operating synergies. However, another popular yet contradictory view is that the acquisition of businesses that differ in fundamental ways can create diversity in a portfolio of businesses, which may lead to financial synergy, as evidenced by reduced risk, higher returns, or both. As Cablevision discovered, these outcomes are difficult to obtain from acquisitions unrelated to the acquiring firm's core business. Most unrelated acquisitions are divested a short time after their purchase and the financial markets view these types of acquisitions unfavorably. We explained why diversifying acquisitions are problematic in Chapter 8. Basically, cultural and management differences are magnified when firms have less in common. Consequently, the sharing of resources and capabilities is constrained. The result is that positive benefits from financial synergy are not enough to offset the negative effects of diversification. We concluded that acquisitions related to the firm's core business are more likely to produce economic value than those that are sought primarily for financial synergy.

Emphasis on Innovation

Innovation success is critical to organizational competitiveness in the global economy. As we discussed in Chapter 9, companies that innovate enjoy the first-mover advantages of acquiring a deep knowledge of new markets and developing strong relationships with key stakeholders in those markets. Innovators are also able to solve many of the most challenging problems associated with changing environments. Organizational innovation can result from using skills and capabilities that are inside the firm (internal innovation) or by acquiring innovation skills or innovative products through purchasing other firms. Many pharmaceutical firms are making acquisitions to add new drugs to existing

product lines. For example, Warner-Lambert acquired Agouron Pharmaceuticals Inc. in large part due to Agouron's research and development expertise in such areas as cancer.

Acquisitions can become a substitute for internal innovation in
companies actively using an acquisition strategy. When this happens,
firms should expect a negative effect on their ability to innovate.
However, firms can counteract this effect through deliberate action.
Many firms continue to emphasize innovation after acquisition, often
through healthy R&D investments. Acquiring firms should have a
specific objective in mind when acquiring innovation so that innovation
and innovative skills can be used efficiently in the combined firm. If
innovation is to be a source of competitive advantage, the sources of
that advantage must be emphasized in the firm's daily operations and
supported through constant reinvestments. Finally, acquiring firms
should maintain a culture that is supportive of innovation. Principles
that help develop a climate that supports innovation include recognizing
that helping others to be innovative is part of everyone's job, fostering
idea sharing to create innovation-related synergy, prizing experimentation, and viewing mistakes as valuable learning experiences.

Cross-Border Mergers and Acquisitions

The number and size of cross-border mergers and acquisitions is growing rapidly. In Chapter 10, we explained that the popularity of these
types of transactions is fueled by the desire to gain increased market
power, overcome entry barriers, reduce or share the cost of new product development, increase speed to market or increase diversification.
Cross-border mergers and acquisitions may also be pursued in response
to environmental threats or opportunities. For example, DaimlerChrysler
was formed, at least in part, due to intense worldwide competition,
global overcapacity in automobile production, and severe downward
pressure on automobile prices.

Organizations that are particularly effective in cross-border transactions have developed a set of valuable, wealth-creating, firm-specific
resources that are difficult for competitors to imitate. Success in cross-
border mergers and acquisitions requires careful identification and evaluation of potential synergies before the deal is initiated. Corporate
executives would be wise to study the cross-border merger and acquisition experiences of competitors prior to embarking on their own acquisition program.

Ethical Concerns/Opportunism

One of the great risks associated with all types of mergers or acquisitions
is that the information received about a target is incorrect, misleading,

or deceptive. Perhaps no other factor can limit the success of an acquisition more than ethical problems. One of the biggest sources of these problems is dishonesty on the part of executives involved in the merger, which is evident when they "cook the books," hide relevant but damaging financial information, or lie about their actual intentions. For instance, CUC padded profits prior to its merger with HFS to form Cendant. The market response to information about the deception reduced Cendant's market value by $29 billion.

In addition to the more obvious ethical problems, executives involved in acquisitions sometimes give disproportionate weight to their own personal interests at the expense of other important stakeholders such as employees or even shareholders. These conflicts of interests can result in problems such as unnecessary layoffs or poor acquisition performance. The inappropriate use of poison pills is another manifestation of self-interested behavior on the part of target firm executives. Chapter 11 encouraged executives of acquiring firms to be thorough and probing in their evaluations of financial information from a potential target. Organizations can also provide incentives such as stock options or cash compensation to managers who take actions consistent with the best interests of the stockholders. The primary responsibility for ensuring ethical behavior falls on the shoulders of a vigilant board of directors.

Each of the chapters identified specific attributes that are associated with either successful or unsuccessful acquisitions. However, in reality, many of these factors work together to either promote or reduce the success of an acquisition. In the next section, we discuss combinations of attributes that lead to success or failure.

Combining the Attributes

There are no simple formulas for success in the business world. Business is complicated and constantly changing, making success difficult to obtain and even more difficult to sustain. This is especially true with mergers and acquisitions. In this book, we have identified a number of important attributes that increase the probability of success in mergers and acquisitions. Furthermore, there are important patterns among these attributes. If an essential element is missing, success is unlikely.

Some of the ingredients of successful acquisitions combine in interesting ways. Specifically, particular attributes must be present for other attributes to be effective.[1] For example, if merging firms enjoy resource complementarity, but the transaction is unfriendly, synergy is unlikely because the creation of synergy requires managers from the combining firms to work together. Cooperation is unlikely in a hostile acquisition. Sometimes what begins as a friendly deal can turn sour during the post-transaction period. For example, Disney's CEO Eisner tried to resolve friction between executives from Disney's production studio and the

ABC TV network that was obtained as a part of the Capital Cities/ABC acquisition. Remarking on the newly combined structure, Eisner stated, "It's disruptive, it's unpleasant, and people don't understand it."[2] Resolving disagreements and keeping the peace are essential to producing the efficiency and creativity that were the intended consequences of Disney's acquisition of ABC.

Another interesting relationship exists between debt and innovation. Low to moderate debt levels increase the probability that innovative activity will continue after the merger. We found both low debt levels and an emphasis on innovation in many mergers and acquisitions, including the acquisition of Anderson Clayton by Quaker Oats, the acquisition of Beech Aircraft by Raytheon, and the acquisition of UCCEL by Computer Associates. Unfortunately, high debt can divert resources away from R&D and cause managers to be more risk averse, which reduces the likelihood that they will promote research projects considered higher in risk. For example, high debt and reduced innovation were observed in the less successful mergers of Ashland Oil with US Filter and US Steel with Marathon Oil.[3] This leads to unattractive performance outcomes for the firms given that innovation is so important in the global economy.

Due diligence has an effect on many other attributes of successful acquisitions. Complete and probing due diligence reduces the probability that ethical problems will surface either during or after the transaction. Furthermore, the information gained during due diligence can help a potential acquirer uncover uniquely valuable synergistic opportunities and determine an appropriate bid price for the target. Due diligence is also an excellent time for an organization to discuss lessons learned from past acquisitions. It is a sort of pre-merger leavening that makes synergy possible.

Organizational learning also can influence each of the other attributes. If experience is documented and learning takes place, firms will be able to more effectively select appropriate financing methods, identify resource complementarities, uncover potential ethical problems, and maintain a friendly acquisition climate. Experience also can teach an organization to avoid diversification away from the firm's core business.

Learning is important during post-acquisition integration also. Union Pacific's acquisition of Southern Pacific led to disastrous results, including safety problems, work stoppages, unhappy customers, and poor financial performance. However, Richard Davidson, CEO, has taken a deliberate approach to learning from mistakes. He decentralized decision-making authority, provided stock options to all employees to make them feel important and committed, implemented new work arrangements to deal with employee fatigue, and sold off unwanted businesses. As a result of these and other actions, efficiency has increased dramatically.[4]

In an acquisition, the size of the premium paid for the target has considerable influence on other attributes. An excessive premium can put pressure on executives to increase margins so that the acquisition appears to be a financial success. Alternatively, the higher margins may be necessary to provide cash to pay for the transaction. Either of these influences can lead executives to be shortsighted, resulting in reduced expenditures in long-term, strategically important activities such as R&D or employee development. High premiums also may lead to higher debt, which could be significant in firms that lack financial slack. The size of the premium is related to the amount of resistance offered by target firm managers. Consequently, friendliness in mergers and acquisitions can greatly enhance financial performance.

In summary, financial success in mergers and acquisitions requires the careful combination of complementary or otherwise related resources, coupled with appropriate financing, a friendly negotiation climate, organizational fit, and managerial actions that help the combined firm realize potential synergies. Opportunism or other ethical problems, high debt, target firm resistance, or straying from the core business can erase potential financial gains. If these latter attributes exist, a merger or acquisition is often unwarranted. Organizations that are facing large hurdles associated with a merger or acquisition may want to consider other types of transactions, such as joint ventures, to accomplish some of the same strategic purposes.

Trends

At the end of 1999, merger mania was fueled by anticipation of the elimination of pooling-of-interests accounting for acquisitions. As we discussed in Chapter 3, pooling of interests allows an acquiring firm to add the target's balance sheet to its own, without any recognition of the sometimes enormous goodwill charges that are reflected in the premiums paid. This accounting technique can artificially inflate return-on-equity, thus making even some poor transactions appear successful. In April 1999, the Financial Accounting Standards Board voted unanimously to eliminate the pooling-of-interests financial accounting method.[5]

The FASB also proposed eliminating the writeoff of target firm in-process R&D (an action that allows firms to take an expense equal to the value of research in progress).[6] These were two of the most popular accounting actions used in mergers and acquisitions during the late 1990s. As their demise drew closer, those interested in completing additional mergers were rushing to make deals under the old rules. However, even after this turn-of-the-century frenzy disintegrates, mergers and acquisitions are likely to remain popular. The elimination of in-process

R&D writeoffs is particularly important to high-tech firms that are committed to significant allocations to R&D, but less important in most other firms, where R&D might account for only a small fraction of operating expenses. Removing pooling of interests as an option is likely to further reinforce the popularity of cash as a medium of exchange in mergers and acquisitions. In addition, cash transactions currently are more highly favored by financial markets.

The trend toward industry consolidation on a global scale shows no signs of slowing. Furthermore, governments worldwide seem to have relaxed their positions with regard to antitrust. For example, in the United States the Federal Communications Commission changed a rule that previously prevented television companies from owning more than one station in the same market. In response, Viacom announced plans to buy CBS for $36 billion and NBC bought a 32 percent stake in Paxson Communications.[7] In France, TotalFina and Elf agreed to merge into the fourth-largest oil company, a deal worth $48.7 billion. Mergers of Exxon and Mobil and British Petroleum, Amoco and Atlantic Richfield occurred previously.[8] Other big consolidating acquisitions include the purchase of Union Carbide by Dow Chemical and the acquisition of Reynolds Metals by Alcoa, which was the world's largest aluminum maker prior to the transaction.[9] Late in 1999, MCI WorldCom and Sprint announced the largest merger ($115 billion) but it was not approved and the two firms called it off.[10] Similar to other countries, in Japan banks continue to consolidate with little government restraint. For example, Dai-Ichi Kangyo, IBJ and Fuji agreed to merge into the world's largest bank.[11]

Another interesting and possibly fleeting development during the final stages of the last century was the increasing popularity of three-way mergers. The sustainability of this trend will depend on the performance of some of the more visible first movers. Already mentioned was the huge merger of three Japanese banks to form the largest financial concern in the world. Other combinations included the merger of Alusuisse Lonza Group with France's Pechiney and Alcan Aluminum of Canada. Also, Banque Nationale de Paris tried to acquire Societe Generale and Paribas.[12] And, of course, America Online's acquisition of Netscape was actually a three-way deal that involved a venture with Sun Microsystems.[13]

Is an end to this merger wave in sight? A dramatic drop in the value of equities in the United States or other industrialized nations could reduce the attractiveness of mergers and acquisitions. Currently, many companies are using their highly valued stock as the medium of exchange for acquisitions. Even if stock is not the medium of exchange, companies can sell stock and use the cash to pay for acquisitions. A large reduction in the valuation in the world's stock markets would make merger financing more difficult. On the other hand, some companies with low stock prices as a result of a crash might be viewed as "good deals," thus offsetting to some degree the financing difficulties.

Even if the current upward trends in merger and acquisition activity flatten or decline over the next few years, they will remain an important strategic approach to firm growth. Although success in these types of activities is difficult to obtain, it is not impossible. We have identified in this book attributes and combinations of attributes that facilitate success in mergers and acquisition and we hope that you have gained a more thorough appreciation of these complex business transactions.

Notes

Chapter 1

Epigraph: *Wall Street Journal Interactive*, October 11, 1999.

1. J. Bennett, 1998. Merger tally hits $626B—But nothing lasts forever. *Wall Street Journal Interactive Edition*, May 11, interactive.wsj.com/archive; L. Cauley, S. Lipin, and J. J. Keller, 1998, AT&T agrees to acquire TCI, creating a telecom behemoth. *Wall Street Journal Interactive Edition*, June 24, interactive.wsj.com/edition; A. Raghavan, S. Lipin, J. J. Keller and S. N. Mehta, 1998. SBC agrees to acquire Ameritech in $61.8 billion stock transaction. *Wall Street Journal Interactive Edition*, May 11, interactive.wsj.com/edition.

2. D. A. Blackmon, 1997. WorldCom's massive bid shakes up little town. *Wall Street Journal*, October 13: B1, B9; P. Elstrom, C. Yang, and S. Jackson, 1997. WorldCom + MCI: How it all adds up. *Business Week*, November 4: 44.

3. R. Blumerstein, S. Lipin, and N. Harris, 1999. MCI-Sprint deal gets cool reception: Stocks decline on fears about delays. *Wall Street Journal Interactive*, October 6, interactive.wsj.com/articles; N. Deogun, 2000. Sprint, WorldCom call of their agreement to merge. *Wall Street Journal Interactive*, July 13, interactive.wsj.com/articles.

4. M. A. Hitt, R. D. Ireland, and R. E. Hoskisson, 1999. *Strategic management: Competitiveness and globalization*. Cincinnati, OH: South-Western Publishing Company.

5. J. Bennett, 1998. Merger tally hits $626B—But nothing lasts forever. *Wall Street Journal Interactive Edition*, May 11, interactive.wsj.com/edition.

6. *BusinessWeek Online*, 1999. Commentary: All of these mergers are great, but . . . , October 9, businessweek.com.

7. M. Hitt, J. Harrison, R. D. Ireland, and A. Best, 1998. Attributes of successful and unsuccessful acquisitions of U.S. firms. *British Journal of Management*, 9: 91–114.

8. W. B. Carper, 1990. Corporate acquisitions and shareholder wealth: A review and explanatory analysis. *Journal of Management*, 16: 807–823; D. K. Datta, G. E. Pinches, and V. K. Narayanan, 1992. Factors influencing wealth creation from mergers and acquisitions: A meta-analysis. *Strategic Management Journal*, 13: 67–84; C. Loderer and K. Martin, 1992. Post acquisition performance of acquiring firms. *Financial Management*, 21: 69–77; M. E. Porter, 1987. From competitive advantage to corporate strategy. *Harvard Business Review*, 67(3):

43–59; D. J. Ravenscraft and R. M. Scherer, 1987. *Mergers, sell-offs and economic efficiency*. Washington, DC: Brookings Institute.

9. M. C. Jensen, 1988. Takeovers: their causes and consequences. *Journal of Economic Perspectives*, 1: 21–48.
10. J. K. Glassman, 1998. Selecting profitable stocks from mergers no slam dunk. *Houston Chronicle*, May 18: 4D.
11. Glassman, 1998. Selecting profitable stocks from mergers no slam dunk.
12. Can Boeing get lean enough, 1999. *Businessweek Online*, August 30, bwarchive.businessweek.com
13. G. Ip, 1999. Megamergers have failed to produce winning stocks. *Wall Street Journal Interactive*, October 11, interactive. wsj.com/articles.
14. Hitt, et al., 1998. Attributes of successful and unsuccessful acquisitions of U.S. firms.
15. M. Gordon, 1998. Merger wave no threat, Greenspan tells senators. *Bryan-College Station Eagle*, June 17: 6C.
16. T. Very, M. Lubatkin, R. Calori, and J. Veiga, 1997. Relative standing and the performance of recently acquired European firms. *Strategic Management Journal*, 18: 593–614.
17. M. A. Hitt, R. E. Hoskisson, and R. D. Ireland, 1990. Mergers and acquisitions and managerial commitment to innovation in M-form firms. *Strategic Management Journal*, 11 (Special Issue): 29–47; M. A. Hitt, R. E. Hoskisson, R. D. Ireland, and J. S. Harrison, 1991. Effects of acquisitions on R&D inputs and outputs. *Academy of Management Journal*, 34: 693–706; M. A. Hitt, R. E. Hoskisson, R. D. Ireland, and J. S. Harrison, 1991. Are acquisitions a poison pill for innovation? *Academy of Management Executive*, 5(4): 22–34; M. A. Hitt, R. E. Hoskisson, R. A. Johnson, and D. D. Moesel, 1996. The market for corporate control and firm innovation. *Academy of Management Journal*, 39: 1084–1119.
18. Hitt et al., 1996. The market for corporate control and firm innovation.
19. K. M. Eisenhardt and S. L. Brown, 1998. Time pacing: Competing in markets that won't stand still. *Harvard Business Review*, 76: 59–69.
20. Mad dogs and mergers, 1997. *The Economist*, November 15: 18.
21. P. Haspeslagh and D. B. Jemison, 1991. *Managing acquisitions*. New York: The Free Press.
22. Big railroad merger quickly goes awry, 1997. *Wall Street Journal*, October 2: A1, A8; D. Machalaba and A. W. Mathews, 1997. Union Pacific tie ups reach across economy. *Wall Street Journal*, October 8: B1, B10; Why those mergers could implode, 1997. *Business Week*, October 20: 170.
23. K. Miller, 1997. How the merger boom will end. *Fortune*, October 27: 279–280.
24. Bloomberg News, 1998. Merger mania likely to continue, Wall Street executives say. *Dallas Morning News*, July 25: F11.
25. Hitt et al., 1999. *Strategic management: Competitiveness and globalization*.
26. Hitt et al., 1998. Attributes of successful and unsuccessful acquisitions of U. S. firms.
27. R. E. Hoskisson and M. A. Hitt, 1994. *Downscoping: How to tame the diversified firm*. New York: Oxford University Press.
28. L. N. Spiro, 1998. They said it would never work. *Business Week*, June 29: 120–121.
29. J. P. Walsh and R. D. Kosnik, 1993. Corporate raiders and their disciplinary role in the market for corporate control. *Academy of Management Journal*, 36: 671–700.
30. P. Holl and D. Kyriazis, 1997. Wealth creation and bid resistance in U.K. takeover bids. *Strategic Management Journal*, 18: 483–498.
31. E. MacDonald, 1998. Ernst & Young blamed for collapse of merger with KPMG

Peat Marwick. *Wall Street Journal Interactive Edition*, February 17, interactive. wsj.com/archive; E. MacDonald, J. S. Lublin, and C. Goldsmith, 1998. Ernst & KPMG canceled merger, citing regulatory, cultural issues. *Wall Street Journal Interactive Edition*, February 16, interactive.wsj.com/archive.

32. R. Langreth and S. Lipin, 1998. SmithKline, Glaxo end talks amid management concerns. *Wall Street Journal Interactive Edition*, February 24, interactive. wsj.com/archive; SmithKline, Glaxo go separate ways, 1998. *Houston Chronicle*, February 23, *www.chron.com/content/chronicle/business*.

33. P. Haspeslagh and D. B. Jemison, 1991. The challenge of renewal through acquisitions. *Planning Review*, March/April: 27–32.

34. J. M. Pennings, H. G. Barkema, and S. W. Douma, 1994. Organizational learning and diversification. *Academy of Management Journal*, 37: 608–640.

35. H. G. Barkema and F. Vermeulen, 1998. International expansion through startup or acquisition: A learning perspective. *Academy of Management Journal*, 41: 7–26.

36. Hitt et al., 1998. Attributes of successful and unsuccessful acquisitions of U. S. firms.

37. D. B. Jemison and S. B. Sitkin, 1986. Corporate acquisitions: A process perspective. *Academy of Management Review*, 11: 145–163.

38. L. G. Franko, 1989. Global corporate competition: Who's winning, who's losing and the R&D factor as one reason why. *Strategic Management Journal*, 10: 449–474.

39. Hitt et al., 1990. Mergers and acquisitions and managerial commitment to innovation in M-form firms; Hitt et al., 1991. Effects of acquisitions on R&D inputs and outputs; Hitt et al., 1996. The market for corporate control and firm innovation.

40. Datta et al., 1992. Factors influencing wealth creation from mergers and acquisitions; C. Markides and P. J. Williamson, 1994. Related diversification, core competences and corporate performance. *Strategic Management Journal*, 15 (Special Issue): 149–165; A. Seth, 1990. Value creation and acquisitions: A reexamination of performance issues. *Strategic Management Journal*, 11: 99–115.

41. R. E. Hoskisson and M. A. Hitt, 1990. Antecedents and performance outcomes of diversification: A review and critique of theoretical perspectives. *Journal of Management*, 16: 461–509.

42. M. L. A. Hayward and D. C. Hambrick, 1997. Explaining the premium paid for large acquisitions: Evidence of CEO hubris. *Administrative Science Quarterly*, 42: 103–127.

43. J. A. Byrne, 1998. How Al Dunlap self-destructed. *Business Week*, July 6: 58–64.

Chapter 2

1. M. L. Sirower, 1998. Constructing a synergistic base for premier deals. *Mergers & Acquisitions*, May/June: 42–49.

2. M. L. Sirower and S. F. O'Byrne, 1998. The measurement of post-acquisition performance: Toward a value-based benchmarking methodology. *Journal of Applied Corporate Finance*, 11: 107–121.

3. A. Barrett and J. Reingold, 1998. The Cendant mess gets messier. *Business Week*, August 3: 68–70.

4. J. Reingold and A. Barrett, 1998. M&A frenzy may be scuttling due diligence. *Business Week*, August 17: 72.

5. Reingold and Barrett, 1998. M&A frenzy may be scuttling due diligence.

6. International business acquisitions: Major legal issues and due diligence, 1997. *George Washington Journal of International Law & Economics*, 31: 173–174.

7. R. C. Byczek, 1997. Are you getting what you pay for in an acquisition? *Mergers & Acquisitions*, July/August: 20–23; S. Lepeak, 1998. How to sabotage a multi-cultural merger? "Ignore it." *Computer World*, 32: 117.

8. R. M. Trottier, 1998. How the successful acquirer keys on market power. *Mergers & Acquisitions*, 32: 30–34.

9. M. A. Hitt, L. Bierman, K. Shimizu, and R. Kochhar, 2001. Moderating effects of human capital on strategy and performance in professional service firms: A resource based perspective. *Academy of Management Journal*, in press.

10. J. R. Carleton, 1997. Cultural due diligence. *Training*, 34: 67–75.

11. W. C. Reed, 1998. Coping with merger-mania: IP's new role. *Health Management Technology*, 19: 38–41.

12. A. Allweiss, 1998. The perils and pitfalls of expanding to Europe. *Commercial Lending Review*, 13: 23–28.

13. W. S. Laufer, 1996. Integrity, diligence and the limits of good corporate citizen-ship. *American Business Law Journal*, 34: 157–181.

14. M. A. Hitt, J. S. Harrison, R. D. Ireland, and A. Best, 1998. Attributes of success-ful and unsuccessful acquisitions of U.S. firms. *British Journal of Management*, 9: 91–114.

15. Hitt, Harrison, Ireland, and Best, 1998. Attributes of successful and unsuccessful acquisitions of U.S. firms.

16. R. L. Simison, 1999. DaimlerChrysler might face rivals in talks with Nissan. *Wall Street Journal Interactive*, January 5, interactive.wsj.com/article.

17. K. Naughton, 1999. Nissan? Drive carefully, Mr. Schrempp. *Business Week*, March 8, 37.

18. L. Revsine, D. W. Collins, and W. D. Johnson, 1999. *Financial Reporting & Analysis*. Englewood Cliffs, NJ: Prentice-Hall.

19. J. Feely, 1996. Risk aspects of mergers and acquisitions. *Accountancy Ireland*, 28: 24.

20. J. K. Glassman, 1998. Selecting profitable stocks from mergers no slam dunk. *Houston Chronicle*, May 18: 4D.

21. M. L. A. Hayward and D. C. Hambrick, 1997. Explaining the premiums paid for large acquisitions: Evidence of CEO hubris. *Administrative Science Quarterly*, 42: 103–127.

22. Mad dogs and mergers, 1997. *The Economist*, November 15: 8.

23. L. Landro and J. L. Roberts, 1993. QVC's $9.5 billion bid for Paramount brings industry titans to fray. *Wall Street Journal*, September 21: A1, A5.

24. D. K. Datta, G. E. Pinches, and V. K. Narayanan, 1992. Factors influencing wealth creation from mergers and acquisitions: A meta-analysis. *Strategic Management Journal*, 13: 67–84.

25. G. Ip, 1999. Megamergers have failed to produce winning stocks. *Wall Street Journal Interactive*, October 11, interactive.wsj.com.articles.

26. J. B. Cahill, 1999. Bank One's McCoy is quitting his posts of Chairman, Chief. *Wall Street Journal Interactive*, December 22, interactive.wsj.com.articles.

27. J. Muller, K. Kerwin, and J. Ewing, 1999. Daimler-Chrysler's Schrempp: Man with a plan. *Businessweek Online*, September 27, businessweek.com.

28. J. Sinkin, 1997. Make your merger/acquisition work. *The CPA Journal*, 67: 68–69.

29. Why those mergers could implode, 1997. *Business Week*, October 20: 170; J. Moreno, 1998. Dow sues railroad over delays. *Houston Chronicle*, March 18: 4C, 8C; D. Ivanovich and J. Moreno, 1998. Union Pacific may have to sell some lines, regulators say. *Houston Chronicle*, April 1: 4C; K. Fairbank, 1998. Gridlock gone, but trains still slow for UP. *Bryan-College Station Eagle*, July 12: E3.

30. S. Lipin, 1998. How Telxon Corp. came to restate earnings. *Wall Street Journal*, December 23: C1.
31. S. Tully, 1998. Merrill Lynch takes over. *Fortune*, April 27: 138–144; P. Shearlock, 1995. The investment picture is shaped by boom in cross-border deals and in U.S. mergers and acquisitions. *The Banker*, February: 16–19; P. Shearlock, 1995. Commercial bank J.P. Morgan is muscling in on the investment bank's territory. *The Banker*, May: 19–21; J. Gray, 1998. M&A takes off with a bang. *The Banker*, March: 31–34.
32. H. M. Bowers and R. E. Miller, 1990. Choice of investment banker and shareholder's wealth of firms involved in acquisitions. *Financial Management*, Winter: 34–44.
33. A. Michel, I. Shaked, and Y.-T. Lee, 1991. An evaluation of investment banker acquisition advice: The shareholder's perspective. *Financial Management*, Summer: 40–49.
34. W. C. Hunter and M. B. Walker, 1990. An empirical examination of investment banking merger fee contracts. *Southern Economic Journal*, 56: 1117–1130.
35. I. F. Kesner, D. L. Shapiro, and A. Sharma, 1994. Brokering mergers: An agency theory perspective on the role of representatives. *Academy of Management Journal*, 37: 703–721.
36. R. M. McLaughlin, 1990. Investment-banking contracts in tender offers. *Journal of Financial Economics*, 28: 209–232.
37. W. P. Barrett, 1990. Less than due diligence? *Forbes*, October 1: 38–41.
38. E. Copulsky, 1996. Investment banking scorecard. *Investments Dealers Digest*, 62: 8.
39. T. J. Chemmanur and P. Fulghieri, 1994. Investment bank reputation, information production and financial intermediation. *Journal of Finance*, 49: 57–79.
40. P. Shearlock, 1998. Behind the merger wheel. *The Banker*, June: 20–24.
41. P. Williams, 1998. Properties for sale. *Oil & Gas Investor*, 18: 48–52.
42. L. Perlmurth, 1996. Who needs M&A bankers? *Institutional Investor*, 30, April: 32.
43. J. Elsen and H. Lux, 1996. New strategy hits merger market: Surfing for M&A deals online. *Investment Dealers' Digest*, February 12: 9.
44. Bowers and Miller, 1990. Choice of investment banker and shareholders' wealth of firms involved in acquisitions.
45. R. Roll, 1986. The hubris hypothesis of corporate takeovers. *Journal of Business*, 59: 197–216.
46. L. Holson, 1999. Accounting for mergers given study. *Houston Chronicle*, February 21: 3D.

Chapter 3

Epigraph: M. H. Lubatkin and P. J. Lane, 1996. Psst ... The merger mavens still have it wrong! *Academy of Management Executive*, 10(1): 21.
1. S. Lipin and E. DeLisser, 1997. First Union to buy Signet in stock swap. *Wall Street Journal*, July 21: A3, A6; B. Orwall, 1997. Hilton to report 4th period loss, mainly due to bally acquisition. *Wall Street Journal*, January 9: B4; M. Siconolfi, 1998. Travelers and Citicorp agree to join forces in $83 billion merger. *Wall Street Journal*, April 7: A1, A8; T. E. Weber, 1998.
2. W. T. Carleton, D. K. Guilkey, R. S. Harris, and J. F. Stewart, 1983. An empirical analysis of the role of the medium of exchange in mergers. *Journal of Finance*, 38: 813–826.
3. Form of payment in M&A deals by price range, 1998. *Mergers and Acquisitions*, April/May: 47.

4. This is Bourgeois' definition as it applies to financial resources. J. Bourgeois, 1981. On the measurement of organizational slack. *Academy of Management Review,* 26: 29–39.

5. D. T. Brown and M. D. Ryngaert, 1991. The mode of acquisition in takeovers: Taxes and asymmetric information. *Journal of Finance,* 46: 653–669.

6. T. M. Burton and S. Lipin, 1998. United Healthcare to acquire Humana. *Wall Street Journal,* May 29; A3, A6; M. Siconolfi, 1998. Travelers and Citicorp agree to join forces in $83 billion merger. *Wall Street Journal,* April 7, A1, A8; G. Steinmetz, C. Goldsmith, and S. Lipin, 1998. BP to acquire Amoco in huge deal spurred by low energy prices. *Wall Street Journal,* August 12: A6, A8.

7. S. Lipin, 1997. H. F. Ahmanson makes offer to acquire Great Western for $6 billion of shares. *Wall Street Journal,* February 18: A3, A10.

8. Brown and Ryngaert, The mode of acquisition in takeovers, 655.

9. W. T. Carleton, D. K. Guilkey, R. S. Harris, and J. F. Stewart, 1983. An empirical analysis of the role of the medium of exchange in mergers. *Journal of Finance,* 38: 813–826; H. Hong, R. S. Kaplan, and G. Mandelker, 1978. Pooling vs. purchase: The effects of accounting for mergers on stock prices. *The Accounting Review,* 53: 31–47.

10. N. Byrnes, R. A. Melcher, and D. Sparks, 1998. Earnings hocus-pocus: How companies come up with the numbers they want. *Business Week,* October 5: 135.

11. Ibid., 134–142.

12. S. Lipin, 1998. Chrysler approves deal with Daimler-Benz; big questions remain. *Wall Street Journal,* May 7: A1, A11.

13. A. Ghosh and W. Ruland, 1998. Managerial ownership, the method of payment for acquisitions and executive job retention. *Journal of Finance,* 53: 785–798.

14. K. J. Martin, 1996. The method of payment in corporate acquisitions, investment opportunities and management ownership. *Journal of Finance,* 51: 12–271246.

15. E. Ramstad and L. Gomes, 1997. Compaq to acquire Tandem Computers. *Wall Street Journal,* June 29: A3, A13.

16. Brown and Ryngaert, The mode of acquisition in takeovers; N. G. Travlos, 1987. Corporate takeover bids, method of payment and bidding firms' stock returns. *The Journal of Finance,* 42: 9439–63; J. W. Wansley, W. R. Lane, and H. C. Yang, 1987. Gains to bidder firms in cash and securities transactions. *The Financial Review,* 22: 4034–14.

17. M. Murray and S. Lipin, 1997. BancOne's costly pact to buy First USA raises doubts. *Wall Street Journal,* January 21: B4.

18. R. G. Hansen, 1987. A theory for the choic of exchange medium in mergers and acquisitions. *Journal of Business,* 60: 759–95.

19. E. DeLisser, 1997. Wachovia agrees to buy Central Fidelity Banks Inc. *Wall Street Journal,* June 27: A3, A10; S.N. Metha, 1998. Bell Atlantic, GTE confirm merger plan. *Wall Street Journal,* July 29: A3, A7; R. Tomsho, 1997. Columbia/HCA agrees to acquire Value Health, Inc. *Wall Street Journal,* May 16: A3.

20. A. Agarwal, J. F. Jaffe, and G. N. Mandelker, 1992. The post-merger performance of acquiring firms: A re-examination of an anomaly. *Journal of Finance,* 47: 16051–621; P. Asquith, R. F. Bruner, and D. W. Mullins, Jr., 1983. The gains to bidding firms from merger, *Journal of Financial Economics,* 11: 121–140; D. K. Datta, G. E. Pinches, and V. K. Narayanan, 1992. Factors influencing wealth creation from mergers and acquisitions: A meta analysis. *Strategic Management Journal,* 13: 678–4; H. Servaes, 1991. Tobin's *q* and the gains from takeovers. *Journal of Finance,* 46: 4094–19; N. G. Travlos, 1987. Corporate takeover bids, methods of payment, and bidding firms' stock returns. *Journal of Finance,* 42:

9439–63; J. W. Wansley, W. R. Lane, and H. C. Yang, 1987. Gains to bidder firms in cash and securities transactions. *The Financial Review*, 22: 403–414.

21. Wansley, Lane, and Yang, Abnormal returns to acquired firms by type of acquisition and method of payment.

22. 12-month moving average stock price, 1998. *Mergers and Acquisitions*, July/August: 55.

23. S. Lippen and S. Warren, 1998. Hercules agrees to acquire BetzDearborn. *Wall Street Journal*, July 30: A3, A12.

24. K. J. Martin, 1996. The method of payment in corporate acquisitions, investment opportunities and management ownership. *Journal of Finance*, 51: 1227–1246.

25. Y. Huang and R. A. Walkling, 1987. Target abnormal returns associated with acquisition announcements: Payment, acquisition form and managerial resistance. *Journal of Financial Economics*, 19: 329–349.

26. S. Chang, 1998. Takeovers of privately held targets, method of payments and bidder returns. *Journal of Finance*, 53: 773–784.

27. S. D. Moore and M. Studer, 1997. Roche Holding to acquire Corange in $11 billion deal. *Wall Street Journal*, May 27: A3, A12.

28. D. Crawford, 1987. The structure of corporate mergers: Accounting, tax and form-of-payment choices. Unpublished dissertation, University of Rochester; K. J. Martin, 1996. The method of payment in corporate acquisitions, investment opportunities and management ownership. *Journal of Finance*, 51: 1227–1246. Contradictory evidence is found in P. K. Chaney, L. M. Lovata, and K. L. Philipich, 1991. Acquiring firm characteristics and the medium of exchange. *Quarterly Journal of Business and Economics*, 30: 55–69.

29. M. C. Jensen, 1988. Agency costs of free cash flow, corporate finance and the market for takeovers. *American Economic Review*: 76: 323–329. Jensen's ideas are supported in empirical research by L. H. P. Lang, R. M. Stulz, and R. A. Walkling, 1991. A test of the free cash flow hypothesis: The case of bidder returns. *Journal of Financial Economics*, 29: 315–335.

30. M. Hitt, J. Harrison, R. D. Ireland, and A. Best, 1998. Attributes of successful and unsuccessful acquisitions of U.S. firms. *British Journal of Management*, 9: 911–114.

31. J. Bourgeois, 1981. On the measurement of organizational slack. *Academy of Management Review*, 26: 29–39.

32. Hitt et al., 1998. Attributes of successful and unsuccessful acquisitions of U.S. firms.

33. Many excellent reviews of this literature exist. Two that may be of particular interest are D. K. Datta, G. E. Pinches, and N. K. Narayan, 1992. Factors influencing wealth creation from mergers and acquisitions: A meta-analysis. *Strategic Management Journal*, 13: 67–84 and M. C. Jensen, and R. S. Ruback, 1983. The market for corporate control: The scientific evidence. *Journal of Financial Economics*, 11: 305–360.

34. J. Barney, 1988. Returns to bidding firms in mergers and acquisitions: Reconsidering the relatedness hypothesis. *Strategic Management Journal*, 9 (Special Issue): 71–78.

35. R. Roll, 1986. The hubris hypothesis of corporate takeovers. *Journal of Business*, 59: 197–216.

36. D. Lohse and E. Beck, 1998. Marsh & McLennan will buy Sedgewick. *Wall Street Journal*, August 25: A3, A14; R. Narisetti, 1997. Cardinal Health agrees to buy Owen in a $484.4 million stock transaction. *Wall Street Journal*, November 29: B3.

37. W. Boston, 1999. Mannesmann resists new vodafone bid—Board unanimously

backs CEO rejection of offer despite rise in value. *Wall Street Journal*, November 29: A23; L. Hays and S. Lipin, 1995. Software landscape shifts as IBM makes hostile bid for Lotus. *Wall Street Journal*, June 6: A1, A10; L. Hays and S. Lipin, 1995. Lotus gives in and accepts IBM offer of $3.52 billion, a sweetened $64 a share. *Wall Street Journal*, June 12: A3, A4; C. McCoy and S. Lipin, 1997. Great Western, white knight set deal. *Wall Street Journal*, March 7: A3; A. Raghavan and Gautam Naik, 1999. Mannesmann CEO rebuffs overture by Vodafone chief. *Wall Street Journal*, December 8: A17.

38. As cited in P. L. Zweig, J. P. Kline, S. A. Forest, and K. Gudridge, 1995. The case against mergers: Even in the 90s, most still fail to deliver. *Business Week,* October 30: 122–130.

39. M & A almanac, 1998. *Mergers & Acquisitions,* May/June: 62.

40. I. F. Kessner, D. L. Shapiro, and A. Sharma, 1994. Brokering mergers: An agency theory perspective on the role of representatives. *Academy of Management Journal*, 37: 703–721.

41. L. Bannon, 1997. Mattel, in post-Tyco revamping, sets $275 million charge, layoffs. *Wall Street Journal*, March 21: B5; R. L. Rundle, 1997. Telnet reports loss on charges tied to OrNda. *Wall Street Journal*, August 1: B5; R. L. Rundle, 1997. Foundation Health will post charges on merger that far exceed estimates. *Wall Street Journal*, August 8: A4.

42. T. L. O'Brien, 1997. Price Communications to acquire Palmer Wireless for $506 million. *Wall Street Journal*, May 27: B4.

43. W. M. Bulkeley, 1997. Westinghouse to buy American Radio. *Wall Street Journal*, September 22: A3, A14; L. Cauley, 1998. AT&T to acquire TCI for $37.3 billion. *Wall Street Journal*, June 25: A3, A16.

44. A. Sharpe, 1998. PhyCor considers going private as option to address depressed price of its shares. *Wall Street Journal*, October 30: B6; M. Brannigan, 1997. PhyCor, MedPartners in $6.98 billion deal. *Wall Street Journal*, October 30: A3, A14.

45. J. Welsh, 1997. JP Foodservice agrees to stock deal for $689.2 million to buy Rykoff-Sexton. *Wall Street Journal*, January 7: A3.

46. M. A. Hitt, R. E. Hoskisson, R. D. Ireland, and J. S. Harrison, 1991. Are acquisitions a poison pill for innovation? *Academy of Management Executive*, 5(4): 26.

47. L. Landro, 1995. It may be Hollywood, but happy endings are unusual in mergers. *Wall Street Journal*, August 2: A1.

48. J. P. Miller, 1997. Millinckrodt-nellcor deal termed strategic but a financial burden. *Wall Street Journal*, July 25: B4.

49. L. Bannon, 1997. Mattel, in post-Tyco revamping, sets $275 million charge, layoffs. *Wall Street Journal*, March 21: B5.

50. M. A. Hitt, R.E. Hoskisson, and R. D. Ireland, 1990. Mergers and acquisitions and managerial commitment to innovation in M-form firms. *Strategic Management Journal*, 11 (special issue): 29–47; M. A. Hitt, R. E. Hoskisson, R. D. Ireland, and J. S. Harrison, 1991. Effects of acquisitions on R&D inputs and outputs. *Academy of Management Journal*, 34: 693–706; M. A. Hitt, R. E. Hoskisson, R. A. Johnson, and D. D. Moesel, 1996. The market for corporate control and firm innovation. *Academy of Mangement Journal*, 39: 1084–1120.

51. M. C. Jensen, 1986. Agency costs of free cash flow, corporate finance and takeovers. *American Economic Review*, 76: 323–329; M. C. Jensen, 1988. Takeovers: Their causes and consequences. *Journal of Economic Perspectives*, 2: 21–48.

52. N. Nohria and R. Gulati, 1996. Is slack good or bad for innovation? *Academy of Management Journal*, 39: 1234–1264.

53. R. A. D'Aveni, 1994. *Hypercompetition*. New York: The Free Press.

54. S. Lipin, 1995. Week's media megadeals put bankers in uncustomary spot: The back seat. *Wall Street Journal*, August 2: A8.

55. J. S. Harrison, 1987. Alternatives to merger—Joint ventures and other strategies, *Long Range Planning*, 20(6): 78–83; G. Steinmetz and M. Marshall, 1997. Krupp suspends hostile bid for Thyssen. *Wall Street Journal*, March 20: A13; A. Sullivan, 1997. Shell Oil, Texaco agree to join units. *Wall Street Journal*, March 19: A3, A8.

56. B. A. Holden, 1997. PG&E agrees to buy unit from Valero. *Wall Street Journal*, February 3: A3, A4; P. McGeehan, 1997. Merrill Lynch expands role running 401(k)s, buys Barclays global unit. *Wall Street Journal*, September 3: C26.

57. Large bonuses for cashing out, 1998. *Mergers & Acquisitions*, March/April: 35.

Chapter 4

Epigraph: (1) D. Pilling, Glaxo and Smith Kline announce merger, *Financial Times*, January 17, 2000, www.ft.com; (2) P. Yip, Optimizing your options, *Dallas Morning News*, January 17, 2000, D1, D2.

1. Oryx Home Page, 1998. Joint News Release. October 15, *www.oryx.com*.

2. Kerr-McGee Home Page, 2000, To Our Stockholders, January 17, www.kerrmcgee.com; K. Yung and D. Solis, 1998. Dallas' Oryx to merge with Kerr-McGee. *Dallas Morning News*, October 15, D1, D10.

3. J. Barney, 1991. Firm resources and sustained competitive advantage. *Journal of Management*, 17: 99–120.

4. D. J. Collis and C. A. Montgomery, 1998. Creating corporate advantage. *Harvard Business Review*, 76 (3): 71–83.

5. C. M. Grimm and K. G. Smith, 1997. *Strategy as action: Industry rivalry and coordination*. Cincinnati: South–Western College Publishing Company, 33.

6. J. S. Harrison, M. A. Hitt, R. E. Hoskisson, and R. D. Ireland, 1991. Synergies and post-acquisition performance: Differences versus similarities in resource allocations. *Journal of Management*, 17: 173–190.

7. M. J. Chen, 1996. Competitor analysis and interfirm rivalry: Toward a theoretical integration. *Academy of Management Review*, 21: 100–134.

8. C. Oliver, 1997. Sustainable competitive advantage: Combining institutional and resource-based views. *Strategic Management Journal*, 18: 697–713.

9. P. C. Davis and A. Kamra, 1998. The value of BIG in banking. *Strategy & Business*, Third quarter, 7–9.

10. W. Glasgall, J. Rossant, and T. Peterson, 1998. Citigroup. *Business Week*, April 20, 35–38.

11. Citigroup Home Page, 2000, Citigroup in the News, January 17, www.citigroup.com.

12. T. J. Flaherty, 1996. Synergies & strategic position. *Public Utilities Fortnightly*, September 1, 30–34; O. Harari, 1997. Curing the merger and acquisition madness. *Management Review*, July/August, 553–556; M. Sikora, 1997. Why the merger and acquisition boom isn't dying down. *Mergers & Acquisitions*, 31 (5): 5–12.

13. B. Wernle, 1997. Republic resumes fast pace for dealership acquisitions. *Automotive News*, November 3, 44.

14. Merger and acquisition roundup, 1997. *Mergers & Acquisitions*, May/June: 49.

15. B. Deener, 1999, Strategy hurt AutoNation, analysts say. *Dallas Morning News*, December 15, D1, D11.

16. M. Goold and A. Campbell, 1998. Desperately seeking synergy. *Harvard Business Review*, 76 (5): 131–143.

17. S. Pulliam, 1995. 'Synergy' fever fuels surge in Chemical, Chase stock. *Wall Street Journal*, August 29, C1, C2.

18. J. Sapsford, 1999, Chase's Shipley cedes chairmanship to Harrison, *Wall Street Journal*, November 17, B12.

19. B. Vlasic, K. Kerwin, D. Woodruff, T. Peterson, and L. N. Spiro, 1998. The first global car colossus. *Business Week*, May 18, 40–43.

20. Chrysler Corporation Home Page, 1998. Merger agreement signed. October 15, www.chrysler.com.

21. Vlasic, Kerwin, Woodruff, Peterson, and Spiro, The first global car colossus, 40.

22. G. McIvor, 1998. Hard work makes big beautiful. *Financial Times*, June 23, 10.

23. J. Calmes, 1998. Administration to study business concentration. *Wall Street Journal*, May 13, A2.

24. M. Sikora, 1998. A throttle on open in the merger and acquisition market. *Mergers & Acquisitions*, March/April: 5–8.

25. What do the trustbusters want? 1998. *Business Week*, March 23, 112.

26. Goold and Campbell, Desperately seeking synergy, 133.

27. Harrison et al., Synergies and post-acquisition performance, 174.

28. E. Alden, 1998. Call-Net to buy Fonorola for C$1.8bn. *Financial Times*, June 27, 19.

29. S. Morriso, 1998. Bigger players come to the fore at US golf courses. *Financial Times*, June 25, 31.

30. The Lex Column, 1998. Johnson & Johnson/Roche. *Financial Times*, July 22, 24.

31. It's got to fit somehow, 1997. *The Economist*, August 16, 53–55.

32. Sirower, *The synergy trap*.

33. R. S. Sisodia, 1995, A goofy deal. *Wall Street Journal*, August 4: A8.

34. R. N. Ashkenas, L. J. DeMonaco, and S. C. Francis, 1998. Making the deal real: How GE Capital integrates acquisitions. *Harvard Business Review*, 76 (1): 165–178.

35. Harari, Curing the merger and acquisition madness.

36. P. L. Zweig, J. P. Kline, S. A. Forest, and K. Gudridge, 1995. The case against mergers: Even in the 90s, most still fail to deliver. *Business Week*, October 30: 122–130.

37. B. Deener, 1999. Mega-deals stifle shares, survey implies, *Dallas Morning News*, November 30, D1, D6.

38. Brand-Name sale bonanza, 1997. *Mergers & Acquisitions*, May/June: 7.

39. A. Lucas, 1996. I want a divorce. *Sales & Marketing Management*, 148 (11): 17.

40. J. Beisler, 1998. Quaker Oats. *Value Line*, August 14, 1489.

41. S. A. Forest and H. Dawley, 1998. Pulp fiction at Kimberly-Clark. *Business Week*, February 23, 90–91.

42. J. Haleblian and S. Finkelstein, 1999. The influence of organizational acquisition experience on acquisition performance: A behavioral learning perspective. *Administrative Science Quarterly*, 44: 29–56.

43. M. A. Hitt, R. D. Ireland, and R. E. Hoskisson, 2001. *Strategic management: Competitiveness and globalization*, 4th ed. Cincinnati, OH: SouthWestern College Publishing, 202–269.

44. D. J. Teece, G. Pisano, and A. Shuen, 1997. Dynamic capabilities and strategic management. *Strategic Management Journal*, 18: 509–533.

45. *Financial Times*, 1998. Learning more by learning together. *Financial Times*, February 13, 6.

46. Collis and Montgomery, Creating corporate advantage, 74.

47. M. A. Hitt, J. S. Harrison, R. D. Ireland, and A. Best, 1998. Attributes of success-

ful and unsuccessful acquisitions in U.S. firms. *British Journal of Management*, 9: 91–114.

48. Teece et al., Dynamic capabilities, 513, 516.
49. F. Leroy and B. Ramanantsoa, 1997. The cognitive and behavioural dimensions of organizational learning in a merger: An empirical study. *Journal of Management Studies*, 34: 871–894.
50. J. P. Liebeskind, 1996. Knowledge, strategy, and the theory of the firm. *Strategic Management Journal*, 17 (Winter Special Issue): 93–107.
51. Hitt et al., Attributes of successful and unsuccessful acquisitions of U.S. firms.
52. E. B. Swort, 1998. Brunswick Corp., *Value Line*, August 28, 1772.
53. Another move for Igloo, 1997. *Mergers & Acquisitions*, May/June: 49.
54. CompUSA Home Page, 2000, CompUSA Inc. Reports second quarter sales, January 18, www.compusa.com; A. Goldstein, 1998. PC culture. *Dallas Morning News*, October 6: D1, D14; CompUSA Home Page, 2000, CompUSA Inc. Reports second quarter sales, January 18, www.compusa.com; A. Goldstein, 1998. PC culture. *Dallas Morning News*, October 6: D1, D14.
55. After the glory days, 1997. *Mergers & Acquisitions*, May/June: 49.
56. L. Siracusano, III, 1998. Clorox Co. *Value Line*, July 17: 955.
57. Addition of a top brand, 1997. *Mergers & Acquisitions*, March/April: 65.
58. A better home, 1997. *Mergers & Acquisitions*, March/April: 65.
59. Exiting in grand style, 1997. *Mergers & Acquisitions*, March/April: 65.
60. E. Rangel, 1998. Room to grow, *Dallas Morning News*, October 7: D1, D10.
61. R. Tomkins, 1998. Wal-Mart launch signals threat to supermarkets. *Financial Times*, October 7: 17.
62. New Wal-Mart chain seen as grocery industry threat, 1998. *Dallas Morning News*, October 7: D10.
63. P. Elstrom, 1998. WorldCom's world-shaker. *Business Week*, January 12: 93.
64. Harrison et al., Synergies and post-acquisition performance, 174.
65. Hitt et al., Attributes of successful and unsuccessful acquisitions, 99.
66. The water industry's "one-stop shop." 1998. *Mergers & Acquisitions*, May/June: 55.

Chapter 5

Epigraph: M. Murray and P. Beckett, 1999. Recipe for a deal: Do it fast—Citigroup's Weill, an M&A vet, offers some tips. *Wall Street Journal*, August 10: B1.

1. S. Lohr and J. Markoff, 1998. Deal is concluded on Netscape sale to America Online. *New York Times*, November 25: A1, C5.
2. K. Swisher, 1998. AOL, Netscape consider partnership, including possible Internet browser deal. *Wall Street Journal*, November 18: B11.
3. Lohr and Markoff, Deal is concluded on Netscape sale to America Online, C5.
4. T. E. Weber, 1998. AOL sets accord to purchase Netscape in a stock transaction for $4.3 billion. *Wall Street Journal*, November 25: A3, A8.
5. S. Callan, 1998. Siebe and BTR agree to $5.67 billion merger. *Wall Street Journal*, November 24: A19.
6. J. S. Lublin and M. Maremont, 1999. Tyco International has CEO with a motto: 'Let's make a deal!' *Wall Street Journal Interactive Edition*, January 28, interactive. wsj.com.
7. Ibid.
8. P. Sherer, 1998. Fenway Partners complete Simmons purchase, in spite of tight environment for financing. *Wall Street Journal*, October 30: C16.

9. T. M. Burton and E. Tanouye, 1998. Another drug industry megamerger goes bust. *Wall Street Journal*, October 14: B1.

10. M. L. Marks and P. H. Mirvis, 1998. How mind-set clashes get merger partners off to a bad start. *Mergers and Acquisitions*, September/October: 29.

11. J. P. Walsh and J. W. Ellwood, 1991. Mergers, acquisitions and the pruning of managerial deadwood. *Strategic Management Journal*, 12, 201–217; J. P. Walsh, 1988. Top management turnover following mergers and acquisitions. *Strategic Management Journal*, 9: 173–184.

12. J. P. Walsh, 1989. Doing a deal: Merger and acquisition negotiations and their impact upon target company top management turnover. *Strategic Management Journal*, 10: 307–322.

13. A. Nahavandi and A. R. Malekzadeh, 1988. Acculturation in mergers and acquisitions. *Academy of Management Review*, 13: 79–90.

14. M. Heitner, 1998. The thorny business of merging rival firms. *Mergers and Acquisitions*, January/February: 18–22.

15. J. Kitching, 1967. Why do mergers miscarry? *Harvard Business Review*, 45 (6): 84–101.

16. Heitner, The thorny business of merging rival firms.

17. Ibid.

18. D. M. Schweiger and A. S. Denisi, 1991. Communication with employees following a merger: A longitudinal field experiment. *Academy of Management Journal*, 34: 110–135.

19. M. Hitt, J. Harrison, R. D. Ireland, and A. Best, 1998. Attributes of successful and unsuccessful acquisitions of U.S. firms. *British Journal of Management*, 9: 91–114.

20. T. Kamm and S. D. Moore, 1998; Hoecst and Rhone-Poulenc strike the deal. *Wall Street Journal*, November 30: A14, A17; S.D. Moore and T. Kamm, 1998. Hoescht and Rhone unveil Aventis unit. *Wall Street Journal*: December 2, A17.

21. J. Welsh, 1998. IP agrees to acquire Union Camp Corp. *Wall Street Journal*, November 25: A3, A6.

22. D. Starkman, 1999. Dillon, the CEO of International Paper, lists goals. *Wall Street Journal*, June 23: B8.

23. R. Blumenstein and L. Gomes, 1999. Ascend board to consider Lucent bid. *Wall Street Journal*, January 12: A3, A6.

24. L. Gomes, 1999. Ascend board accepts buyout offer from Lucent. *Wall Street Journal*, January 13: A3, A10.

25. J. Cole, 1994. Merger of Lockheed and Martin Marietta pushes industry trend. *Wall Street Journal*, August 30: A1, A5; J. Cole and A. Pasztor, 1994. Lockheed-Marietta merger sends industry scrambling. *Wall Street Journal*, August 31: A3, A4.

26. J. Cole, 1999. Lockheed could shed some core assets. *Wall Street Journal*, November 12: A3, A4.

27. Hitt et al., Attributes of successful and unsuccessful acquisitions of U.S. firms.

28. Reuters, 1998. WHX announces a friendly deal for Handy & Harman. *New York Times*, March 3: D4.

29. Corporate News, 1991. *The Wall Street Journal Index*, 310.

30. L. Perlmuth, 1997. Premium patterns. *Insitutional Investor*, 31 (4): 32.

31. G. F. Davis, 1991. Agents without principles? The spread of the poison pill through the intercorporate network. *Administrative Science Quarterly*, 36: 583–613; R. D. Kosnik, 1987. Greenmail: A study of board performance in corporate governance. *Administrative Science Quarterly*, 32: 163–185; T. A. Turk, 1992. Takeover resistance, information leakage and target firm value. *Journal of Management*, 18: 503–522.

32. Turk, Takeover resistance, information leakage and target firm value.
33. E. Beck, 1999. JIL wins battle for Sears PLC after submitting higher bid. *Wall Street Journal Interactive Edition*, January 22, interactive.wsj.com.
34. Turk, Takeover resistance, information leakage and target firm value.
35. T. Carlisle, 1997. Canadian Occidental to acquire Wascan, topping Talisman bid. *Wall Street Journal*, March 19: B4.
36. A. W. Mathews and D. Machalara, 1997. CSX and Conrail move to revise accord. *Wall Street Journal*, March 3: A3, A12.
37. S. D. Moore, 1998. Zeneca, Astra make deal, but some see suitors. *Wall Street Journal*, December 10: A17.
38. Turk, Takeover resistance, information leakage and target firm value.
39. Davis, Agents without principles?
40. Y. Amihud and B. Lev, 1981. Risk reduction as a managerial motive for conglomerate mergers. *Bell Journal of Economics*, 12: 650–657; R. A. Walkling and M. S. Long, 1984. Agency theory, managerial welfare and takeover bid resistance. *Rand Journal of Economics*, 15: 54–68.
41. Davis, Agents without principles?; J. Pound, 1987. The effects of antitakeover amendments on takeover activity: Some direct evidence. *Journal of Law and Economics*, 30: 353–367. C. Sundaramurthy, 1996. Corporate governance within the context of antitakeover provisions. *Strategic Management Journal*, 17: 377–394.
42. Davis, Agents without principles?
43. B. Martinez, 1999. REIT Interest: Poison pills become popular for many real-estate firms. *Wall Street Journal Interactive Edition*, January 27, interactive.wsj.com.
44. Sundaramurthy, Corporate governance within the context of antitakeover provisions.
45. Turk, Takeover resistance, information leakage and target firm value.
46. C. Binkley and S. Lipin, 1997. ITT plans to split into three companies. *Wall Street Journal*, July 17: A3, A10.
47. P. H. Malatesta and R. A. Walkling, 1988. Poison pill securities: Stockholder wealth, profitability and ownership structure. *Journal of Financial Economics*, 20: 347–376; Pound, The effects of antitakeover amendments on takeover activity.
48. J. M. Mahoney and J. T. Mahoney, 1993. An empirical investigation of the effect of corporate charter antitakeover amendments on stockholder wealth. *Strategic Management Journal*, 14: 17–31.
49. C. Mollenkamp, 1999. After Drummond is spurned, some ask if Citation is worth its price. *Wall Street Journal Interactive Edition*, February 10, interactive.wsj.com.
50. Davis, Agents without principles?; E. S. Herman, 1981. *Corporate control, corporate power*. New York: Cambridge University Press; Kosnik, Greenmail: A study of board performance in corporate governance; H. Singh and F. Harianto, 1989. Management-board relationships, takeover risk and the adoption of golden parachutes. *Academy of Management Journal*, 32: 7–24; M. Zeitlin, 1974. Corporate ownership and control: The large corporation and the capitalist class. *American Journal of Sociology*, 79: 1073–1119.
51. P. H. Malatesta and R. A. Walkling, 1988. Poison pill securities: Stockholder wealth, profitability and ownership structure. *Journal of Financial Economics*, 20: 347–376
52. Mahoney and Mahoney, An empirical investigation of the effect of corporate charter antitakeover amendments on stockholder wealth.
53. Datta, Pinches, and Naranyanan, Factors influencing wealth creation from mergers and acquisitions; Y. Huang and R. A. Walkling, 1987. Target abnormal

returns associated with acquisition announcements: Payment, acquisition form and managerial resistance. *Journal of Financial Economics*, 19: 329–349.

54. Datta, Pinches, and Naranyanan, Factors influencing wealth creation from mergers and acquisitions.

55. Ibid.

56. This evidence is summarized in M. C. Jensen and R. S. Ruback, 1983. The market for corporate control: the scientific evidence. *Journal of Financial Economics*, 11: 5–50.

57. C. Loderer and K. Martin, 1992. Postacquisition performance of acquiring firms. *Financial Management*, 19, 69–79; P. R. Rau and T. Vermaelen, 1998. Glamour, value and the post-acquisition performance of acquiring firms. *Journal of Financial Economics*, 49: 223–253.

58. K. L. Fowler and D. R. Schmidt, 1989. Determinants of tender offer post-acquisition financial performance. *Strategic Management Journal*, 10: 339–350; J. P. Walsh, 1989. Doing a deal: Merger and acquisition negotiations and their impact upon target company top management turnover. *Strategic Management Journal*, 10: 307–322.

59. D. B. Jemison and S. B. Sitkin, 1986. Corporate acquisitions: A process perspective. *Academy of Management Review*, 11: 145–163.

60. P. M. Sherer and A. Barrett, 1999. Stealthy takeover of Gucci makes poison pill look good. *Wall Street Journal Interactive Edition*, January 29, interactive.wsj.com.

61. S. Lipin, 1998. Limited 'dead hand' poison pill faces test in a Delaware court. *Wall Street Journal*, November 5: B21; see also S. Lipin, 1998. Court in quickturn case throws out limited 'dead hand' antitakeover plan. *Wall Street Journal*, December 3: A8.

62. S. Lipin, 1999. Pennsylvania law threatens AlliedSignal profit from bid. *Wall Street Journal Interactive Edition*, January 26, interactive.wsj.com.

63. Dow Jones Newswire, 1999. TRW wins bidding for LucasVarity as Federal-Mogul withdraws offer. *Wall Street Journal Interactive Edition*, February 10.

64. J. S. Lublin and M. Maremont, 1999. Tyco International has CEO with a motto: 'Let's make a deal!' *Wall Street Journal Interactive Edition*, January 29, interactive.wsj.com.

Chapter 6

Epigraph: (1) Integration strategies and the scope of the company, *Financial Times* (Mastering Strategy, Part II), December 6, 1999, 8–10. (2) M&A—the challenge of learning to integrate, *Financial Times* (Mastering Strategy, Part II), December 6, 1999. 14–15.

1. Packet Engines Home Page, 1999. Alcatel completes acquisition of Packet Engines, March 26, *www.packetengines.com*.

2. J. Files, 1998. Alcatel to buy network firm, extend reach in U.S. market. *Dallas Morning News*, October 13: D1, D2.

3. Packet Engine Home Page, 2000, About Enterprise Internetworking, January 19, *www.packetengines.com*; Packet Engines Home Page, 1999, Alcatel, March 23, www.packetengines.com.

4. J. E. Harrison and C. St. John, 1997. *Strategic management of organizations and stakeholders*. St. Paul: West Publishing Company.

5. E. Berkovitch and M. P. Narayanan, 1993. Motives for takeovers: An empirical investigation. *Journal of Financial and Quantitative Analysis*, 28: 347–361.

6. J. Landers, 1999. Business without borders is the way of the world. *Dallas Morning News*, March 29: D1, D4.

7. R. Wolffe, 1998. The new rules of competition. *Financial Times*, October 10: 6.

8. A. Rappaport, 1998. Calculating the value-creation potential of a deal. *Mergers & Acquisitions*, July/August: 33–44.
9. A. R. Lajoux and J. F. Weston, 1998. Do deals deliver on postmerger performance? *Mergers & Acquisitions*, September/October: 34–37; M. L. Sirower, 1998. Imagined synergy: A prescription for a no-win deal. *Mergers & Acquisitions*, January/February: 23–29; A. Campbell, 1995. Vertical integration: Synergy or seduction? *Long Range Planning*, 28(2): 126–128.
10. U. Harnischfeger, 1999. Deutsche plans $3.4bn war chest for acquisitions. *Financial Times*, March 19: 1.
11. P. Betts, 1999. Italian banks move to join European merger wave. *Financial Times*, March 22: 1.
12. P. Betts, 1999. Miracles never cease. *Financial Times*, March 22: 17.
13. N. Knox, 1999. Oil companies confirm talks. *Dallas Morning News*, March 30: D1, D4; M. White, 1999. Arco, BP make deal official. *Dallas Morning News*, April 2: D1, D11.
14. Associated Press, 1999. BP Amoco, Arco close to announcing merger. *Dallas Morning News*, March 29: D1, D4.
15. A. S. Hoffman, 1998. How consolidating industries forge an m&a power base. *Mergers & Acquisitions*, July/August: 10–17.
16. M. Goold and A. Campbell, 1998. Desperately seeking synergy. *Harvard Business Review*, 76(5): 131–143.
17. Goold & Campbell, Desperately seeking synergy, 132.
18. M. L. Sirower, 1997. *The synergy trap*. New York: Free Press.
19. Ibid., 133; Jackson, Culture crucial to synergy creation; M. L. Sirower, *The synergy trap*.
20. J. S. Harrison, M. A. Hitt, R. E. Hoskisson, and R. D. Ireland, 1991. Synergies and post-acquisition performance: Differences versus similarities in resource allocations. *Journal of Management*, 17: 173–190.
21. Goold and Campbell, 133.
22. P. M. Healy, K. G. Paelpu, and R. S. Ruback, 1997. Which takeovers are profitable? Strategic or financial? *Sloan Management Review*, Summer: 45–57.
23. The water industry's 'one stop shop.' 1998. *Mergers & Acquisitions*, May/June: 55.
24. Harrison and St. John, *Strategic management of organizations and stakeholders*.
25. M. L. Marks and P. H. Mirvis, 1997. Revisiting the merger syndrome: Dealing with stress. *Mergers & Acquisitions*, May/June: 21–27.
26. D. Solis, 1998. Halliburton laying off 8 percent of workforce. *Dallas Morning News*, October 15: D1, D11.
27. RPM, Inc. Home Page, Company Overview, January 19, 2000, www.rpminc.com; S. Einhorn, J. Christiansen, and T. Myers, 1995. Mergers: The search for synergism. *American Paint & Coatings Journal*, April 24: 21–22.
28. Sirower, *The synergy trap*, 35.
29. What's Japanese for "synergy"? 1997. *The Economist*, November 4: 2.
30. A. Lucas, 1996. I want a divorce. *Sales & Marketing*, November: 17.
31. R. N. Ashkenas, L. J. DeMonaco, and S. C. Francis, 1998. Making the deal real: How GE Capital integrates acquisitions. *Harvard Business Review*, 76(1): 165–178.
32. T. J. Galpin and D. E. Robinson, 1997. Merger integration: The ultimate change management challenge. *Mergers & Acquisitions*, January/February: 24–28.
33. W. J. Altier, 1997. A method for unearthing likely post-deal snags. *Mergers & Acquisitions*, January/February: 33–35.
34. K. W. Smith and S. E. Hershman, 1997. How M&A fits into a real growth strategy. *Mergers & Acquisitions*, September/October: 38–42.

35. Ashkenas, DeMonaco, and Francis, Making the deal real, 167.
36. Harrison and St. John, *Strategic management of organizations and stakeholders*, 180.
37. D. Pilling and T. Burt, 1998. Pharmaceuticals find right chemistry. *Financial Times*, December 9: 21.
38. W. Lewis, T. Burt, and D. Pilling, 1998. Zeneca and Astra set to merge. *Financial Times*, December 9: 1.
39. Associated Press, 1998. British Aerospace plans European merger deal. *Dallas Morning News*, October 13: D4.
40. A. Barrett and C. Yang, 1997. The math behind this $34.5 billion deal. *Business Week*, October 13: 30.
41. J. Jowit, 1998. Glynwed makes $298m German purchase. *Financial Times*, October 7: 23.
42. J. Harrison, 1998. Childcare providers are poised for growth. *Mergers & Acquisitions*, July/August: 51–52.
43. A. Raghavan and S. Lipin, 1999. Vivendi is set to purchase U.S. Filter. *Wall Street Journal*, March 22: A3, A12.
44. D. Owen and R. Waters, 1999. Acquisitive Vivendi may list in US. *Financial Times*, March 23, 22.
45. L. Tanner, 1998. Adding spice. *Dallas Morning News*, February 2: D4.
46. A. Nicoll, 1999. Helicopter makers' moment of truth has yet to arrive. *Financial Times*, March 19: 29.
47. A. Nicoll and J. Blitz, 1999. Westland and Agusta to merge. *Financial Times*, March 19: 23.
48. S. Brostoff, 1996. Will mega-mergers provide 'synergies'? *National Underwriter*, May 18: 11.
49. New England Business Service Home Page, 1999. Welcome to NEBS Online!, April 3, www.nebs.com.
50. Acquisitions bolster a firm's reinvention, 1998. *Mergers & Acquisitions*, May/June: 50.
51. A. Rawsthorn and F. Studemann, 1998. Traditional booksellers assail online Amazon. *Financial Times*, October 8: 18.
52. EFTC Corp. Home Page, 1999. Corporate Information, April 4, www.eftc.com.
53. Carving out a niche through acquisitions, 1998. *Mergers & Acquisitions*, May/June: 54.
54. M. L. Marks and P. H. Mirvis, 1998. How mind-set clashes get merger partners off to a bad start. *Mergers & Acquisitions*, September/October: 28–33.
55. Harrison and St. John, *Strategic management of organizations and stakeholders*.
56. Harrison, Child care providers are poised for growth, 51.
57. The *Economist* Books, 1998. *Pocket strategy*. London: Profile Books, 25.
58. Harrison and St. John, *Strategic management of organizations and stakeholders*, 199.
59. D. McNees and L. M. Chase, 1998. The deal breaker threatening bank-brokerage unions. *Mergers & Acquisitions*, July/August: 45–47.
60. Jackson, Culture crucial to synergy equation.
61. E. MacDonald and J. S. Lublin, 1998. In the debris of a failed merger: Trade secrets. *Wall Street Journal*, March 20: B4.
62. Associated Press, 1998. Monsanto, American Home call off merger. *Dallas Morning News*, October 14: D2.
63. Ibid., D2.
64. MacDonald and Lublin, In the debris.
65. Marks and Mirvis, Revisiting the merger syndrome: Dealing with stress, 23.

66. M. L. Marks and P. H. Mirvis, 1997. Revisiting the merger syndrome: Crisis management, 34–40.
67. M. N. Clemente and D. S. Greenspan, 1997. Keeping customers satisfied while the deal proceeds. *Mergers & Acquisitions,* July/August: 24–28.
68. Carving out a niche, 38.
69. Marks and Mirvis, Revisiting the merger syndrome: Crisis management, 39.
70. Marks and Mirvis, How mind-set clashes, 33.
71. A. Campbell, 1995. Vertical integration: Synergy or seduction? *Long Range Planning,* 28(2): 126–128.
72. Going for broke with massive deals, 1998. *Mergers & Acquisitions,* July/August: 53–57.
73. Sirower, *The synergy trap,* 5, 14.
74. Culture crucial to synergy equation.
75. Vivendi, 1999. *Financial Times,* March 23: 20.
76. M. A. Hitt, J. S. Harrison, R. D. Ireland, and A. Best, 1998. Attributes of successful and unsuccessful acquisitions of U.S. firms. *British Journal of Management,* 9: 91–114.
77. S. J. Paltrow, 1999. Are there cracks in Conseco's house of acquisitions? *Wall Street Journal,* March 23: C1, C2.

Chapter 7

Epigraph: A. Kleiner and G. Roth, 1997. How to make experience your company's best teacher. *Harvard Business Review.* September/October: 172.
 1. Honor roll of the most active acquirers, 1999. *Mergers and Acquisitions,* March/April: 43–44.
 2. Honor roll of the most active acquirers, 1998. *Mergers and Acquisitions,* March/April: 43–44.
 3. A conversation with Roberto Goizueta and Jack Welch, 1995. *Fortune,* December 11: 97.
 4. S. Challis, 1997. A tale of two cultures. *ReActions,* December: 22–23.
 5. D. Lei and M. A. Hitt, 1995. Strategic restructuring and outsourcing: The effect of mergers and acquisitions and LBOs on building firm skills and capabilities. *Journal of Management,* 21: 835–859.
 6. R. C. Gott, 1956. Integrating and consolidating company acquisitions. In *Long-range planning in an expanding economy.* New York: American Management Association, 48.
 7. J. P. Walsh, 1988. Top management turnover following mergers and acquisitions. *Strategic Management Journal,* 9, 173–184; J. P. Walsh and J. W. Ellwood, 1991. Mergers, acquisitions and the pruning of managerial deadwood. *Strategic Management Journal,* 12: 201–217.
 8. R. Frank and S. Liesman, 1999. While BP prepares new U.S. acquisition, Amoco counts scars. *Wall Street Journal,* March 31: A1, A8.
 9. P. C. Haspeslagh and D. B. Jamison, 1991. *Managing acquisitions: Creating value through corporate renewal,* New York: The Free Press.
10. M. Hitt, J. Harrison, R. D. Ireland, and A. Best, 1998. Attributes of successful and unsuccessful acquisitions of US firms. *British Journal of Management,* 9: 91–114.
11. D. K. Datta and J. H. Grant, 1990. Relationships between type of acquisition, the autonomy given to the acquired firm and acquisition success: An empirical analysis. *Journal of Management,* 16: 29–44.
12. C. K. Prahalad and G. Hamel, 1990. The core competence of the corporation. *Harvard Business Review,* 68(3): 85.

13. Thomas and Betts: Think acquisitions, 1997. *Mergers and Acquisitions*, July/August: 49.
14. W. M. Cohen and D. A. Levinthal, 1990. Absorptive capacity: A new perspective on learning and innovation. *Administrative Science Quarterly*, 35: 128–152.
15. M. Brannigan, 1999. Quintiles seeks mother lode in health 'data mining'— Costly acquisition may lead to adapting 'Wal-Mart' style to pharmaceuticals. *Wall Street Journal*, March 2: B4; D. Morse, 1998. Quintiles to buy Envoy in $1.4 billion stock deal. *Wall Street Journal*, December 17: A3, A6.
16. M. Hitt, J. Harrison, R. D. Ireland, and A. Best, 1998. Attributes of successful and unsuccessful acquisitions of US firms. *British Journal of Management*, 9: 91–114.
17. K. L. Fowler and D. R. Schmidt, 1989. Determinants of tender offer post-acquisition financial performance. *Strategic Management Journal*, 10: 339–350; Hitt, Harrison, Ireland, and Best, Attributes of successful and unsuccessful acquisitions of US firms; J. B. Kusewitt, Jr., 1985. An exploratory study of strategic acquisition factors relating to performance. *Strategic Management Journal*, 6: 151–169; M. H. Lubatkin, 1982. *A market model analysis of diversification strategies and administrative experience on the performance of merging firms*. Knoxville: University of Tennessee; J. M. Pennings, H. Barkema, and S. Douma, 1994. Organizational learning and diversification. *Academy of Management Journal*, 37: 608–640.
18. Hitt, Harrison, Ireland, and Best, Attributes of successful and unsuccessful acquisitions of US firms.
19. J. Haleblian and S. Finkelstein, 1999. The influence of organizational acquisition experience on acquisition performance: A behavioral perspective. *Administrative Science Quarterly*, 44: 29–56.
20. J. B. Quinn, 1992. *The intelligent enterprise*. New York: The Free Press.
21. J. S. Lublin and M. Maremont, 1999. Tyco International has CEO with a motto: 'Let's make a deal!' *Wall Street Journal Interactive Edition*, January 28, interactive. wsj.com.
22. G. P. Huber, 1991. Organizational learning: The contributing processes and the literatures. *Organization Science*, 2: 88–115.
23. D. Epple, L. Argote, and R. Devadas, 1991. Organizational learning curves: A method for investigating intra-plant transfer of knowledge acquired through learning by doing. *Organization Science*, 2: 58–70.
24. T. L. Amburgey and A. S. Miner, 1992. Strategic momentum: The effects of repetitive, positional and contextual momentum on merger activity. *Strategic Management Journal*, 13: 335–348.
25. J. B. Cahill, 1999. Earnings at National City, KeyCorp, BankBoston and PNC top forecasts. *Wall Street Journal*, July 16: A4; M. Murray, 1998. National City is no longer just a big midwestern bank. *Wall Street Journal*, February 5: B4.
26. D. Suss, 1996. The acquisition tango. *Communication World*, September: 30–32.
27. J. G. March, 1991. Exploration and exploitation in organizational learning. *Organization Science*, 2: 71–87.
28. R. Berner, 1998. Safeway to acquire Dominick's for $1.2 billion. *Wall Street Journal*, October 14: A4; C. Y. Coleman, 1998. Albertson's plans to buy American Stores. *Wall Street Journal*, August 4: A3, A4.
29. M. Feldman, 1989. *Order without design: Information production and policy making*. Stanford, CA: Stanford University Press.
30. G. P. Huber, 1982. Organizational information systems: Determinants of their performance and behavior. *Management Science*, 28: 135–155; W. H. Starbuck and F. J. Milliken, 1988. Executives' perceptual filters: What they notice and how they make sense. In D. Hambrick (ed.), *The executive effect: concepts and methods for studying top managers*. Greenwich, CT: JAI Press, 35–66.

31. Huber, Organizational information systems.
32. B. Levitt and G. March, 1988. Organizational learning. *Annual Review of Sociology*, 14: 319–340.
33. Hitt, Harrison, Ireland, and Best, Attributes of successful and unsuccessful acquisitions of US firms.
34. A. C. Inkpen, 1996. Creating knowledge through collaboration. *California Management Review*, 39(1): 123–140.
35. This information comes from personal experience with this client.
36. G. P. Huber, 1991. Organizational learning: The contributing processes and the literatures. *Organization Science*, 2: 88–115.
37. R. Daft and K. W. Weick, 1984. Toward a model of organizations as interpretation systems. *Academy of Management Review*, 9: 294.
38. F. Leroy and B. Ramanantsoa, 1997. The cognitive and behavioural dimensions of organizational learning in a merger: An empirical study. *Journal of Management Studies*, 34: 886.
39. Ibid.
40. P. Huber, 1991. Organizational learning: The contributing processes and the literatures. *Organization Science*, 2: 88–115.
41. H. A. Simon, 1991. Bounded rationality and organizational learning. *Organization Science*, 2: 125–134.
42. Huber, Organizational learning.
43. Haleblian and Finkelstein, The influence of organizational acquisition experience on acquisition performance.

Chapter 8

Epigraph: *Downscoping*: How to tame the diversified firm. New York: Oxford University Press, 1994.

1. A. Barrett, 1999. Allied well at Honeywell. *Business Week*, June 21, 42G. Fairclough, 1999. AlliedSignal to acquire Honeywell in $14 billion stock transaction. *Wall Street Journal Interactive Edition*, June 7, interactive.wsj.com/articles; G. Fairclough, 1999. Investors cheer AlliedSignal's deal to buy Honeywell in stock swap. *Wall Street Journal Interactive Edition*, June 8, interactive.wsj.com/articles; *The Economist*, 1999. Honeywell and AlliedSignal: Old-world charm. June 12, 59–60.
2. A. Chakrabarati, J. Hauschildt, and C. Suverkrup, 1994. Does it pay to acquire technological firms? *R&D Management*, 24(1): 47–56; M. A. Hitt, R. D. Ireland, and R. D. Hoskisson, 2001. *Strategic management: Competitiveness and globalization*. Cincinnati, OH: SouthWestern Publishing Co.
3. Ibid.; D. Deneffe and P. Wakker, 1996. Mergers, strategic investments and antitrust policy. *Managerial and Decision Economics*, 17: 231–240.
4. D. Ivanovich, 1998. Climate encourages mergers: High stocks, easy borrowing help. *Houston Chronicle*, May 12: 1C, 7C; J. Peters, 1993. On growth. *Management Decision*, 31(6): 18–20.
5. *Journal of Business Strategies*, 1997. After the ink dries. 18(3): 4.
6. L. Hall and J. Sweeney, 1998. Profitability of mergers in food manufacturing. *Applied Economics*, 18: 709–727.
7. C. Markides, 1994. Shareholder benefits from corporate international diversification: Evidence from U.S. international acquisitions. *Journal of International Business Studies*, 25: 343–367.
8. C. Whelan, 1998. Blending cable, retailing. *Electronic News*, 44(2206), 43–45.
9. Cablevision Systems Corporation reports second quarter 1999 financial results, 1999. Cablevision News Release, August 12, Cablevision.com/cvhome/

cvabout/news; E. Lesly, 1997. Cablevision loses its tunnel vision. *BusinessWeek Online*, October 20, businessweek.com.

10. G. G. Dess, J. C. Picken, and J. J. Janney, 1998. Subtracting value by adding businesses. *Business Horizons*, 41(1): 9–19.

11. *M&A Almanac*, 1999. Divestiture activity in 1998. March/April: 53–54.

12. D. D. Bergh, 1997. Predicting divestiture of unrelated acquisitions: An integrative model of ex-ante conditions. *Strategic Management Journal*, 18: 715–731.

13. R. E. Hoskisson and M. A. Hitt, 1994. *Downscoping: How to tame the diversified firm.* New York: Oxford University Press.

14. D. D. Bergh and G. F. Holbein, 1997. Assessment and redirection of longitudinal analysis: Demonstration with a study of the diversification and divestiture relationship. *Strategic Management Journal*, 18: 557–571.

15. Hoskisson and Hitt, *Downscoping.*

16. Hitt, Ireland, and Hoskisson, *Strategic management.*

17. C. J. Loomis, 1996. AT&T has no clothes. *Fortune*, February 5: 78–80.

18. Fairclough, Investors cheer AlliedSignal's deal to buy Honeywell and stock swap.

19. Hitt, Ireland, and Hoskisson, *Strategic management.*

20. D. E. Kalish, 1998. AT&T purchase of TCI merges technologies. *Bryan-College Station Eagle*, June 25: 1A–2A.

21. L. Cauley, 1998. AT&T to buy TCI for $37.3 billion: Move opens up local-phone market. *Wall Street Journal Interactive Edition*, June 25, interactive.wsj.com/edition; S. Hansell, 1998. Analysis: AT&T-TCI merger is driven by the Internet. *The New York Times on the Web*, June 25, NYTimes.com/library/tech.

22. E. Shapiro, 1998. TCI chairman John Malone prepares for new life as pa Bell. *Wall Street Journal Interactive Edition*, June 25, interactive.wsj.com/edition.

23. S. Schiesel, 1998. With cable deal, AT&T makes move to regain empire. *The New York Times on the Web*, June 25, NYTimes.com/library/tech.

24. S. N. Mehta, 1998. AT&T faces hurdles and plan to use TCI as platform for communications network. *Wall Street Journal Interactive Edition*, June 25, interactive.wsj.com/edition.

25. C. Cooper and S. Liesman, 1998. BP to acquire Amoco in huge deals spurred by low energy prices. *Wall Street Journal*, August 12: A1, A6.

26. S. Liesman, 1999. ExxonMobil to cut 14,000 jobs, expect $3.8 billion in savings, December 16. interactive.wsj.com; ExxonMobil expects bigger job cuts, cost savings from merger. December 15, 1999. Ca.dailynews.yahoo.com/ca/h.

27. J. D. Elizondo, Jr. 1998. Debate rings out over Bell, GTE merger effects. *Bryan-College Station Eagle*, August 16: E1; E8; M. Mills, 1998. Bell Atlantic and GTE get static on merger. *Washington Post*, July 29, washingtonpost.com/wp-s.

28. H. Durgin, 1998. Halliburton to alter balance: Dresser addition gives firm ability to dominate trade. *Houston Chronicle*, February 27: 1C, 8C; S. Lipin and P. Fritsch, 1998. Halliburton to buy Dresser in $7.7 billion stock deal. *Wall Street Journal Interactive Edition*, February 26, interactive.wsj.com/edition.

29. S. Lipin and S. N. Mehta, 1999. Vodafone Group makes an offer to buy AirTouch for $45 billion. *Wall Street Journal Interactive Edition*, January 5, interactive.wsj.com/articles; *Wall Street Journal Interactive Edition*, 1999. Vodafone agrees to buy AirTouch in $56 billion cash-and-stock deal. January 15, interactive.wsj.com/articles.

30. Vodafone to make formal Mannesmann offer around Christmas. 1999, DowJones Newswires, December 16, interactive.swj.com; W. Boston, G. Naik, and S. Calian, 1999. Mannesmann rejects Vodafone offer but chairman leaves the door open, *Wall Street Journal Interactive*, November 22, interactive.wsj.com.

31. R. L. Simison and A. Latour, 1999. Ford to buy Volvo's auto unit in a deal worth

$6.45 billion. *Wall Street Journal Interactive Edition*, January 28, interactive. wsj.com/articles.

32. C. W. L. Hill, 1988. Internal capital market controls and financial performance in multidivisional firms. *Journal of Industrial Economics*, 37: 67–83.

33. R. E. Hoskisson and M. A. Hitt, 1990. Antecedents and performance outcomes of diversification: A review and critique of theoretical perspectives. *Journal of Management*, 16: 461–509; R. E. Hoskisson and M. A. Hitt, 1988. Strategic control systems and relative R&D investment in large multiproduct firms. *Strategic Management Journal*, 9: 605–621.

34. Hoskisson and Hitt, *Downscoping*.

35. *The Economist*, 1992. ICI: Asunder. August 1, 60–61; R. Heller, 1995. Thickness needn't be bad for you. *Management Today*, July: 23.

36. M. A. Hitt, R. D. Ireland, and R. E. Hoskisson, 1995. *Strategic management: Competitiveness and globalization*. St. Paul, MN: West Publishing Co.

37. M. A. Hitt, R. D. Ireland, and R. E. Hoskisson, 1997. *Strategic management: Competitiveness and globalization*. 2nd edition. Cincinnati, OH: SouthWestern Publishing Co.

38. V. Matthews, 1995. Guardian of the high ground. *Marketing Week*, March 24: 38–39; Sears reports third quarter 1999 results. 1999, Sears, Roebuck and Co. Investor Relations, October 21, corporate-ir.net.

39. C. Farrell and R. A. Melcher, 1997. The lofty price of getting hitched. *Business Week*, December 3, businessweek.com/1997.

40. T. Aeppel and W. M. Bulkeley, 1997. Westinghouse to buy American Radio. *Wall Street Journal*, September 22: A3–A4; T. Aeppel, 1997. How Westinghouse's famous name simply faded away. *Wall Street Journal*, November 10: B4.

41. K. Miller, 1997. How the merger boom will end. *Fortune*, October 27: 279–280.

42. A. Sullivan and N. Templin, 1998. Styles, strategies of chiefs differ like oil and water. *Wall Street Journal Interactive Edition*, November 30, interactive.wsj.com/archive.

43. E. MacDonald, J. S. Lublin, and C. Goldsmith, 1998. Ernst and KPMG cancel merger, citing regulatory, cultural issues. *Wall Street Journal Interactive Edition*, February 16, interactive.wsj.com/archive; E. MacDonald, 1998. Ernst & Young blamed for collapse of merger with KPMG Peat Marwick. *Wall Street Journal Interactive Edition*, February 17, interactive.wsj.com/archive.

44. R. Langreth and S. Lipin, 1998. SmithKline, Glaxo end talks amid management concerns. *Wall Street Journal Interactive Edition*, February 24, interactive.wsj.com/archive.

45. R. Winslow, 1998. Drug stock skyrocket; more mergers are possible. *Wall Street Journal Interactive Edition*, February 3, interactive.wsj.com/archive.

46. S. D. Moore, 1998. U.K. drug giants reap rewards of the industry's merger talks. *Wall Street Journal Interactive Edition*, February 19, interactive.wsj.com/archive.

47. Qwest Communications and U.S. West appoint Cliff Dodd executive vice president of systems integration. 1999. Qwest Communications Investor Relations. December 1, qwest.com/press/story; Global Crossing completes merger with Frontier. 1999. Global Crossing Investor Relations, September 28, globalcrossing.com/pressreleases.

48. R. Blumenstein and S. N. Mehta, 1999. Quest's hostile U.S. West, Frontier offers start bidding war with Global Crossing. *Wall Street Journal Interactive Edition*, June 14, interactive.wsj.com/archive; S. Schiesel, 1999. Quest tries to beat foe for U.S. West Frontier. *Houston Chronicle*, June 14: 10A; S. N. Mehta, 1999. Quest's stock declines sharply following announcement of deal. *Wall Street Journal Interactive Edition*, June 15, interactive.wsj.com/articles; R. Blumenstein, S. N. Mehta, and S. Thurm, 1999. Quest officials are trying to calm jitters about 25

percent stock decline. *Wall Street Journal Interactive Edition*, June 17, interactive. wsj.com/articles.

49. J. M. Pennings, H. G. Barkema, and S. Douma, 1994. Organizational learning and diversification. *Academy of Management Journal*, 37: 608–633.

50. H. G. Barkema and F. Vermeulen, 1998. International expansion through start-up or acquisition: A learning perspective. *Academy of Management Journal*, 41: 7–20.

51. M. A. Hitt, R. E. Hoskisson, and H. Kim, 1997. International diversification: Effects on innovation and firm performance in product-diversified firms. *Academy of Management Journal*, 40: 767–798.

Chapter 9

Epigraph: (1) Toward a reconciliation of the definitional issues in the field of corporate entrepreneurship. *Entrepreneurship: Theory & Practice*, 23(3), 1999: 11–27. (2) Entrepreneurship and Cross-Functional Fertilization: Activation, Process and Disintegration of a New Product Design Team, *Entrepreneurship: Theory & Practice*, 23(3) 1999: 145–167.

1. D. J. Collis and C. A. Montgomery, 1998. Creating corporate advantage. *Harvard Business Review*, 76(3): 70–83.

2. C. H. Deutsch, 1998. Newell buying Rubbermaid in $5.8 billion deal. *Financial Times*, October 22: C1.

3. Newell to pay $6bn for toy maker. 1998. *The London Times*, October 22: C5.

4. Deutsch, Newell buying Rubbermaid, C1.

5. Newell Rubbermaid Home Page, 1999. Newell and Rubbermaid in $14 billion combination; creates consumer products powerhouse, September 14, www.newellco.com.

6. Ibid.

7. Newell Rubbermaid Home Page, 1999. Newell completes Rubbermaid acquisition, September 14, www.rubbermaid.com.

8. S. W. F. Omta and J. M. L. van Engelen, 1998. Preparing for the twenty-first century. *Research-Technology Management*, January-February: 31–35.

9. S. A. Zahra. 1999. The changing rules of global competitiveness in the twenty-first century. *Academy of Management Executive*, 13(1): 36–42.

10. R. M. Kanter, 1999. From spare change to real change. *Harvard Business Review*, 77(3): 123–132.

11. P. Drucker, 1973. *Management: Tasks, responsibilities and practices*. New York: Harper & Row.

12. N. Capon, J. J. Farley, D. R. Lehmann, and J. M. Hulbert, 1992. Profiles of product innovators among large U.S. manufacturers. *Management Science*, 38: 157–169; J. Clemens, 1998. Bank mergers would foster new technologies. *The Montreal Gazette*, September 14: B3.

13. S. A. Buckler, 1997. The spiritual nature of innovation. *Research-Technology Management*, March-April: 43–47.

14. R. Nobel and J. Birkinshaw, 1998. Innovation in multinational corporations: Control and communication patterns in international R&D operations. *Strategic Management Journal*, 19: 479–496.

15 A. D. James, L. Georghiou, and J. S. Metcalfe, 1998. Integrating technology into merger and acquisition decision making. *Technovation*, 18(8/9): 563–573.

16. J. H. Meyer, 1997. Revitalize your product lines through continuous platform renewal. *Research-Technology Management*, March-April: 17–28.

17. PR Newswire Association, Inc. 1999. Sybron International Corporation announces acquisition and divestiture. January 22.
18. N. Capon, J. U. Farley, and J. M. Hulbert, 1988. *Corporate strategic planning.* New York: Columbia University Press; F. Damanpour, 1996. Organizational complexity and innovation: Developing and testing multiple contingency models. *Management Science*, 42: 693–716.
19. M. A. Mone, W. McKinley, and V. L. Barker, III, 1999. Organizational decline and innovation: A contingency framework. *Academy of Management Review*, 23: 115–132.
20. S. Shane, S. Venkataraman, and I. MacMillan, 1995. Cultural differences in innovation championing strategies. *Journal of Management*, 21: 931–952.
21. Zahra, The changing rules, 36.
22. P. W. Roberts, 1999. Product innovation, product-market competition and persistent profitability in the U.S. Pharmaceutical industry. *Strategic Management Journal*, 20: 655–670.
23. R. Pouder and C. H. St. John, 1996. Hot spots and blind spots: Geographical clusters of firms and innovation. *Academy of Management Review*, 21: 1192–1225.
24. Mone, McKinley, and Barker, Organizational decline, 117.
25. L. S. Edelheit, 1998. GE's R&D strategy: Be vital. *Research-Technology Management*, March-April: 21–30.
26. M. A. Glynn, 1996. Innovative genius: A framework for relating individual and organizational intelligences to innovation. *Academy of Management Review*, 21: 1081–1111.
27. F. Damanpour, 1991. Organizational innovation: A meta-analysis of effects of determinants and moderators. *Academy of Management Journal*, 34: 555–590.
28. Damanpour, Organizational complexity, 694.
29. M. H. Morris and D. L. Sexton, 1996. The concept of entrepreneurial intensity: Implications for company performance. *Journal of Business Research*, 36: 5–13.
30. D. Dougherty and C. Hardy, 1996. Sustained product innovation in large, mature organizations: Overcoming innovation-to-organization problems. *Academy of Management Journal*, 39: 1120–1153.
31. D. H. Lester, 1998. Critical success factors for new product development. *Research-Technology Management*, January-February: 36–43.
32. Damanpour, Organizational innovation, 561.
33. J. E. Ettlie and E. M. Reza, 1992. Organizational integration and process innovation. *Academy of Management Journal*, 35: 795–827.
34. Damanpour, Organizational innovation, 561.
35. APCOA, Inc. Standard Parking to Merge, Creating a leader in systems innovation and customer service. 1998. January 27.
36. M. A. Hitt, R. D. Ireland, and R. E. Hoskisson, 2001. *Strategic management: Competitiveness and globalization*, 4th Ed. Cincinnati, OH: SouthWestern College Publishing, 242–245.
37. E. W. Barnholt, 1997. Fostering business growth with breakthrough innovation. *Research-Technology Management*, March–April: 12–16.
38. A. L. Frohman, 1998. Building a culture for innovation. *Research-Technology Management*, March-April: 9–12.
39. J. Barney, 1995. Looking inside for competitive advantage. *Academy of Management Executive*, 9: 49–61 as reported in Roberts, Innovation and persistent profitability, 657.
40. P. Marsh, 1997. Same aims, different strategies. *Financial Times*, December 23: 10.

41. PSA Peugeot Citroen, 1998. Annual Report, 3.
42. J. K. Shank and V. Govindarajan, 1992. Strategic cost analysis of technological investments, *Sloan Management Review*, 34(Fall): 39–51.
43. G. Marcotti, 1998. Technology innovation: Eight out of 10 new products are commercial failures. *Financial Times*, March 31: 21.
44. Innovation, 1998. Special Advertising Section: *Fortune*, March 30: S2.
45. G. Nairn, 1999. Vendors aim to combine the best of both worlds: Equipment for IP telephony. *Financial Times*, March 18: 6.
46. Omta and van Engelen, Preparing for the twenty-first century, 31.
47. A. Page, 1993. Assessing new product development practices and performance: Establishing crucial norms. *Journal of Product Innovation Management*, 10: 273–290.
48. E. H. Kessler and A. K. Chakrabarti, 1996. Innovation speed: A conceptual model of context, antecedents, and outcomes. *Academy of Management Review*, 21: 1143–1191.
49. M. A. Hitt, R. E. Hoskisson, R. A. Johnson, and D. D. Moesel, 1996. The market for corporate control and firm performance. *Academy of Management Journal*, 39: 1084–1119.
50. D. Pilling, 1998. The facts of life: Chemical and pharmaceutical companies see their future in biological innovation. *Financial Times*, December 9: 21.
51. A. Barrett, 1999. Warner-Lambert needs a refill. *Business Week*, March 29: 60.
52. Johnson & Johnson buying biotech firm for $4.9 billion, 1999. *Wall Street Journal*, July 22: B5.
53. Baxter to acquire Somatogen, 1998. *PR Newswire*, February 24.
54. Inex Pharmaceuticals acquires a leading position in development of antisense therapeutics, 1998. *Canada NewsWire*, February 5.
55. Nairn, Vendors aim to combine, 6.
56. TAS/NoiseCom acquisition finalized; TAS buys NoiseCom wireless and satellite test equipment business, 1999. March 15,
57. M. A. Hitt, R. E. Hoskisson, and R. D. Ireland, 1990. Mergers and acquisitions and managerial commitment to innovation in M-form firms. *Strategic Management Journal* (Summer Special Issue), 11: 29–47.
58. J. Constable, 1986. Diversification as a factor in U.K. industrial strategy. *Long Range Planning*, 19: 52–60.
59. M. A. Hitt, R. E. Hoskisson, R. D. Ireland, and J. S. Harrison, 1991a. Effects of acquisitions on R&D inputs and outputs. *Academy of Management Journal*, 34: 693–706; M. A. Hitt, R. E. Hoskisson, R. D. Ireland, and J. S. Harrison, 1991b. Are acquisitions a poison pill for innovation? *Academy of Management Executive*, 5(4): 22–34.
60. Hitt, Hoskisson, Johnson, and Moesel, The market for corporate control.
61. C. Reidy and G. Staff, 1998. Hasbro unit pays $5m for Atari arcade game rights. *The Boston Globe*, March 17: C6.
62. R. Burgelman, 1986. Managing corporate entrepreneurship: New structures for implementing technological innovation, *Academy of Management Review*, 8: 61–70.
63. Hitt, Hoskisson, Johnson, and Moesel, The market for corporate control.
64. Hitt et al., Mergers and acquisitions.
65. M. Hitt, J. Harrison, R.D. Ireland, and A. Best, 1998. Attributes of successful and unsuccessful acquisitions of US firms. *British Journal of Management*, 9: 91–114.
66. Capon, Farley, Lehmann, and Hulbert, Profiles of product innovators.
67. Frohman, Building a culture, 9.

Chapter 10

Epigraph: (1) Europe sets the stage for more megamergers. *Wall Street Journal*, January 4, 2000: A17. (2) Dialing up big deals, *Waco Tribune-Herald*, January 2, 2000: B4.

1. Birth of a global company. 1999. DaimlerChrysler Home Page. www. daimlerchrysler.com/specials/81117birth, July 20.
2. H. Simonian, 1998. Chrysler/Daimler-Benz merger. *Financial Times*, May 14: 19.
3. T. Burt, 1999. DaimlerChrysler gears up for common car assembly. *Financial Times*, July 16: 15.
4. Lex Column, 1998. Valuing synergies. *Financial Times*, May 21: 30.
5. J. Hughes, 1998. Chrysler, Daimler merger could reshape auto industry. *The Toronto Sun*. May 10: D13.
6. J. Ball, 1999. DaimlerChrysler frets over loss of U.S. shareholders. *Wall Street Journal*, March 24: B13.
7. Ibid., B13.
8. P. C. Haspeslagh and D. B. Jemison, 1991. *Managing acquisitions: Creating value through corporate renewal.* New York: The Free Press.
9. P. Morosini, S. Shane, and H. Singh, 1998. National cultural distance and cross-border acquisition performance. *Journal of International Business Studies*, 29 (1): 137–158.
10. H. G. Barkema and F. Vermeulen, 1998. International expansion through start-up or acquisition: A learning perspective. *Academy of Management Journal*, 41: 7–26; M. A. Hitt, R. D. Ireland, and R. E. Hoskisson, 2001. *Strategic management: Competitiveness and globalization,* 4th Ed. Cincinnati, OH: SouthWestern College Publishing Company.
11. T. Burt, 1999. Volvo 'would consider' any serious bids. *Financial Times*, July 16: 17.
12. K. Naughton, 1999. The global six. *Business Week*, January 25: 68–72.
13. N. Tait, 1999. GM chief sees more industry consolidation. *Financial Times*, June 8: 18.
14. DaimlerChrysler merger already paying off in operations, Stallkamp says. 1998. *Financial Times*, December 29: 17.
15. Naughton, The global six.
16. Hitt, Ireland, and Hoskisson, *Strategic management.*
17. M.J. Rouse and U. S. Daellenbach, 1999. Rethinking research methods for the resource-based perspective: Isolating sources of sustainable competitive advantage. *Strategic Management Journal*, 20: 487–494.
18. G. Dutton, 1999. Building a global brain. *Management Review*, May: 23–30.
19. Ibid., 26.
20. D. Owen, 1999. Vivendi chief urges Europe to think big. *Financial Times*, May 10: 23.
21. D. White, and A. Nicoll, 1999. DaimlerChrysler wins fight for Spain's Casa. *Financial Times*, June 12/13: 24.
22. G. Stein, 1999. Mergers, acquisitions on record pace in '99. *Dallas Morning News*, July 2: D1, D10.
23. A. Lebis, 1999. Foremost on cross-border dealmakers' list of concerns? Integrating cultures. *Securities Data Publishing*, May 31.
24. Cross-border spending continues to rise. *Financial Times*, June 10: viii.
25. B. Coleman, 1997. EU antitrust officials brace themselves for merger wave. *Wall Street Journal Interactive*, October 15, interactive.wsj.com.

26. G. Holmes, 1999. A vintage year for European M&A: Deregulation and the imminence of unification drove the deal flow. *Securities Data Publishing*, April 1.
27. Corporate News, 1999. Announced European M&A volume exceeds $345 billion in 1Q99. www.secdata.com/news/news_corp/archive/1999press, April 6.
28. M&A Compendium, 1999. *Chemical Week*, April 28: S2.
29. G. Graham,1999. HSBC buys banking group in $10bn deal. *Financial Times*, May 11: 1.
30. Barkema and Vermeulen, International expansion, 10.
31. A. Harney, 1999. Denso gears up to compete. *Financial Times*, June 22: 22.
32. Associated Press. GM likely to buy rest of Saab. *Dallas Morning News*, July 31: F3.
33. D. Angwin and B. Savill, 1997. Strategic perspectives on European cross-border acquisitions: A view from the top European executives. *European Management Review*, 15: 423–435.
34. Holmes, A vintage year for European M&A.
35. Stein, Mergers, acquisitions.
36. A. Raghavan and S. Lipin, 1999. Europeans are learning mergers the American way. *Wall Street Journal*, April 23: A12.
37. Ibid.
38. Holmes, A vintage year for European M&A.
39. Hitt, Ireland, and Hoskisson, *Strategic competitiveness*, 217.
40. K. Ramaswamy, 1997. The performance impact of strategic similarity in horizontal mergers. *Academy of Management Journal*, 40: 697–715.
41. A. Nicoll and D. Owen, 1999. Thomson takes aim at defence sector. *Financial Times*, June 16: 10.
42. J. Authers, 1999. York to buy Sabroe in $590m cash deal. *Financial Times*, March 29: 22.
43. M. Dickie and R. Taylor, 1999. Taiwanese chipset producer to buy Cyrix. *Financial Times*, July 1: 14.
44. Via Technologies Home Page, 2000, About Us, January 22, www.viatech.com.
45. K. Brown and G. Cramb, 1999. British Steel announces Hoogovens merger. *Financial Times*, June 8: 15.
46. J. Croft, 1999. British Steel in merger talks. *Financial Times*, June 21: 21.
47. E. Frey, 1999. VA Stahl wants no part in mergers. *Financial Times*, June 14: 22.
48. A. Edgecliffe-Johnson, 1999. Safeway buys Randall's in Texas. *Financial Times*, July 24/25: 23.
49. D. Solis, 1999. Texas Utilities changes its name after expansion. *Dallas Morning News*, May 15: F1, F3.
50. TXU, 1999. Our family of companies. www.txu.com/html.asp?section, July 19.
51. Lex Column, 1999. Suez/Nalco. *Financial Times*, June 29: 14.
52. C. H. Deutsch, 1999. Big French water company to acquire Nalco Chemical. *The New York Times*, June 29: 2.
53. Lex Column, Suez/Nalco, 14.
54. Hitt, Ireland, and Hoskisson, *Strategic Management*, 241.
55. Ibid.
56. E. Robinson, 1999. Unilever busy Beijing tea producer for $15m. *Financial Times*, May 26: 22.
57. Vodafone Home Page. 1999. About Vodafone. www.vodafone.com, July 28.
58. A. Cane and W. Lewis, 1999. Vodafone pays $764m for US cellular company. *Financial Times*, July 20: 13.

59. S. Lipin, 1999. More big firms are ripe for hostile takeover bids. *Wall Street Journal*, November 22: B10.

60. A. Taylor, 1998. Enron steps into global water market. *Financial Times*, July 25: 19.

61. Enron Home Page, 1999. www.enron.com. July 29.

62. M. A. Hitt, R. E. Hoskisson, and H. Kim, 1997. International diversification: Effects on innovation and firm performance in product-diversified firms. *Academy of Management Journal*, 40: 767–798; M. A. Hitt, R E. Hoskisson, and R. D. Ireland, 1994. A mid-range theory of the interactive effects of international and product diversification on innovation and performance. *Journal of Management*, 20: 297–326.

63. M. A. Hitt, R. E., Hoskisson, R. A. Johnson, and D. D. Moesel, 1996. The market for corporate control and firm innovation. *Academy of Management Journal*, 34: 693–706.

64. S. Glain, 1995. Going for growth: Korea's Samsung plans very rapid expansion into autos, other lines. *Wall Street Journal*, March 2: A1, A6.

65. J. Burton, 1999. Samsung to put car group in receivership. *Financial Times*, July 1: 1.

66. Ibid., 1.

67. J. Dempsey, 1999. TI buys Israeli high-tech group. *Financial Times*, June 21: 21.

68. Bloomberg News. 1999. Bio-Rad offers $210 million for Sanofi-Synthelabo Unit. *The New York Times*, June 18: C3.

69. Bio-Rad Home Page, 1999. www.biorad.com. July 29.

70. K. F. McCardle and S. Viswanathan, 1994. The direct entry versus takeover decision and stock price performance around takeovers. *Journal of Business*, 67: 1–43.

71. A. Raghavan and S. Callan, 1997. Merrill's $5.3 billion global bet. *Wall Street Journal*, November 20: C1, C22.

72. C. Bobinski and G. Graham, 1999. Allied Irish in $582m deal for Polish bank. *Financial Times*, June 25: 15.

73. J. Willman and I. Bickerton, 1999. Heineken wins race for Spain's largest brewer. *Financial Times*, June 11: 17.

74. D.D. Bergh, 1997. Predicting divestiture of unrelated acquisitions: An integrative model of *ex ante* conditions. *Strategic Management Journal*, 18: 715–731.

75. S. Morrison, 1999. Weyerhaeuser in $2.45bn deal. *Financial Times*, June 22: 21.

Chapter 11

1. K. Bryceland and T. Porter, 1999. Citing numerous setbacks, Sunbeam reports net loss for year, 4th quarter. *HFN the Weekly Newspaper for the Home Furnishing Network*, April 26: 62; R. D. Santa, 1998. Chain saw ECR. *Supermarket Business*, July 1998: 3; M. Schifrin, 1998. The unkindest cuts: Despite Al Dunlap's radical surgery, Sunbeam Corp. has been a recent disaster. It is likely to get worse. *Forbes*, May 4: 44–45; D. Weimer, G. DeGeorge, and L. N. Spiro, 1998. Chainsaw Al goes to Camp Coleman. *BusinessWeek Online*, March 16, bwarchive. businessweek.com.

2. T. Porter, 1999. Sunbeam's acquisitions help raise sales. *HFN the Weekly Newspaper for the Home Furnishing Network*, June 14: 48.

3. H. J. Reitz, J. A. Wall, Jr., and M. S. Love, 1998. Ethics in negotiation: Oil and water or good lubrication? *Business Horizons*, 41(3), 5–14; A. F. Buono and J. L.

Bowditch, 1990. Ethical considerations in merger and acquisition management: A human resource perspective. *Advanced Management Journal,* 55(4): 18–23.

4. Reitz, Wall, and Love, Ethics in negotiation.

5. Buono and Bowditch, Ethical considerations in merger and acquisition management.

6. F. K. Achampong and W. Zemedkun, 1995. An empirical and ethical analysis of factors motivating managers' merger decision. *Journal of Business Ethics,* 14: 855–865.

7. R. Morck, A. Shleifer, and R. W. Vishny, 1990. Do managerial objectives drive bad acquisitions? *Journal of Finance,* 45: 31–48.

8. J. A. Teresa, 1991. Corporate restructuring and incentive effects of leverage and taxes. *Managerial & Decision Economics,* 12: 461–472.; J. A. Teresa, 1986. Mergers and investment incentives. *Journal of Financial & Quantitative Analysis,* 21: 393–413.

9. P. J. Lane, A. A. Cannella, Jr., and M. H. Lubatkin, 1998. Agency problems as antecedents to unrelated mergers and diversification: Amihud and Lev reconsidered. *Strategic Management Journal,* 19: 555–578.

10. O. J. Blanchard, F. Lopez-de-Silanes, and A. Shleifer, 1994. What do firms do with cash windfalls? *Journal of Financial Economics,* 36: 337–360.

11. S. V. Mann and N. W. Sicherman, 1991. The agency costs of free cash flow: Acquisition activity and equity issues. *Journal of Business,* 64: 213–227.

12. J. E. Bethel, J. P. Liebeskind, and T. Opler, 1998. Block share purchases and corporate performance. *Journal of Finance,* 53: 605–634.

13. P. Elkind, 1998. A merger made in hell. *Fortune,* November 9: 134–135.

14. M. Pacelle and E. MacDonald, 1999. Ernst & Young woes continue despite Cendant settlement, *Wall Street Journal Interactive,* December 20, interactive. wsj.com/articles.

15. J. Folpe, W. Woods, and P. Meering, 1999. Lies, damned lies, and managed earnings: The crackdown is here. The nations top earnings cop has put corporate America on notice: Quit cooking the books. Cross the line, you may do time. *Fortune,* August 2: 74–76.

16. N. L. Meade and D. Davidson, 1993. The use of shark repellents to prevent corporate takeovers: An ethical perspective. *Journal of Business Ethics,* 12: 83–92.

17. M. Kahan and M. Klausner, 1993. Antitakeover provisions in bonds: Bondholder protection or management enrichment? *UCLA Law Review,* 40: 931–982.

18. J. Wade, C. A. O'Reilly, III, and I. Chandratat, 1990. Golden parachutes: CEOs and the exercise of social influence. *Administrative Science Quarterly,* 35: 587–603.

19. R. A. D'Aveni and I. F. Kesner, 1993. A study of elite social networks and target firm cooperation during takeovers. *Organization Science,* 4: 123–151.

20. C. J. Chipello, 1999. Air Canada adopts poison pill in an effort to stall Onex bid. *Wall Street Journal Interactive,* September 1, interactive.wsj.com/articles.

21. T. Carlisle, 1999. Canadian Airlines gets 'fair' offer from Air Canada, but seeks more. *Wall Street Journal Interactive,* November 30, interactive.wsj.com/archive.

22. W. Beaver, 1995. Corporations' misguided obsession with shareholder wealth. *Business and Society Review,* 95: 49–53.

23. R. J. Giuffra, Jr., 1986. Investment bankers' fairness opinions in corporate control transactions. *The Yale Law Journal,* 96(1): 119–141.

24. J. Evans, T. H. Noe, and J. H. Thornton, Jr., 1997. Regulatory distortion of management compensation: The case of golden parachutes for bank managers. *Journal of Banking and Finance,* 21: 825–848.

25. J. A. Byrne, 1998. At least chainsaw Al knew how to hire a board. *Business Week Online*, June 29, bwarchive.businessweek.com.

26. D. D. Bergh, 1995. Size and relatedness of units sold: An agency theory and resource-based perspective. *Strategic Management Journal*, 16: 221–239.

27. R. G. Hubbard and D. Palia, 1995. Benefits of control, managerial ownership, and the stock returns of acquiring firms. *Rand Journal of Economics*, 26: 782–792.

28. G. Petry and J. Settle, 1991. Relationship of takeover gains to the state of owners in the acquiring firms. *Journal of Economics & Business*, 43(2): 99–114.

29. S. Green, 1992. Managerial motivation and strategy in management buyouts: A cultural analysis. *Journal of Management Studies*, 29: 513–535.

30. R. T. King, Jr., 1999. Scandal fells McKesson's top executives. *Wall Street Journal*, June 22: A3, A6.

31. S. Lipin and M. Pacelle, 1999. Price of a scandal? Cendant Corp. stock is weighed down by potential liability. *Wall Street Journal*, August 31: C1,C2.

32. R. Almeder and D. Carey, 1991. In defense of sharks: Moral issues in hostile liquidating takeovers. *Journal of Business Ethics*, 10: 471–484.

33. J. Franks and C. Mayer, 1996. Hostile takeovers and the direction of managerial failure. *Journal of Financial Economics*, 40: 163–181.

34. S. Bhagat, A. Shleifer, and R.W. Vishny, 1990. Hostile takeovers in the 1980s: The return to corporate specialization. *Brookings Papers on Economic Activity*, 1–84.

35. J. G. Gillis and J. L. Casey, 1985. Ethical considerations in takeovers. *Financial Analysts Journal*, 41(March-April): 10–12.

36. K. Hanly, 1992. Hostile takeovers and methods of defense: A stakeholder analysis. *Journal of Business Ethics*, 11: 895–913.

37. L. H. Newton, 1988. Charting shark-invested waters: Ethical dimensions of the hostile takeover. *Journal of Business Ethics*, 7: 81–87.

38. A. Trounson, 1999. Delta Gold launches hostile bid for competitor Acacia Resources. *Wall Street Journal Interactive*, September 2, interactive.wsj.com.

39. J. M. Ramseyer, 1987. Takeovers in Japan: Opportunism, ideology and corporate control. *UCLA Law Review*, 35(1): 1–64.

40. T. Kamm, 1999. Behind the competition for luxury-goods firm is a new European ethic. *Wall Street Journal*, March 22: A1, A10.

41. A. Raghavan and G. Naik, 1999. How lone-wolf CEO let Telecom Italia fall into Olivetti's grip. *Wall Street Journal*, July 12: A1, A10.

42. V. di Norcia, 1988. Mergers, takeovers and a property ethic. *Journal of Business Ethics*, 7; 109–116.

43. T. M. Ginter, L. E. Swayne, and W. J. Duncan, 1992. When merger means death: Organizational euthanasia and strategic choice. *Organizational Dynamics*, 20(Winter): 21–33.

44. P. H. Werhane, 1988. Two ethical issues in mergers and acquisitions. *Journal of Business Ethics*, 7: 41–45.

45. S. D. Makar, A. Tervaiz, and M. A. Pearson, 1996. Earnings management: The case of political costs over business cycles. *Business and Professional Ethics Journal*, 15(Summer): 33–50.

46. D. G. Chase, B. J. Byrnes, and G. A. Claypool, 1997. A suggested ethical framework for evaluating corporate mergers and acquisitions. *Journal of Business Ethics*, 16: 1753–1763.

47. J. R. Cohen, L. W. Pant, and D. J. Sharpe, 1993. Cultural-based ethical conflicts confronting multinational accounting firms. *Accounting Horizons*, 7(3), 1–13.

48. S. A. Rhodes, 1998. The efficiency effects of bank mergers: An overview of case

studies of nine mergers. *Journal of Banking and Finance*, 22: 273–291; A. Greenspan, 1998. Merger efficiencies, pro and con. *Banking Strategies*, 74 (September/October): 72.

49. J.D. Richman, 1984. Merger decision making: An ethical analysis and recommendation. *California Management Review*, 27(Fall), 177–184.

Chapter 12

Epigraph: C. A. de Kluyver, 2000. *Strategic thinking: an executive perspective*. Upper Saddle River, NJ: Prentice-Hall: 101.

1. M. Hitt, J. Harrison, R. D. Ireland, and A. Best, 1998. Attributes of successful and unsuccessful acquisitions of US firms. *British Journal of Management*, 9: 91–114.
2. K. Pople and B. Orwall, 1999. Merger of Disney's production studio with ABC TV network sparks unrest. *Wall Street Journal*, August 25: A3.
3. Hitt, Harrison, Ireland, and Best, Attributes of successful and unsuccessful acquisitions of US firms.
4. D. Machalaba, 1999. After crippling chaos, Union Pacific can see the proverbial light. *Wall Street Journal*, August 25: A1, A8.
5. S. Tully, 1999. It's time for Merger Mania II. *Fortune*, June 7: 231–232.
6. E. MacDonald, 1999. SEC crackdown on merger write-off may make some deals more difficult. *Wall Street Journal*, January 5: A4.
7. S. Beatty, 1999. NBC agreement to buy stake in Paxson reflects big networks' bid to diversify. *Wall Street Journal*, September 17: B5.
8. T. Kamm and B. Bahree, 1999. French oil giants agree to $48.7 billion merger. *Wall Street Journal*, September 14: A14.
9. R. G. Matthews, S. Warren, and B.Wystock, Jr. , 1999. Alcoa-Reynolds Union bears stamp of deals rocking commodities. *Wall Street Journal*, August 20: A1, A5.
10. R. Blumenstein, S. Lipin, and N. Harris, 1999. Investors greet MCI-Sprint deal coolly. *Wall Street Journal*, October 6: A3, A10.
11. P. Landers, 1999. Japanese banks to form colosus. *Wall Street Journal*, August 20: A7.
12. R. Simon, 1999. At M&A altar, three may be a crowd, but that's just how some suitors like it. *Wall Street Journal*, August 25: C1, C2.
13. T. E. Weber, 1998. AOL sets accord to purchase Netscape in a stock transaction for $4.3 billion. *Wall Street Journal*, November 25.

Index